"Piercing the links between crime and money requires vigilance and the constant adaption of strategies. Finance undergirds much modern evil – from corruption, fraud and tax evasion to trafficking in drugs and the sex-trafficking of children. To achieve any measure of success in harnessing evil, intervention must be grounded on a solid understanding. This series of essays offers rich insight on crime and criminal financing. Amidst a range of topics, the series examines financial institutions and their complicity in human rights violations in the context of authoritarian regimes; digital intermediaries and their role in facilitating sex trafficking; modern technological innovations such as open banking and the connection to terrorist financing; offshore transparency, beneficial ownership and illicit funds; and corruption as an endemic feature of societies as well as a problem once resisted through adequate financial laws. Offering a global portrait forged of jurisdictions stretching from the United Kingdom and the United States to Hong Kong and Bulgaria, this collection will be of interest to practitioners, scholars and professionals."

Michelle Gallant PhD, *Professor of Law, Faculty of Law, University of Manitoba, Canada*

"*Contemporary Economic Crime* is a must read for anyone interested in financial crime and corporate criminal liability. The book offers excellent insights and analysis of corporate financial crimes and enforcement methods used against culpable companies in different jurisdictions. This edited collection presents a selection of unique and insightful perspectives into corporate wrongdoing and sanctions enforced against corporate bodies. It will be of great interest to both practitioners and academics."

Diana Johnson PhD, *Senior Lecturer, Bristol Law School, University of the West of England, United Kingdom*

"One of the tremendous benefits of this book is that it is responsive to the needs of different audiences. To people relatively unfamiliar with the broad topic of economic crime, the chapters collectively provide an introduction to a number of important areas (from fraud-based offences in the UK, to the contours of how a corporation can be held liable for *mens rea* crimes, to cyber-criminality through the lens of sex trafficking, among others). This introduction gives the neophyte an easy entry into some difficult areas of law. For those who open this book with a moderate understanding of some of these issues, the chapters also discuss potential issues that will likely arise going forward, and/or make recommendations for how the law under consideration could potentially be improved. As an academic working outside of Europe, a collection like this one can bring important thinkers to my attention that I might otherwise have missed. The footnotes and bibliographies in the various chapters offer a number of starting points for further research. Among others, people who want to use a comparative approach in research about economic should definitely read this volume."

Darcy L. MacPherson, *Professor, Faculty of Law, University of Manitoba, Research Director, Marcel A. Desautels Centre for Private Enterprise and the Law*

"*Contemporary Economic Crime – Issues and Challenges* situates the phenomenon of corporate criminality within a comparative framework and with reference to various jurisdictions and specific crimes. While the chapters are varied and diverse in terms of subject matter and focus, they all share the same assumption, that corporations/corporate entities are not only the abstract legal fictions of doctrinal debates and criminal law theory, but are indeed actors with significant commercial, trade and political influence and impact. The value of this volume, then, is in the application of well-known and sometimes contested theory to increasingly complex criminal phenomena. The work will be of interest to an audience beyond the United Kingdom. Indeed, the work shows how interrelated legal frameworks have become in the age of corporate and financial globalisation."

Gerhard Kemp, *Professor of Criminal Law,*
University of the West of England,
Bristol, UK

Contemporary Economic Crime

This edited collection explores the culpability of corporate bodies and international organisations and examines the different responses to economic offences such as money laundering, bribery and corruption, cybercrime, market manipulation, insider trading and market abuse. In a world where corporations wield legal personhood, the legal intricacies of corporate criminal liability come to the forefront. While national and international lawmakers attempt to rein in corporate power, the ever-evolving landscape demands a re-evaluation of the current normative framework.

The heart of this book lies in its dual mission – firstly, to compare the different jurisdictional approaches to crimes committed by corporations, and secondly, to propose solutions to some of the challenges faced by lawmakers, policymakers and law enforcement. Expert contributors embark on a global journey from North America to the Asia Pacific via Europe, from Common Law jurisdictions to Civil Law ones, unravelling the diverse approaches to corporate and institutional crime. The challenges facing lawmakers, policymakers and law enforcement are explored throughout this book, alongside solutions to the complex issues they face, whether this involves money laundering, bribery and corruption, fraud, cybertrafficking and corporate involvement in human rights violations.

Contemporary Economic Crime: Issues and Challenges is an indispensable resource for anyone captivated by the dynamic dominion of white-collar and corporate wrongdoing. It will be of interest to academics, legal practitioners, lawmakers, policymakers and law enforcement navigating the complex terrain of financial and corporate crime.

Michala Meiselles is senior law lecturer at Derby University's Law School. She sits on the RASSO and hate crimes scrutiny panels for the Crown Prosecution Service in the East Midlands and has advised UNESCO on online safety and digital rights. Moreover, she is Director of an inter-institutional think tank dedicated to corporate crime which explores white-collar crime, cybercrime and modern slavery. Her research and teaching activities focus inter alia on financial crime, cybercrime and the role of digital providers in the fight against cybercrime.

Nicholas Ryder is a Professor of Financial Crime at Cardiff University's School of Law and Politics and has played advisory roles both nationally (e.g. for the Home Office, the Home Affairs Select Committee the Law Commission, Transparency International, the Foreign and Commonwealth Office) and internationally (e.g. NATO, United Nations, Cepol, Europol). He has created and edits Routledge's *Law of Financial Crime Series*.

Penelope Giosa is Lecturer in Law at the University of Reading and Part-time Associate Lecturer at Oxford Brookes University. She is also Member of the Advisory Board of the George Washington University Competition and Innovation Lab and Convenor of the Comparative Law Section in the Society of Legal Scholars (SLS).

Routledge Studies in Crime and Society

Youth Involvement in Street Gangs in California's Central Valley
Huan Gao

Pauline Tarnowsky's Les Femmes Homicides
Part I
Edited by Lin Huff-Corzine and Kayla Toohy
Translated by Kayla Toohy and Boniface Noyongoyo

Crime, Violence and Masculinities
Research Paths and Understanding
Stephen Tomsen

Learning from Victims' Family Narratives
The Impact of Offline and Online Harm in Cases of Intimate Partner Homicide
Morag C. Kennedy

Juvenile Delinquency, Victimization, and Justice in Chinese Societies
Edited by Yue Zhuo and Hua Zhong

The Social Construction of Kidnapping
A Critical Perspective
Camilo Tamayo Gomez

Contemporary Economic Crime
Issues and Challenges
Edited by Michala Meiselles, Nicholas Ryder, and Penelope Giosa

For more information about this series, please visit: www.routledge.com/Routledge-Studies-in-Crime-and-Society/book-series/RSCS

Contemporary Economic Crime
Issues and Challenges

Edited by
Michala Meiselles, Nicholas Ryder, and Penelope Giosa

Routledge
Taylor & Francis Group
LONDON AND NEW YORK

First published 2026
by Routledge
4 Park Square, Milton Park, Abingdon, Oxon OX14 4RN

and by Routledge
605 Third Avenue, New York, NY 10158

Routledge is an imprint of the Taylor & Francis Group, an informa business

British Library Cataloguing-in-Publication Data
A catalogue record for this book is available from the British Library

ISBN: 9781032350042 (hbk)
ISBN: 9781032350059 (pbk)
ISBN: 9781003324843 (ebk)

DOI: 10.4324/9781003324843

Typeset in Sabon
by codeMantra

From Michala Meiselles: In Loving Memory of Denise (Daliah) Meiselles (1948–2022)

Contents

Contributors

Georgia Bufton is currently pursuing a PhD at Cardiff University's School of Law and Politics. Her doctoral research focuses on the Economic Crime and Corporate Transparency Act 2023, with particular emphasis on the newly introduced "failure to prevent fraud" offence. Her thesis examines the implications of this legislative reform, exploring its potential to enhance corporate governance, deter fraudulent activity and strengthen compliance frameworks within organisations. An evaluation of *how* the "failure to prevent fraud" offence fits into the broader landscape of corporate criminal liability is evaluated while offering practical insights to inform policymaking and the development of effective compliance strategies.

Dolapo Fakuade (Dolas) is a "pracademic" with over a decade of teaching, training and working experience in different academic institutions and public sector organisations in the United Kingdom (UK), New Zealand, the United States of America (USA), Australia, Singapore, Turkey, the United Arab Emirates (UAE) and Germany, to mention a few. Through collegiality, she has contributed to security, safety and humanitarian assistance discourse around the world. Her security and disaster management qualifications and expertise have been beneficial in informing policy and practice in the UK, New Zealand, Singapore and ASEAN countries. She leads the Intelligence, Security and Disaster Management MSc at the University of Derby and serves as external examiner for humanitarian postgraduate degrees in UK universities. Her versatility, energy and solution-driven approaches make her a delight to work with.

Paul Gilmour is a senior lecturer in Economic Crime at the University of Portsmouth. He has presented and written extensively on the subject of corporate transparency and has consulted the Financial Action Task Force (FATF) on amendments to Recommendation 24 on the transparency and beneficial ownership of legal persons. He served for nearly 20 years in the UK police service, most recently as a detective specialising in criminal investigations. He is an Accredited Counter Fraud Specialist and Certified Fraud Examiner. His research focuses on issues of financial secrecy, offshore finance, freeports and beneficial ownership. He is intrigued with understanding the characteristics of offshore jurisdictions, the methods used to conceal beneficial ownership and how governments and regulatory bodies attempt to control illicit offshore activities and markets.

Penelope Giosa is Lecturer in Law at the University of Reading and Part-time Associate Lecturer at Oxford Brookes University. She is also Member of the Advisory Board of the George Washington University Competition and Innovation Lab and Convenor of the Comparative Law Section in the Society of Legal Scholars (SLS).

Doron Goldbarsht is an Associate Professor at Macquarie Law School, where he teaches banking and financial crime. He is the Academic Head of the Graduate Certificate in Financial Integrity Law and the Director of the Financial Integrity Hub (FIH). He is an authority on anti-money laundering and counter-terrorist financing (AML/CTF) regulations, with expertise in the related fields of compliance and financial innovation, with over 20 years of experience. His recent publications focus on international AML/CTF standards and the mechanisms for their effective implementation and compliance at the national level.

David C. Hicks has worked with enforcement, intelligence, nongovernment and government institutions in Canada. He is currently senior lecturer in Criminology at the University of Derby and programme leader for the MSc Financial Investigation and Digital Intelligence and the MSc Criminal Investigation. He has previously taught at Cardiff University and the University of Ottawa.

Branislav Hock is an Associate Professor in Economic Crime and Compliance at the University of Portsmouth. He is a passionate interdisciplinary researcher who thrives in both an academic environment and practice contributing to the knowledge that exists in the area of economic crime and compliance. With a rapidly developing international reputation for excellence in policy-oriented research, Dr Hock has played advisory roles both nationally (Home Office, Synectic Solutions, Crowe) and internationally (EU Commission, European Court of Auditors, OECD, United Nations). Branislav has established an annual Winter Economic Crime Symposium and is the co-editor in chief of the *Journal of Economic Criminology*.

Flora Huang is Professor of Law and Business at the University of Derby in the UK and Central Asian Legal Research Fellow at the Tashkent State University of Law in Uzbekistan. Her extensive academic and professional background has cultivated a profound understanding of economic systems, sustainability, business law and trade and investment policies. Her most recent monograph explores a novel market trading mechanism, giving mutual market access to Chinese and international investors.

Craig Hughes worked within law enforcement for over 30 years, the last 20 of which he was a financial investigator and manager at local, regional and national levels for the Police and Home Office departments including the Assets Recovery Agency and Serious Fraud Office. He is former Head of Policing at the School of Law and Social Sciences, College of Business, Law and Social Sciences, University of Derby, UK.

Michala Meiselles is senior law lecturer at Derby University's Law School. She sits on the scrutiny panel for the Crown Prosecution Service in the East Midlands and has advised UNESCO on online safety and digital rights. Moreover, she is Director of an inter-institutional think tank dedicated to corporate crime which explores white-collar crime, cybercrime and modern slavery. Her research and teaching activities focus inter alia on financial crime, cybercrime and the role of digital providers in the fight against cybercrime.

J. S. Nelson is a leading voice on issues of business ethics, white-collar crime, compliance and corporate misconduct. She brings a deep, diverse background to her work, bridging both business and law school. She is currently a Professor of Law at the University of Pittsburgh. She previously taught at Harvard Business School and was a visiting researcher at Harvard Law School. Her work concentrates on the way that legal rules shape ethical behaviour within business organisations and the impact of different frameworks on large-scale corporate wrongdoing. Her work has a broad scholarly and public impact. She has contributed to over 120 publications through scholarship and media. Her scholarship has been published in both legal and business journals, and her chapters are in academic books.

Samuel Orchard is a lawyer at Arnold Bloch Leibler. Samuel graduated from Macquarie University with a Bachelor of Arts (Psychology) and Laws (Honours) in 2022 and is currently a research assistant to the Financial Integrity Hub (FIH) at Macquarie Law School. Samuel has a broad research interest in the legal structures upholding Australia's anti-money laundering and counter-terrorism financing framework, specifically as it applies to new and emerging financial products and services.

Yudy Paola Pinzon Fernandez is a qualified lawyer in Colombia since 2009 with considerable experience in the public and private sector, working as a litigator, corporate legal adviser, government official and contractor. Her academic background is composed of a postgraduate diploma in Commercial Law and a five-year bachelor's degree (Colombia), where she received the academic excellence award for outstanding performance. Additionally, in 2018, Yudy Paola was awarded with the Chancellor´s Scholarship by the University of the West of England for postgraduate studies and achieved her LL.M. in Commercial Law with distinction in 2020. Over the course of her career, Yudy Paola had the opportunity to manage disciplinary procedures against government officials, getting to know more closely the networks used by corruption and the bad practices that lead to it. Accordingly, she has developed a special interest in researching more effective ways to tackle corruption, and by doing so, Yudy Paola dedicated her master's thesis to carry out a comparative law study on the United Kingdom and Colombian approaches towards corporate anti-bribery policies.

Stephen Schneider is a Professor in the Department of Criminology at Saint Mary's University in Halifax, Canada. His areas of interest include organised crime, policing and law enforcement, crime prevention and corporate crime. Dr Schneider is the author of seven books. His chapter in the current book is informed by a larger research project exploring unethical and unlawful activities by multinational financial institutions.

Radosveta Vassileva is an Adjunct Senior Research Fellow at UCD Sutherland School of Law, Ireland. She holds a PhD in Law from University College London (the UK), a master's degree in Economic Law from Sciences Po Paris (France), a master's degree in Global Business Law from Université de Paris 1 Panthéon-Sorbonne (France) and a BA in International Relations from Tufts University (the USA). She publishes extensively in the areas of comparative private law, international commercial law and the rule of law, and she has recently authored *Bulgarian Private Law at Crossroads*, which was published by Intersentia in 2022. In addition to being a legal scholar, Dr Vassileva is also a social advocate. She runs a blog on the rule of law and human rights and on occasion publishes articles in various media. Moreover, for several years, she has served as a reporter on the non-implementation of CJEU judgements in Bulgaria for the "Justice Delayed and Justice Denied: Non-Implementation of European Courts' Judgments and the Rule of Law" project of the European Implementation Network (EIN) and Democracy Reporting International (DRI). She was interviewed by the Delors Institute as part of their Study informing the Mid-term Evaluation of the Recovery and Resilience Facility in the EU in 2023. She was also interviewed by the Organization for Security and Co-operation in Europe and the Council of Europe as part of their monitoring of the parliamentary elections in Bulgaria in 2021.

Horace Yeung is Associate Professor in Commercial Law at the University of Leicester in the UK and Central Asian Legal Research Fellow at the Tashkent State University of Law in Uzbekistan. His research interests lie closely with the teaching he is doing surrounding commercial law (very broadly defined). His research has a distinctive global comparative and interdisciplinary approach especially underlining the role of law in economic development. He was a recipient of the Confucius Institute Highly Commended Prize for his research in Chinese law.

Introduction

Corporations are juridical persons that through the legal process of incorporation are endowed with a legal identity, which distinguishes them from their creators. The common law provides that corporations are qualified to breach certain offences under the criminal law largely because of this legal procedure.[1] A number of common law rules have evolved in order to limit disproportionate abuse of power by corporations, including breaches of criminal law.[2] Corporate financial crime has been referred to as a 'complex subject on many levels and efforts at strict definitional exactitude rapidly become self-defeating'.[3] Since the seminal definition of white-collar crime by Sutherland, financial crime has attracted a great deal of research and commentary. For instance, detailed research and related literature have been published on money laundering,[4] terrorist financing,[5] fraud,[6] market manipulation[7] and more recently bribery.[8] However, there is a deficiency of literature on corporate financial crime within the UK. Most of the literature in this area initially concentrated on the development of the doctrine of corporate criminal responsibility.[9] Subsequent literature has focused on the liability of corporations for breaching the Corporate Manslaughter and Corporate Homicide Act 2007,[10] the creation of the failure to prevent bribery offences under the Bribery Act 2010[11] and the use of DPAs by the SFO.[12] There is little published research on the Ministry of Justice (MoJ) call for evidence which has only recently been covered by Wells and less on the Law Commissions Discussion Paper.[13] The international profile of corporate financial crime has substantially increased during the last three decades. This is due, in part, to instances of corporate financial crime in the US including the Savings and Loans Crisis,[14] the collapse of several large corporations including Enron and WorldCom,[15] the Bernard Madoff Ponzi fraud scheme[16] and the 'Great Wall Street Rip-Off'.[17] Similarly, the UK has experienced wide-scale corporate financial crime including Barlow Clowes International,[18] the Bank of Credit and Commerce International,[19] Barings Bank,[20] market manipulation by financial institutions[21] and money laundering.[22] In the twelve-month period leading up to September 2020, there were over 5,000 convictions in England and Wales of legal persons including companies for activities ranging from regulatory offences (such as breaches of environmental or trading regulations) to offences including bribery, manslaughter, money laundering and fraud.[23] There is a recognition that the law on corporate criminal liability is not always capable of properly criminalising and punishing corporate misbehaviour, especially when large and dispersed entities are involved; moreover some suggest that it is extremely hard to prosecute such entities for economic crimes committed by and on their behalf.[24] The identification principle currently in use in England and Wales requires proof of a specific state of mind by the company's 'directing mind and will'; whilst it may be easier to prove this requisite state of mind when the

DOI: 10.4324/9781003324843-1

company is small and the decision-making process more centralised, there is concern that the principle is unfit to tackle misconduct conducted on a larger scale, by and on behalf of companies with multifaceted decision-making configurations.[25] Other jurisdictions use more contemporary liability models; in Australia, for example, companies can be found criminally liable if there is a culture of non-compliance or the misconduct endorsed by senior management.[26] More recently, Parliament has introduced a new family of 'failure to prevent' offences; companies that fail to prevent bribery or tax evasion by persons associated with them (employees, agents and even commercial counterparts) may be found liable unless they can demonstrate that they have adequate procedures in place to prevent such conduct. There is a suggestion that similar offences may be introduced to cover economic crimes such as fraud.[27] Each 'failure to prevent' offence is accompanied by government guidance setting out the steps that companies should take in order to prevent persons associated with them from engaging in bribery or tax evasion; though merely optional, a failure to follow such guidance may make it harder for the company under investigation to demonstrate that it had adequate procedures in place ('comply or explain').[28] It is within this context that this edited collection seeks to address the disparity in the financial crime literature.

The purpose of this collection and the earlier one – published in 2024 – is to provide a unique commentary on the response to corporate crime across several jurisdictions.[29] These edited collections seek to contribute to this vast area of law by providing a unique review from a wide range of experts from academia and practice.

In Chapter 1 (Open Banking in Australia: Anti-Money Laundering and Counter-Terrorism Financing Considerations), Goldbarsht and Orchard focus on Open Banking and how it is designed to give customers more control over their financial data, allowing them to request their bank to securely share product, pricing and transaction data with other banks or authorised third party providers. This chapter discusses how open banking relies on application programming interfaces (APIs) – the bridge that allows two systems to communicate and share data without an intermediary via a common language. The authors argue that this will put banks domestically and internationally in competition with a range of new players, from fintech start-ups to technology companies. However, the authors argue that implementation of broad data-sharing arrangements, and opening systems to access by APIs, may raise questions about whether open banking exposes banks to significantly more money laundering and terrorism financing risk. This is an assessment that all banks will need to conduct when launching or implementing any kind of new business practice, service or developing technology and would feed into the overall enterprise-wide assessment of money laundering and terrorist financing risks faced by the bank. This chapter aims to shed light on the implications of open banking regimes for money laundering and terrorist financing risks, with a view to providing recommendations for enhancing financial integrity in the Australian financial sector.

In Chapter 2 (Money Laundering Challenges in the United Kingdom), Hughes and Hicks focus on how money laundering is consistently acknowledged not only as a significant criminal offence but also as a major threat to the United Kingdom and international financial architecture. This chapter critically examines the efficacy of the UK money laundering legislation in terms of enforcement strategies to implement domestic and international policies. The central question is whether or not policy translates into effective practice across UK law enforcement. The parallel challenge is to determine whether existing money laundering powers are well used or effective and to assess the symbolic and practical implications of calls for additional powers such as unexplained wealth orders.

This work also examines whether current UK anti-money laundering regulations, policy and practice are robust and inclusive enough to tackle the issue of an emerging and relatively unknown threat environment of the twenty-first century. For instance, criminals are presented with new opportunities in the digital environment while multiple creations of largely unregulated cryptocurrencies present global money laundering challenges for law enforcement. This critical evaluation is expected to indicate areas of good practice in enforcement strategies which may point to recommendations for research pathways and policy development.

In Chapter 3 (Illicit Offshore Finance: Examining the Measures Adopted by the United Kingdom to Enhance Corporate Transparency), Gilmour and Hock provide a critical insight into illicit offshore finance and the key challenges facing governments in tackling money laundering through offshore jurisdictions. The secretive world of offshore finance has come under increasing scrutiny since recent exposés. The 'Pandora Papers' and similar leakages highlighted the apparent widespread misuse of offshore jurisdictions for tax evasion and money laundering purposes. Focusing on the UK's anti-money laundering regime, this chapter explores the legal and practical measures adopted by the UK in its effort to enhance corporate transparency. The UK has responded to such controversies by introducing registers of beneficial owners, an Economic Crime plan and new Economic Crime and Corporate Transparency laws. However, many view the UK's approach to tackling money laundering as costly and ineffective. This chapter concludes by analysing the success of the UK's measures to strengthen beneficial ownership transparency and disrupt illicit offshore flows.

Chapter 4 ("Help at Any Cost" – Impacts and Enablers of Corruption in Humanitarian Sector) by Fakuade focuses on the issue of corruption in the humanitarian sector. It identifies and examines forms and enablers of corruption in this sector and discusses the implications of enablers of corruption in providing humanitarian assistance in countries dependent on aid. Drawing from patterns of humanitarian work, the perception that corruption is an unethical weapon that may hinder investment in humanitarian aid is unravelled to refute the notion that humanitarian assistance ought to be "help at any cost".

Fernandez in Chapter 5 (Critical Analysis of the Legal Framework for Corporate Anti-Bribery Policies: The United Kingdom and Colombian Approaches) explores the anti-bribery self-regulation approaches of the United Kingdom and Colombia. It analyses the legal frameworks of both countries, focusing on their compliance with international standards, the government's support for corporations in developing and implementing corporate anti-bribery policies (CAB-policies) and the mechanisms used to monitor and enforce these policies. The comparative analysis reveals that corporations have substantial control over the design and monitoring of CAB-policies, with case studies showing that these policies are assessed only within the context of criminal investigations. As a result, the author highlights the importance of understanding corporate anti-bribery self-regulation as a complement to formal regulations and explores some of the challenges corporations face in developing and implementing CAB-policies. This chapter concludes that both countries share similar approaches towards CAB-policies and identifies areas where their legal frameworks could complement each other. Additionally, it proposes an institutional strategy that, despite certain limitations, would enable governments to adopt a more proactive approach towards this self-regulation tool.

In Chapter 6 (The End of a Corruption-Free Era? The Story of Hong Kong), Yeung and Huang explore the anti-corruption strategies in Hong Kong and focus on the Independent Commission Against Corruption (ICAC). This chapter discusses how following the handover of sovereignty in 1997, the level of corruption in Hong Kong has been perceived as worsening by the general public, according to the data from the Hong Kong Public Opinion Research Institute. This chapter discusses how the establishment of the ICAC, together with the enactment of the Prevention of Bribery Ordinance, in the 1970s has enabled Hong Kong to control corruption effectively. Furthermore, this chapter concerns whether this institutional advantage of Hong Kong, inherited from its colonial past, may have faded away in the decades after the handover.

In Chapter 7 (Is It Possible to Fight Corruption in a Post-Communist Captured State? The Case of Bulgaria), Vassileva argues that Bulgaria had developed its anti-corruption bodies in bad faith. Bulgaria created the false impression it had the political will to fight corruption, which was important vis-à-vis the Cooperation and Verification Mechanism (CVM). However, not only did it dilute responsibility and make sure these bodes are susceptible to political influences, but also it diverted attention from one of its longstanding rule of law challenges – the over-powerful Prosecutor's Office, which is seen by experts as a major source of corruption and blackmail, because it shields those in power from criminal liability and attacks their opponents.

In Chapter 8 (Civil False Claims Act: An Effective Anti-Corporate Fraud Remedy?), Giosa evaluates the effectiveness of the False Claims Act (FCA) in addressing fraud committed by companies against the federal government of the United States. It reviews the history and theoretical underpinnings of the FCA in the US and investigates when liability arises and what are the various forms false claims can take. It then discusses how the Fraud Enforcement and Recovery Act (FERA) of 2009 has increased accountability for the corporate frauds and examines to what extent the current qui tam provisions promote whistleblowing against corporate fraud.

Chapter 9 (Unethical and Unlawful Behaviour by Global Banks: Implications for Human Rights) by Schneider focuses on how global banks and other multinational financial service providers have come under scrutiny for conducting business in countries with abysmal human rights records. This includes transactions with correspondent banks and other private sector companies accused of supporting terrorist groups. The cases examined in this chapter reveal that several of the world's largest Multinational Financial Institutions (MFIs) have failed to meet the basic litmus test set by the United Nations Guiding Principles on Business and Human Rights, making them complicit in human rights abuses.

In Chapter 10 (A Critique of Corporate Criminal Liability in the US: How Fraud Swallows Everything: Policing What Corporations *Say* Instead of What They *Do*), Nelson focuses on the approach towards policing fraud and large corporations. This chapter discusses how focusing prosecutions on what companies say creates additional incentives for lying and volatile results that more substantive and solidly consistent regulation based on companies' underlying actions would not. This chapter notes that there should be a broader discussion about whether this is an effective way for the US to design and administer its enforcement system.

In Chapter 11 (Corporate Criminal Liability: Shifting the Burden of Cost to the Private Sector), Bufton focuses on the introduction of the failure to prevent offences under the Bribery Act 2010 and the Criminal Finances Act 2017 before moving on to examine the impact of the Economic Crime and Corporate Transparency Act 2023.

In the final chapter (Are Traditional Laws Fit for Purpose? A Critique of International Law Governing the Criminal Liability of Digital Providers for Cyber-Sex-Trafficking), Meiselles asks whether it is time to revisit the international legal framework we currently use, so we can address the role and responsibilities of digital providers for CST (cyber-sex-trafficking)? To answer this question, this chapter explores the ways in which traffickers exploit the digital ecosystem, before critically assessing the current international legal framework. It concludes by drawing out the key challenges that lawmakers and policymakers face in their fight against CST.

Notes

1 Ministry of Justice Corporate Liability for Economic Crime Call for Evidence (Ministry of Justice: London, 2017) at 10. See generally Salomon v. Salomon [1897] A.C. 22.
2 See generally R. v. P&O European Ferries (Dover) Ltd (1991) 93 Cr. App. R. 72, 83.
3 T. Edwards House of Commons Library Briefing Paper – Corporate Economic Crime: Bribery and Corruption, Number 7359, 22 March 2017, at 3.
4 See generally P. Alldridge, *Money Laundering Law: Forfeiture, Confiscation, Civil Recovery, Criminal Laundering the Taxation of the Proceeds of Crime* (Hart: Oxford, 2003) and M. Gallant, *Money Laundering and the Proceeds of Crime: Economic Crime and Civil Remedies* (Edward Elgar: Cheltenham, 2005).
5 See generally J. Gurule, *Unfunding Terror: The Legal Response to the Financing of Global Terrorism* (Edward Elgar: Cheltenham, 2010).
6 See A. Doig, *Fraud* (Routledge: London, 2006) and M. Levi, *Regulating Fraud: White-Collar Crime and the Criminal Process* (Routledge: London, 1987).
7 See J. Austin, *Insider Trading and Market Manipulation: Investigating and Prosecuting across Borders* (Edward Elgar: Cheltenham, 2017) and J. Markham, *Law Enforcement and the History of Financial Market Manipulation* (Routledge: London, 2015).
8 See A. Palmer, *Countering Economic Crime a Comparative Analysis* (Routledge: London, 2017) and D. Chaikin and J. Sharman, *Corruption and Money Laundering a Symbiotic Relationship* (Palgrave: New York, 2009).
9 There are several contrasting views on the doctrine of corporate criminal liability. See, for example, A. Visconti, 'Corporate Manslaughter and Corporate Violence Victims Rights in Italy: A Long and Winding Road' in M. Meiselles, N. Ryder and A. Visconti (eds), *Corporate Criminal Liability and Sanctions: Current Trends and Policy Changes* (Routledge: London, 2024), 37; S. Lontai, 'Corporate Compliance Choices in the Italian Legal System: Organisational Models and Internal Investigations' in M. Meiselles, N. Ryder and A. Visconti (eds), *Corporate Criminal Liability and Sanctions: Current Trends and Policy Changes* (Routledge: London, 2024), 8; G. Almkvist, 'Corporate Criminal Liability: Two Nordic Solutions' in M. Meiselles, N. Ryder and A. Visconti (eds), *Corporate Criminal Liability and Sanctions: Current Trends and Policy Changes* (Routledge: London, 2024), 51; C. Wells, *Corporations and Criminal Responsibility* (Oxford University Press: Oxford, 2001); E. Wlogast, *Ethics of an Artificial Person: Lost Responsibility in Professions and Organisations* (Stanford University Press: Stanford, CA, 1992).
10 See generally S. Griffin, 'Corporate Killing – The Corporate Manslaughter and Corporate Homicide Act 2007' (2009) 1 *Lloyd's Maritime and Commercial Law Quarterly* 73; D. Ormerod and R. Taylor, 'The Corporate Manslaughter and Corporate Homicide Act 2007' (2008) 8 *Criminal Law Review* 589 and J. Gobert, 'The Corporate Manslaughter and Corporate Homicide Act 2007 – Thirteen Years in the Making But Was It Worth the Wait?' (2008) 7 *Modern Law Review* 413.
11 See generally C. Wells, 'Who's Afraid of the Bribery Act 2010?' (2012) 5 *Journal of Business Law* 420 and S. Gentle, 'The Bribery Act 2010: Part 2: The Corporate Offence' (2011) 2 *Criminal Law Review* 101.
12 See C. Grasso, 'Peaks and Troughs of the English Deferred Prosecution Agreement: The Lesson Learned from the DPA between the SFO and ICBC SB Plc' (2016) 5 *Journal of Business Law* 388.
13 See C. Wells, 'Corporate Failure to Prevent Economic Crime - A Proposal' (2017) 6 *Criminal Law Review* 426 and Law Commission, *Corporate Criminal Liability A Discussion Paper* (Law Commission, 2021).

14 The savings and loans crises in the 1980s and 1990s resulted in the financial collapse of over 1,000 savings institutions due to the excessive fraud committed by the institutions senior officials.
15 The collapse of Enron and WorldCom are associated with wide-scale elements of control fraud and several high-ranking associates in both firms received long custodial sentences. For example, Jeffrey Skilling was initially sentenced to 24 years imprisonment for his role in the collapse of Enron, but this was later reduced to 14 years following an agreement with the DoJ.
16 In June 2009, Bernard Madoff was convicted for orchestrating the US largest Ponzi fraud schemes and was sentenced to 150 years' imprisonment. See United States v. Bernard L. Madoff, 2009, 29 June 2009, United States District Courts.
17 This is referred to the illegal conduct of many financial institutions before and during the 2007/2008 Financial Crisis.
18 Barlow Clowes went into liquidation in 1988 after amassing £190m after misleading 20,000 investors. Peter Clowes was eventually convicted of fraud and sentenced to ten years imprisonment.
19 BCCI is the most infamous banking collapses in the UK when it went into liquidation in 1991 following allegations of fraud and money laundering.
20 The collapse of Barings Bank is associated with the illegal activity of the 'rogue trader' Nick Leeson who was convicted of fraud for his role in the collapse of the then UKs oldest merchant bank in 1995.
21 Market manipulation is associated with the LIBOR and FOREX scandals following the 2007/2008 Financial Crisis and have resulted in many financial institutions being heavily fined in the US and UK. It has also resulted in a few low-level traders being convicted for fraud. See R v. Tom Alexander William Hayes [2015] EWCA Crim 1944.
22 In January 2017 Deutshce Bank was fined £163.1m by the FCA (Financial Conduct Authority) for breaching its money laundering regulations. See Financial Conduct Authority, 'FCA Fines Deutsche Bank £163 Million for Serious Anti-Money Laundering Controls Failings', 31January 2017, available from https://www.fca.org.uk/news/press-releases/fca-fines-deutsche-bank-163-million-anti-money-laundering-controls-failure (accessed 27 March 2025).
23 Law Commission, Corporate Criminal Liability: An Options Paper (2022), para 1.1, available from https://webarchive.nationalarchives.gov.uk/ukgwa/20250109172659mp_/https://s3-eu-west-2.amazonaws.com/cloud-platform-e218f50a4812967ba1215eaecede923f/uploads/sites/30/2022/06/Corporate-Criminal-Liability-Options-Paper_LC.pdf (accessed 27 March 2025).
24 Law Commission, Corporate Criminal Liability: An Options Paper (2022), para 1.2–1.3. See also https://www.lawcom.gov.uk/law-commission-seek-views-on-corporate-criminal-liability/ (accessed 22 June 2021).
25 Law Commission, Corporate Criminal Liability: An Options Paper (2022), para 1.2, 1.23. See also https://www.lawcom.gov.uk/law-commission-seek-views-on-corporate-criminal-liability/ (accessed 22 June 2021).
26 Law Commission, Corporate Criminal Liability: An Options Paper (2022), para 6.3–6.6.
27 Law Commission, Corporate Criminal Liability: An Options Paper (2022), para 8.1.
28 Law Commission, Corporate Criminal Liability: An Options Paper (2022), para 8.1–8.17.
29 M. Meiselles, N. Ryder and A. Visconti (eds), *Corporate Criminal Liability and Sanctions: Current Trends and Policy Changes* (Routledge: London, 2024).

Part One

Money Laundering

1 Open Banking in Australia

Anti-Money Laundering and Counter-Terrorism Financing Considerations

Doron Goldbarsht and Samuel Orchard

1 Introduction

'Open banking' is an emerging financial services model which has been touted as a watershed moment for consumers in the fight against the profiteering of banks via the exploitation of customer data.[1] Significant technological advancements in data collection, processing and analytics have resulted in the financial sector becoming increasingly reliant on customer data as a critical resource to the products and services it offers.[2] Whilst without precise legislative definition,[3] the term 'open banking' refers to the implementation of a regulatory system focusing on the portability and open availability of customer data held by financial institutions,[4] placing ownership and control of an individual's transaction and account data in their hands. The potential benefits of open banking have been recognised globally and have resulted in the implementation of pioneering regulatory regimes across Australia, the United Kingdom, the European Economic Area, Canada, the United States, Brazil, Chile and India. Under an open banking model, customers are empowered by the ability to authorise the efficient transferral of their account and transaction information between financial institutions and authorised third-party service providers (TPPs), for the purpose of achieving beneficial financial outcomes. The process of data transferral is facilitated via application programming interfaces (APIs) that allow software applications to communicate via a common language, enabling the secure transferral of customer data across providers without an intermediary.[5]

Open banking has gained significant attention globally, from legislators and academics alike, reflecting an industry-wide recognition that financial innovation benefits the economy[6] and an individual's banking data is a valuable commodity rightfully owned and controlled by the customer, rather than an existing data holder (such as a bank).[7] Customer banking data is able to provide significant insight into the financial affairs of customers, such as their spending habits, financial management practices and how they use financial services; such data can then be leveraged by the bank to enhance the personalisation of financial services by means of improved data analytics.[8] The sharing of customer banking data has been touted as a 'public good',[9] as individual customers ought to be able to reap the benefits of their data by having it shared in a manner most beneficial to themselves. In doing so, open banking seeks to challenge the 'bottleneck' problem inherent in the traditional opacity of financial and transaction data, owned and essentially 'locked in' by large banks with which customers have existing relationships.[10] Open banking fosters increased openness, inclusion and transparency by empowering nimble entrants into the market, such as FinTechs,[11] as it allows for both the cohesion of previously separated products and services into innovative new offerings as well as

DOI: 10.4324/9781003324843-3

the deconstruction of traditionally bundled banking products into specific and severable services and functionalities.[12] The increased saturation of financial service providers and the fragmentation of financial markets have transformed the competitive landscape and fundamentally changed the character and structure of business models through the introduction of new sources of value creation.[13] However, as consumers rely on an increasing number of financial service providers to facilitate their everyday financial activities, there is a corresponding reduction in the level of oversight such entities are afforded. Furthermore, inherent in the increase in competition which has emerged in response to the new opportunities for value creation made available in an open banking model is an increase in the number of entities responsible for maintaining appropriate anti-money laundering and counter-terrorism financing (AML/CTF) protections. Accordingly, consideration needs to be given to the appropriate legislative requirements imposed upon such organisations in order to ensure that the benefits presented by open banking are balanced against any increased AML/CTF risks.

Research into open banking has typically been analysed through either a regulatory, technical or managerial lens, focusing on the legislation supporting open banking as well as the rationale and strategic implications from the regulators' and financial services providers' perspective,[14] the underlying infrastructure and technical implementation issues and, more recently, structural changes in the demand and supply of financial services in the retail banking market and consumer perspectives.[15] Academic and regulatory criticism of Australia's open banking regime has focused on issues concerning competition,[16] data privacy,[17] access, security and portability.[18] This chapter aims to extend previous discussion[19] into the AML/CTF risks posed by open banking to Australia's financial services ecosystem by illuminating how the increased distribution of customer data and diffusion of oversight, as a product of open banking, may undermine the fundamental tenants of AML/CTF, namely, customer due diligence (CDD) and know your customer (KYC) protocols.

The structure of this chapter is as follows. Section 2 outlines the implementation of open banking across the Australian market. Section 3 highlights the money laundering and terrorism financing (ML/TF) risks posed by open banking. Section 4 sets out Australia's current AML/CTF regime that relates to open banking. Section 5 concludes by demonstrating several implications of open banking for risk assessments conducted by internal AML/CTF compliance specialists in the banking market.

2 Introduction of Open Banking to the Australian Market

A generalised definition of open banking was articulated by Briones de Araluze and Cassinello Plaza as 'a generally regulated framework that enables banking consumers to share their data with third parties, commonly through standardised interfaces such as APIs, to increase competition in the financial sector'.[20] In Australia, Farrell summarised the purpose of open banking as 'giving customers the ability to instruct that their banking data be securely shared with parties they trust to unlock the value in that data'.[21] In this sense, open banking comprises three elements: first, consumers are granted greater access to and control over their banking data; second, banks are required to share product and consumer data with their customers; and finally, consumers are able to request that their bank shares their product and customer data with accredited third parties.

2.1 Open Banking in Australia

Open banking was introduced in Australia as part of an economy-wide recognition as to the necessity for consumers to obtain value from their data, increase customer control and to encourage innovation and competition in the banking ecosystem, as the first step in standardising the sharing of data and services across sectors.[22] In 2019, the Australian Government implemented a mandatory framework for data sharing through the introduction of the Consumer Data Right (CDR).[23] This mandatory regime necessitates that banks and TPPs who collect or receive data under the regime must share their independently collected data, regardless of their size or bank status.[24] Further, due to the single legislative structure, customers in Australia are able to share their data across sector boundaries and are not 'siloed' in a particular sector.[25] However, under the CDR, the transferral of data requires the explicit consent of the customer, limiting the use of such data to activities in accordance with such consent.[26]

The right to transfer data applies to 'CDR data' as defined in the *Competition and Consumer Act*,[27] and includes consumer, transaction and product data. Relevantly, the term 'product' is broad and encompasses goods and services offered or supplied in connection with taking money on deposit, making advances of money or other financial activities included in the definition of 'banking business' in the *Banking Act 1959* (Cth).[28]

In September 2022, the Commonwealth Department of Treasury proposed to expand the CDR to enable third-party action initiation (TPAI).[29] TPAI requires existing data holders to perform actions, including making payments or closing an account, in accordance with valid instructions received from third-party accredited action initiators as if they came directly from a customer.[30] The draft legislation seeks to establish 'Accredited Action Initiators' (AAIs), authorised to instruct Action Service Providers (ASPs) to carry out actions on behalf of a customer and ASPs, required to act on valid instructions received from AAIs. The Treasury flagged that whilst AAIs and ASPs may be protected from liability in certain circumstances, such would not extend to breaches of the AML/CTF Act.[31] In addition, the introduction of TPAI will not prevent existing data holders from applying security or other (presumably, CDD) checks, insofar as existing laws and practices that govern the performance of actions are intended to continue unaffected.[32]

3 Money Laundering and Terrorism Financing Risks in Open Banking

Whilst the ML/TF risks associated with providing customer data through APIs under Australia's open banking regime would appear to be low, regulatory challenges can arise when considering correspondent banking relationships and open banking broadly, including by reason of the significant economic pressure placed upon market entrants to offer streamlined onboarding services to customers and the reduction of oversight each institution is able to have over its customers' financial behaviour.

Open banking and TPAI were introduced to create efficiencies and enable the banking industry to reduce some of the costs associated with conducting CDD and fulfilling AML/CTF obligations and, in this sense, must be viewed in the economic context in which it operates.[33] The elimination of switching costs removes a powerful disincentive to customers utilising a range of service providers for their discrete financial activities. For example, under an open banking model, customers are more likely to separate their investing and share trading activities from their portfolio, dividend and capital gains tax tracking, to receive the most streamlined and informative service for each activity. Accordingly, as incumbent firms increasingly compete with nimble entrants for market share, there is likely to be increased pressure on identification data to be collected, analysed and verified within a shorter period of time. However, implicit in the desire for firms to streamline their onboarding process in order to attract and retain customers is a corresponding risk of the reduction of their AML/CTF obligations, such as conducting appropriate CDD and sanctions checks. In addition, as recent market entrants may lack a physical presence, such as a local branch, customer identity verification is, in such circumstances, typically achieved by requiring customers to upload photographs of their identification documents, resulting in an increased separation between customer and service provider. Accordingly, an increase in market pressure to streamline onboarding processes may result in weakened customer identification procedures, which are a fundamental tenant of Australia's AML/CTF legislative regime.

The reduced ability of reporting entities to effectively conduct CDD may become exacerbated by the reduction or dilution of oversight a single institution has over the banking activities, transaction history and financial relationships of its customers. The ability of a bank to understand the business relationship between itself and its client base is a core tenant of the risk-based model promulgated by the Financial Action Task Force and may be undermined by the increased complexity of end-to-end processing chains involved in open banking.[34] As customers utilise an increasing number of independent providers for their financial services, exacerbated through the introduction of TPAI and the effective elimination of switching costs for customers, banks, once the primary method of regulatory control and identification of money laundering and terrorism financing activity in the Australian financial market,[35] will have minimal observation of the financial activities of its customers. In this sense, savvy criminals may be able to refuse consent for the transferral of their data, rendering new banking providers essentially blind to prior suspicious transaction behaviour, and effectively undermining its ability to identify suspicious or unusual transaction behaviours of its customers with reference to their transaction history.

Accordingly, in order to maintain relevance in an ever-increasingly saturated market, banks will be forced to place significant reliance on the risk-management strategies employed by third parties, such as FinTechs. Such entities cannot be expected to have implemented sophisticated customer identification verification or transaction monitoring protocols comparable to those in place at major financial services providers. However, customer banking behaviours will increasingly take place via AAIs and ASPs, necessitating that market participants enter into complex webs of correspondent banking relationships and, accordingly, undermining the comprehensiveness of CDD procedures in favour of a desire for ease of customer onboarding.

Correspondent banking relationships facilitated via the authorised transferral of customer data through an ASP would likely involve two layers of separation between an incumbent service provider and customer. For example, the process of opening a bank account with a new service provider would involve the customer holding an existing account with a bank (Bank A or the data holder), opened via engrossing an online application form and providing a photo of a driver's licence or other identity document, lacking any form of in-person or verbal interaction. The customer would then request the data holder to provide their customer and financial data to a third-party provider, such as a product that compares interest rates between various high-interest long-term bank accounts offered by several banks (the accredited data recipient). The customer would then authorise an AAI to open an account with a bank that best matches their financial circumstances (Bank B) utilising the data obtained from Bank A and facilitate the transferral of their assets from Bank A to Bank B. Clearly, both Bank A and Bank B provide designated services and accordingly are subject to the CDD requirements contained in the AML/CTF Act. However, in this instance, Bank B would be able to rely on the CDD procedures conducted by Bank A, in circumstances where they do not have access to the customer's transaction history or having independently verified the customer's identification documents, provided that Bank A and Bank B have entered into a CDD arrangement. In these circumstances, Bank B would be operating effectively blind to the purpose and nature of a future transaction in the context of the customer's transaction history or banking relationships.

The ability of Bank B to undertake a risk-based appraisal of the ML/TF risks presented by such a transaction is fundamentally undermined by the considerable separation imposed between the reporting entity and customer by the mandatory open banking regime and introduction of TPAI. As the banking market continues to be saturated with new entrants, reporting entities will be forced to become increasingly reliant on correspondent banking relationships to maintain compliance with their CDD obligations and remain competitive. Reporting entities entering into several correspondent banking relationships, including foreign entities subject to varying degrees of AML/CTF regulatory protections, are required to be satisfied that each respondent entity continues to maintain an appropriate risk-based system to mitigate ML/TF risks. Consistent comprehension of the measures implemented by several correspondent institutions to mitigate their own unique money laundering risks is unsustainable in a market which is increasingly rewarding of streamlined onboarding processes. Accordingly, given the significant financial benefits involved in entering into several correspondent banking arrangements, particularly in circumstances where open banking and TPAI are expected to significantly increase the flow of data between banks and the transferral of customer accounts, questions remain as to whether weakening CDD requirements is an appropriate step in protecting Australia's banking ecosystem against ML/TF exploitation.

Whilst the oversight a single institution has over the banking history of a single customer is reduced, the total amount of transaction data required to be analysed will dramatically increase. CDD and transaction monitoring require substantial ongoing financial investment to facilitate, first, the purchase and/or development of sophisticated technology to facilitate the onboarding process and analyse the substantial amount of transaction data and, second, human 'second line' review of machine-collated data flagged as suspicious. By mandating open banking and dramatically reducing the switching costs through TPAI, potential entrants to the banking market may be locked out by the significant AML/CTF compliance requirements in order to avoid facing substantial financial penalties for non-compliance.

4 AML/CTF Regime in Australia: Recommendations

Australia's AML/CTF regime is set out within the *Anti-Money Laundering and Counter-Terrorism Financing Act 2006* (Cth) (AML/CTF Act) and the *Anti-Money Laundering and Counter-Terrorism Financing Rules Instrument 2007 (No. 1)* (Cth),[36] and is centred around the requirement for regulated businesses who provide 'designated services', known as reporting entities, to establish, implement and maintain an AML/CTF compliance programme before providing a designated service to a customer. Such programmes must reflect the specific risk profile of the business and must include ongoing CDD processes in order to verify the identification of customers in accordance with KYC obligations. CDD is an integral part of combating ML/TF and, depending on the level and sophistication of the risks faced by the organisation, requires the collection and verification of all relevant customer information in order to ensure the customer is who they claim to be, as well as to understand the nature and purpose of the customer's business on an ongoing basis, known as KYC. A reporting entity is prohibited from providing a designated service if customer identification procedures cannot be performed, except in specific circumstances. Reporting entities are required to conduct ongoing CDD to ensure information collected about a customer or beneficial owner is accurate and up to date and to determine whether extra CDD information should be collected and verified. In the context of open banking, financial services providers must be required to maintain a robust process of customer identification verification and, where appropriate, undertake additional steps to ascertain the identity of their customers via a risk-based appraisal of their correspondent banking relationships.

The decision to undertake enhanced CDD (ECDD) is to be made according to a risk-based approach. The risk-based approach necessitates consideration of the risk profile of the entity and the purpose of its business relationship with its customers. Reporting entities must consider the specific type of ML/TF risks they might reasonably face, the source of individual customer wealth and the manner in which they provide the services they do. In circumstances where there is an identifiably higher risk of ML/TF activity occurring, the entity is required to collect and verify more information to ensure they are reasonably satisfied that their customers are who they claim to be and that they are effectively managing their ML/TF risk. As such, firms must also ensure adequate processes are implemented to properly manage and incorporate their correspondent banking relationships into their risk-based assessments.

The *Anti-Money Laundering and Counter-Terrorism Financing and Other Legislation Amendment Act 2020* (Cth) (the Amendment Act) expanded the circumstances under the AML/CTF Act in which reporting entities can rely on another party's CDD procedures.[37] The Amendment Act allows reporting entities to rely on CDD performed by another reporting entity subject to a written agreement or arrangement (CDD arrangement) and affords reliant parties a safe harbour from liability from relevant breaches of the AML/CTF Act.[38] Where a reporting entity has reasonable grounds to believe that each of the AML/CTF requirements has been satisfied by the correspondent party at the time of entering into the agreement, it can rely on applicable CDD procedures carried out by them.[39] The reporting entity must regularly assess the agreement and terminate it if there are no reasonable grounds to believe that each of the relevant requirements is being applied.[40] Importantly, a reporting entity will generally have reasonable grounds to believe that the relevant requirements are being met where they have previously reached this conclusion and they are not aware of any circumstances that could bring this conclusion into significant doubt, such as the detection of a significant breach, relevant adverse media or inadequate communication. The existence of safe harbour provisions arguably weakens the regulatory protections afforded by the Amendment Act and may incentivise a reduced critical appraisal of one's business partners in order to maintain profitable relationships.

Reporting entities are also required to conduct transaction monitoring in order to detect suspicious matters that must be reported to Australia's financial intelligence unit, the Australian Transaction Reports and Analysis Centre (AUSTRAC).[41] Transactions may be designated as suspicious if they originate from illegal activities, are unusually large or have no lawful explanation. Analysis of customer and transaction data typically takes into account the purpose for which the account has been opened and used, the source of funds, location of the account holder and the risks associated with the products and services the customer generally uses. Thus, in order to effectively mitigate against ML/TF risks, a bank is expected to have complete knowledge about a client's business purposes, present and anticipated activities and destination of money transacted to ensure that the institution is not facilitating any suspicious activities.

The AML/CTF Act imposes significant requirements upon reporting entities to disclose confidential information to AUSTRAC whilst prohibiting disclosure of the fact that a reporting entity has given, or is required to give, a report to the client and, accordingly, eliminating the requirement for customer consent.[42] There has been academic discussion as to the extent to which the principles of open banking are inconsistent with the reporting obligations imposed upon designated entities and whether flagging suspicious activities to a customer would infringe the 'tipping off' offence.[43] Whilst the Attorney General has indicated the potential amendment of the tipping-off offence to provide greater flexibility in meeting the challenges of new business models and risk-management approaches to financial crime, such is outside the scope of this chapter.

5 Conclusion

Mandatory reporting and compliance obligations under the AML/CTF Act are likely to impose significant burdens on new entrants to the financial services market as they attempt to provide innovative offerings at a competitive price point. The benefits of an open banking system must be balanced against the necessity for a robust AML/CTF enforcement mechanism. The increased portability of customer data, in combination with the introduction of TPAI, is likely to dramatically reduce the switching costs for banking customers. As customers switch frequently between providers in search of the most beneficial financial outcome, those responsible for imposing AML/CTF measures must avoid regarding compliance as a mere tick-box exercise and ensure that adequate appraisal is given to the novel risks across the banking ecosystem posed by open banking and TPAI.[44] Clearly, increased separation between service provider and customer, or a lack of visibility as to a customer's transaction history, is a relevant consideration when conducting a risk-based appraisal. Accordingly, the desire to increase the development of the market for alternate banking products in pursuit of increased customer financial wellbeing must not overtake the necessity to maintain a high level of AML/CTF compliance across the banking sector.

Acknowledgement

We gratefully acknowledge the support of the Financial Integrity Hub at Macquarie Law School in New South Wales, Australia for partly funding this research.

Notes

1 Ruben Sandino Kremers, "Hack/Make the Bank': The Everyday Politics of Fintech' (Ph.D. Thesis, University of Warwick, 2021).

2 Christoph Frei, 'Open Banking: Opportunities and Risks', in Thomas Walker, Elaheh Nikbakht and Maher Hooli (eds), *The Fintech Disruption: How Financial Innovation is Transforming the Banking Industry* (Springer Nature, 2023) 167–189; Ross Buckley, Natalia Jevglevskaja and Scott Farrell, 'Australia's Data-Sharing Regime: Six Lessons for the World' (2022) 33(1) *King's Law Journal* 61.

3 See Competition and Consumer (Consumer Data Right) Rules 2020 (Cth) (AUS); Competition and Consumer Act 2010 (Cth) (AUS).

4 Emma Leong, 'Open Banking: The Changing Nature of Regulating Banking Data-A Case Study of Australia and Singapore' (2020) 35(3) *Banking & Finance Law Review* 443; Ana Badour

and Dominic Presta, 'Open Banking: Canadian and International Developments' (2018) 34(1) *Banking & Finance Law Review* 41.

5 Natalia Jevglevskaja and Ross Buckley, 'A World-Leading Sanitation System for Our Digital Economy: The Consumer Data Right' (2023) *UNSW Law Research Paper*, 9, https://papers.ssrn.com/sol3/papers.cfm?abstract_id=4505135.

6 Doron Goldbarsht and Louis de Koker, 'From Paper Money to Digital Assets: Financial Technology and the Risks of Criminal Abuse', in D. Goldbarsht and L. de Koker (eds), *Financial Technology and the Law: Law, Governance and Technology Series* (vol. 47, Springer, 2022) 7.

7 Oscar Borgogno and Giuseppe Colangelo, 'Consumer Inertia and Competition-Sensitive Data Governance: The Case of Open Banking' (2020) 9 *Journal of European Consumer and Market Law* 143, 150.

8 Doron Goldbarsht, Baskaran Balasingham and Jeremy Moller, 'Open Banking in Australia: Competition and Money Laundering, Risks and Benefits' (2021) 32(2) *Journal of Banking and Finance Law and Practice* 59, 60; Daniel Gozman, Jonas Hedman and Kasper Sylvest, 'Open Banking: Emergent Roles, Risks & Opportunities' (26th European Conference on Information Systems, University of Portsmouth, 2018), https://research.cbs.dk/en/publications/open-banking-emergent-roles-risks-amp-opportunities.

9 David Kreps, *A Course in Microeconomic Theory* (Princeton University Press, 2020) 168.

10 Scott Farrell, 'Designing Data Rights for Canadian Open Banking: Lessons from Banking Law in Australia and the United Kingdom' (2022) 85 *Saskatchewan Law Review* 165, 166; Leong (n 6) 443–444.

11 Wendy Currie, Daniel Gozman and Jonathan Seddon, 'Calculative Tensions in the Pre-and Post-Crisis Financial Markets: A Longitudinal Study of Regulatory Technology' (2018) 33(4) *Journal of Information Technology* 304; Gozman, Hedman and Sylvest (n 10).

12 Borgogno and Colangelo (n 9) 150; Ariadne Plaitakis and Stefan Staschen, 'Open Banking: How to Design for Financial Inclusion' (2020) Consultative Group to Assist the Poor (CGAP) Working Paper, 8, https://documents1.worldbank.org/curated/en/351881625136775280/pdf/Open-Banking-How-to-Design-for-Financial-Inclusion.pdf.

13 Wendy Currie and Thomas Lagoarde-Segot, 'Financialization and Information Technology: Themes, Issues and Critical Debates-Part I' (2017) 32(3) *Journal of Information Technology* 211, 214.

14 Sophie Guibaud, 'How to Develop a Profitable, Customer-Focused Digital Banking Strategy: Open Banking Services and Developer-Friendly APIs' (2016) 1(1) *Journal of Digital Banking* 6; Svetlana Krivoruchko and Valerii Lopatin, 'The Impact of the Open Banking Implementation on the Development of the National FinTech Sector'
(2018) 11(6) *Economics Taxes & Law* 80; Yvon Moysan and Margaux Rudnicki, 'Open Banking: Towards Platform and Modular Banking' (2019) 4(2) *Journal of Digital Banking* 131; Boumediene Ramdani, Ben Rothwell and Elias Boukrami, 'Open Banking: The Emergence of New Digital Business Models' (2020) 17(5) *International Journal of Innovation and Technology Management* 2050033.

15 Gorka Koldobika Briones de Araluze and Cassinello Plaza, 'Open Banking: A Bibliometric Analysis-Driven Definition' (2022) 17(1) *PloS One* 3.

16 See Goldbarsht, Balasingham and Moller (n 10); Suman Podder, 'Australian Open Banking: The Regulatory Dilemma of Balancing Different Policy Objectives' (2021) 29(1) *Australian Journal of Competition and Consumer Law* 15.

17 See Jevglevskaja and Buckley (n 7).

18 See Farrell (n 12).

19 See Goldbarsht, Balasingham and Moller (n 10); Suman Podder, 'Leveraging the Provisions of Open Banking to Fight Financial Crime', in Doron Goldbarsht and Louis de Koker (eds), *Financial Technology and the Law Combating Financial Crime* (Law, Governance and Technology Series, vol. 47, Springer, 2022) 19–46.

20 Briones de Araluze and Plaza (n 17) 13.

21 Commonwealth Department of Treasury, 'Review into Open Banking in Australia – Final Report' (2017) 8.

22 Goldbarsht, Balasingham and Moller (n 10); see Commonwealth Department of Treasury (n 23).

23 Treasury Laws Amendment (Consumer Data Right) Act 2019 (Cth) (AUS) which was applied to the banking sector under the Consumer Data Right (Authorised Deposit Taking Institutions) Designation 2019 (Cth) (AUS).

24 Competition and Consumer (Consumer Data Right) Rules 2020 (Cth) Sch 3 (AUS).
25 Bertin Martens, 'JRC Technical Report: An Economic Perspective on Data and Platform Market Power' (10 February 2021) JRC Digital Economy Working Paper No. 2020-09, 7, https://papers.ssrn.com/sol3/papers.cfm?abstract_id=3783297.
26 Podder (n 21) 21.
27 Competition and Consumer Act 2010 (Cth) s 56AI (AUS).
28 Banking Act 1959 (Cth) s 4(2) (AUS).
29 Australian Department of Treasury, 'Consumer Data Right – Exposure Draft Legislation to Enable Action Initiation' (September 2022).
30 Australian Department of Treasury (n 31) 3.
31 Australian Department of Treasury (n 31) 7.
32 Australian Department of Treasury (n 31).
33 Explanatory Memorandum to the Anti-Money Laundering and Counter-Terrorism Financing Amendment Bill 2024, para 14.
34 Deloitte, 'How to Flourish in an Uncertain Future-Open Banking' (20 June 2017), https://www2.deloitte.com/content/dam/Deloitte/global/Documents/Financial-Services/gx-fsi-open-banking-florish-uncertain-future.pdf.
35 Podder (n 21) 20.
36 Anti-Money Laundering and Counter-Terrorism Financing Act 2006 (Cth) (AML/CTF Act); Anti-Money Laundering and Counter-Terrorism Financing Rules Instrument 2007 (No. 1) (Cth) (AUS).
37 Anti-Money Laundering and Counter-Terrorism Financing and Other Legislation Amendment Act 2020 (Cth) (AUS).
38 AML/CTF Act s 37A, 38.
39 AML/CTF Act s 37A.
40 AML/CTF Act s 37B.
41 AML/CTF Act s 41(2)
42 Disclosure by a reporting entity to a customer that the entity has given, or is required to give a report under section 41, 43 or 45 of the AML/CTF Act would constitute a breach of s 123 of the AML/CTF Act and an offence under s 124(11) of the AML/CTF Act.
43 See Goldbarsht, Balasingham and Moller (n 10); Podder (n 21).
44 Podder (n 18).

Bibliography

Arun, T, and others, 'The evolution and current state of open banking in India and UK' (August 2024) Policy Paper 4 – UK India Trust in Fintech & Fintech-Enabled Services, https://papers.ssrn.com/sol3/papers.cfm?abstract_id=4924965.

Australian Department of Treasury, 'Consumer Data Right – Exposure draft legislation to enable action initiation' (September 2022).

Badour, A, and Presta, D, 'Open banking: Canadian and international developments' (2018) 34(1) *Banking & Finance Law Review* 41.

Borgogno, O, and Colangelo, G, 'Consumer inertia and competition-sensitive data governance: The case of open banking' (2020) 9 *Journal of European Consumer and Market Law* 143.

Briones de Araluze, GK, and Cassinello Plaza, N, 'Open banking: A bibliometric analysis-driven definition' (2022) 17(1) *PloS One* 1–19.

Buckley, R, Jevglevskaja, N, and Farrell, S, 'Australia's data-sharing regime: Six lessons for the world' King's Law Journal' (2022) 33(1) *Kings Law Journal* 61.

Commonwealth Department of Treasury, 'Review into open banking in Australia – Final report' (2017).

Currie, W, Gozman, D, and Seddon, J, 'Calculative tensions in the pre-and post-crisis financial markets: A longitudinal study of regulatory technology' (2018) 33(4) *Journal of Information Technology* 304.

Currie, W, and Lagoarde-Segot, T, 'Financialization and information technology: Themes, issues and critical debates-part I' (2017) 32(3) *Journal of Information Technology* 211.

Deloitte, 'How to flourish in an uncertain future-open banking' (20 June 2017), https://www2.deloitte.com/content/dam/Deloitte/global/Documents/Financial-Services/gx-fsi-open-banking-florish-uncertain-future.pdf.

De Pascalis, F, and Brener, A, *Open Banking: Global Development and Regulation* (Taylor & Francis, 2024).

Farrell, S, 'Designing data rights for Canadian open banking: Lessons from banking law in Australia and the United Kingdom' (2022) 85 *Saskatchewan Law Review* 165.

Frei, C, 'Open banking: Opportunities and risks', in T Walker, E Nikbakht, and M Hooli (eds), *The Fintech Disruption: How Financial Innovation is Transforming the Banking Industry* (Springer Nature, 2023) 167–189.

Goldbarsht, D, Balasingham, B, and Moller, J, 'Open banking in Australia: Competition and money laundering, risks and benefits' (2021) 32(2) *Journal of Banking and Finance Law and Practice* 59.

Goldbarsht, D, and de Koker, L, 'From paper money to digital assets: Financial technology and the risks of criminal abuse', in D Goldbarsht, and L de Koker (eds), *Financial Technology and the Law* (Law, Governance and Technology Series, vol. 47, Springer, 2022) 1–15.

Gounari, M, and others, 'Harmonizing open banking in the European Union: An analysis of PSD2 compliance and interrelation with cybersecurity frameworks and standards' (2023) 5 *International Cybersecurity Law Review* 79.

Gozman, D, Hedman, J, and Sylvest, K, 'Open banking: Emergent roles, risks & opportunities' (26th European Conference on Information Systems, University of Portsmouth, 2018), https://research.cbs.dk/en/publications/open-banking-emergent-roles-risks-amp-opportunities.

Guibaud, S, 'How to develop a profitable, customer-focused digital banking strategy: Open banking services and developer-friendly APIs' (2016) 1(1) *Journal of Digital Banking* 6.

Jevglevskaja, N, and Buckley, R, 'A world-leading sanitation system for our digital economy: The consumer data right' (2023) *UNSW Law Research Paper*, 9, https://papers.ssrn.com/sol3/papers.cfm?abstract_id=4505135.

Kremers, RS, 'Hack/make the bank': The everyday politics of Fintech (Ph.D. thesis, University of Warwick 2021).

Kreps, DM, *A Course in Microeconomic Theory* (Princeton University Press, 2020).

Krivoruchko, S, and Lopatin, V, 'The impact of the open banking implementation on the development of the National FinTech Sector' (2018) 11(6) *Economics Taxes & Law* 80.

Leong, E, 'Open banking: The changing nature of regulating banking data - A case study of Australia and Singapore' (2020) 35(3) *Banking & Finance Law Review* 443.

Martens, B, 'JRC technical report: An economic perspective on data and platform market power' (10 February 2021) JRC Digital Economy Working Paper No. 2020-09, https://papers.ssrn.com/sol3/papers.cfm?abstract_id=3783297.

Moysan, Y, and Rudnicki, M, 'Open banking: Towards platform and modular banking' (2019) 4(2) *Journal of Digital Banking* 131.

Plaitakis, A, and Staschen, S, 'Open banking: How to design for financial inclusion' (2020) Consultative Group to Assist the Poor (CGAP) Working Paper, 8, https://documents1.worldbank.org/curated/en/351881625136775280/pdf/Open-Banking-How-to-Design-for-Financial-Inclusion.pdf.

Podder, S, 'Australian open banking: The regulatory dilemma of balancing different policy objectives' (2021) 29(1) *Australian Journal of Competition and Consumer Law* 15.

Podder, S, 'Leveraging the provisions of open banking to fight financial crime', in D Goldbarsht and L de Koker (eds), *Financial Technology and the Law Combating Financial Crime* (Law, Governance and Technology Series, vol. 47, Springer, 2022) 19–46.

Ramdani, B, Rothwell, B, and Boukrami, E, 'Open banking: The emergence of new digital business models' (2020) 17(5) *International Journal of Innovation and Technology Management* 2050033.

2 Money Laundering Challenges in the United Kingdom (UK)

Craig Hughes and David C. Hicks

1 Money Laundering Offences under UK Law

Within the UK, offences of money laundering are defined within the Proceeds of Crime Act 2002.[1] Its origins lie in the drug trafficking legislation of the late twentieth century as well as the recommendations issued from 1990 by an intergovernmental organisation that sets standards on money laundering and terrorist funding, the Financial Action Task Force (FATF).[2] Since 2002 in the UK, money laundering can be investigated and prosecuted as stand-alone offences (broadly defined to include criminal offences or regulatory offences) without being dependent on those underlying (or predicate) offences. The money laundering offences and the powers seem intended to be applied by generalist investigators and, apart from asset recovery, specialist knowledge is not required. Money laundering is not limited to cash or funds, but instead applies broadly to interactions with criminal property such as a house, boat, car as well as data in the emerging environment of digital device and internet criminality.

The extent of the money laundering problem in the UK lacks reliable empirical data.[3] Money laundering in London is estimated to be no less than £100 billion.[4] It is noted that[5]:

> Economic crime is a broad category of illegal activity, including fraud, corruption, money laundering, and tax evasion…The overall scale of economic crime [in the UK] is estimated to be £14.4 billion per year.

Estimates of the scale of the problem, whether as a total for money laundering in its generic form or scaled down to specific typologies of criminality, seem to be 'best guesses' and unsubstantiated,[6] a situation apparently unimproved upon over time.[7]

2 Challenges Posed by the UK's Approach to Money Laundering

As money laundering is consistently acknowledged as a significant criminal offence at governmental, strategic, tactical and practice levels[8] and a potential threat to national security (the weakening of UK financial architecture), several questions must be considered,[9] including whether: (a) existing powers are effectively and broadly utilised by UK law enforcement; (b) the standards of training available to investigators are fit-for-purpose (generalists and specialists); (c) detected money laundering offences are accurately recorded as offences; (d) offences are robustly prosecuted; and (e) governmental and policing policy drive the fight against the recognised money laundering problem.

DOI: 10.4324/9781003324843-4

This should also include consideration of regulatory measures currently in place to combat money laundering, their effectiveness and whether mandatory compliance elements such as suspicious activity reports (SARS), submitted by private sector businesses, are perceived as useful by law enforcement.[10] The digital environment presents new (and largely unregulated) money laundering opportunities for criminals and this chapter will consider the UK response to this emerging threat. Anticipated outcomes will often 'guide' the focus of investigations, thus uptake of money laundering prosecutions and the position of UK courts will be integral to enhancing efforts to tackle money laundering. That said, this does not (necessarily) inhibit law enforcement from utilising money laundering powers for all relevant investigations.

As a significant threat to financial architecture and national security,[11] it is odd that there is currently no central money laundering enforcement unit in the UK (one which solely targets the perceived problem such as the Serious Fraud Office targeting fraud). Stand-alone and pro-active money laundering investigations (where no other criminal offences are charged) seem not to be the preference of law enforcement or prosecutors.[12] The guidelines are unclear as to what innumerable methods will be considered and at what level due to the broad nature of UK legislative definitions. This chapter focuses on four key areas to help guide the reader: the practice level (how the legislation is used and by whom); proceeds of crime legislation; government policy and strategic level of law enforcement as the driver for applying money laundering powers and the integration of them within national and international parameters; and prosecution of money laundering offences.

2.1 Practice Level

Much has been written about money laundering, usually from the perspective of addressing serious and organised crime.[13] At the routine level of policing (in its wider sense), there appears to be a scarcity of research regarding the training of uniform and criminal investigation department (CID) investigators and the application of money laundering powers, who applies them and how effective is the prosecution of offences.

Little data appears to be available explaining how money laundering offences are recorded and how accurate the recording system might be. Scant data is available to help determine which offences merited a crime number and which did not (and why), at what point money laundering investigations commence, who conducts them, the number of reactive money laundering investigations stemming from so-called predicate offending (underlying criminality) and the number of pro-active money laundering investigations undertaken. There is a need to go beyond unpublished efforts,[14] to generate reliable published data (including decision-making rationales) on how many times money laundering offences are charged (or not charged), the reason for either and how many such offences attract some degree of plea bargain (or are discontinued) once inside the court prosecution framework.

Routine investigator (generalist) knowledge of money laundering and application of these powers is under-researched. Money laundering powers are not only the domain of accredited financial investigators (AFIs) (specialists), but these were also made available to all constables (generalists) and Her Majesty's Revenue and Customs (HMRC) under the 2002 Act. Other law enforcement agencies such as Trading Standards have access to the powers through subsequent legislative measures. How the powers have been applied since 2002 does not appear well recorded and a reliable picture of the money laundering threat remains absent.

2.2 *Proceeds of Crime Legislation (Money Laundering)*

Money laundering is defined broadly to include any criminal property, possessed, altered or concealed and the investigative powers can be applied to any criminal or regulatory offences. The lack of training offered and undertaken by baseline investigators is curious given the utility of money laundering powers. The UK government's drive to increase the number of police recruits does not have proceeds of crime legislation scheduled for the first two years of training in a police constable's career. There does not currently appear to be any training available to generalists (including detectives) which is specific to addressing the generally perceived money laundering threat or to distinguish between the different levels of it. Governmental recognition of this shortfall[15] has not been met with subsequent efforts to alter the basic training landscape.[16] Money laundering may well be perceived by generalists to be a complex and complicated area of investigation due to the lack of training exposure as well as the myth of specialisation.

Despite the legislation being intended for generalists to use, if supervisors submit to the specialist-only perception, then money laundering cannot become a routine avenue of investigation as it will not be considered in the tactical planning stages. Without consistent use at all levels across law enforcement it is difficult to understand how money laundering powers can assist the goal of crime reduction. Lack of knowledge and direction or reluctance from supervisors at the general investigation level, in addition to a requirement for better knowledge and direction from strategic managers may well prove to be two key inhibitors to more effective application of money laundering powers.

These points may begin to explain why the comprehensive array of (under-utilised) powers available under proceeds of crime legislation does not dissuade continued lobbying for more.[17] UK money laundering definitions apply to all property derived from criminal conduct,[18] essentially any conduct in the UK (or internationally) which constitutes an offence from which a benefit is acquired, directly or indirectly.[19] Money laundering powers, coupled with the advantage of civil recovery legislation which does not require a criminal conviction and is designed to target assets, should therefore be sufficient to deal with any criminal property generated in the UK as well as any funds entering the UK in suspicious or unclear circumstances. These existing powers did not prevent calls for more draconian measures in the form of an unexplained wealth order (UWO) as created under the Criminal Finances Act 2017. An UWO is a specialist tool available to the Serious Fraud Office, HMRC, National Crime Agency (NCA), Financial Conduct Authority (FCA) and the Crown Prosecution Service (CPS) if the asset value under investigation is £50,000 or more and there is reasonable suspicion that the property directly or indirectly originated from criminality. A UWO produces evidence for civil (not criminal) proceedings to lead to forfeiture of assets unexplained by legal and transparent audit trails, which have been applied to both suspicious foreign investment as well as serious crime suspects.[20]

2.3 *Policy*

Calls for new powers do not necessarily originate in the halls of government; policies are sometimes shaped by outside commentators with no direct investigation responsibilities but whose views are considered by policymakers and legislators. In the case of money laundering, particularly the problem of funds from outside the UK being invested in the London property market, involvement of independent agencies such as Transparency International

(TI-UK) may have influenced government thinking.[21] A case seems to have been made for UWOs as a civil asset recovery tool based upon an analysis of suspicious activity reports (information mandatorily supplied to the NCA under anti-money laundering regulations) concerning what TI-UK termed grand corruption.[22] It is a term regularly used internationally but in the UK, bribery and corruption are the offences within the Bribery Act 2010. Such reports contributed to a cross-party government effort to tackle corruption in the UK, specifically the commission of bribery nationally and internationally and the abuse of positions by individuals to create benefits for themselves. It is unclear whether money laundering and civil recovery powers from 2002 have been effectively applied and prosecuted to deal with corruption. Indeed, UWOs have only been used in a handful of cases which raises questions about continuing calls for further (and more draconian) powers.

Terms such as money laundering and terrorism financing do not seem helpful in clarifying what exactly is being discussed. It is interesting that three strategic priorities in addressing money laundering were identified at governmental level in the year preceding the introduction of UWOs.[23] First, it was argued that law enforcement needs a more robust (aggressive powers and capabilities) approach to money laundering. Second, that the supervisory regime requires reform to target facilitators and enablers. Third, that the international reach of the UK required extending regarding foreign funds entering the UK. Further, it is noted that to accomplish these three objectives depends on the 'efforts of law enforcement and prosecutorial agencies…'.[24] The objectives are underpinned by other UK national strategies[25] but the lack of clarity on routine (generalist and specialist) application of money laundering powers persists alongside the generalised absence of training and a 'best guess' approach to empirical data.[26]

Any attempt to reform the existing company supervisory regime presumably must address SARs and the over-burden resulting from UK and international anti-money laundering regulations.[27] Submissions from the financial sector have increased from 15,000 (in 2000) to over 640,000 (in 2020).[28] SARs are issued by businesses within what is termed the regulated sector including banks, solicitors, estate agents, casinos and many more. The lack of clarity on what is deemed suspicious may explain why SARs vary in length, detail and quality of information.[29] SARs are submitted to the UK Financial Investigation Unit (UKFIU), embedded within the NCA and then made available to relevant law enforcement agencies. A SAR is deleted if there is confirmation of no suspicious activity or if it has existed for six years, which still leaves 2.25 million reports available to law enforcement.[30]

Any assumption that SARs are only available to members of a law enforcement agency's financial investigation unit[31] seems misleading. SARs are recognised as a valuable intelligence resource for routine policing (containing dates of birth, names, addresses, telephone numbers as well as more obvious data such as bank accounts and transaction details).[32] Generalist investigators can access the information in a SAR (despite it being treated as sensitive material) by approaching an intelligence office or a financial investigation unit. There is evidence to indicate that generalists know very little about SARs and their potential for investigations.[33] Any assumption at strategic or government level that SARs are routinely used may be an unreliable one (raising the issue of training again) and a key area for more research.

The potential for SARs to be effective against so-called cybercrime (expansion of criminality using digital pathways) remains unknown, the digital theatre only recently being included under the anti-money laundering regulations by way of European directive (Directive (EU) 2018/843).[34] There appears to be no clear understanding of how the digital environment facilitates money laundering, nor any reliable information concerning the potential profiles of individuals likely to take advantage of it.[35] Cryptocurrencies and cryptoassets seem to be considered by law enforcement as a serious emerging threat. This directive brings cryptoexchanges dealing with cryptocurrencies and assets into line with other financial transactions and will require the issue of a suspicious activity report if illicit investments are suspected. If digital pathways are more frequently used by criminals or their sophisticated internet enablers, national policy should be questioning how policy should drive money laundering application at strategic, tactical and practice levels. The scarcity of empirical data on these matters suggests they are immediate areas for research to inform and drive such policy and effect the change towards robustness that the government requires.[36]

2.4 *Prosecution of Money Laundering*

This chapter advocates that money laundering investigations can only be effective if an integrated approach is taken by all agencies concerned and including support for the prosecution of offences. There is some evidence that money laundering offences have faced inhibitors within the prosecution and court system environments.[37] Previous research has highlighted a degree of reluctance on the part of the CPS to charge offenders with money laundering offences if other offences were already clearly identified.[38] A 'marked reluctance (or lack of understanding)' was identified by investigators in the pursuit of money laundering offences by the CPS as "stand-alone" cases.[39] This could originate from the CPS policy concerning money laundering, one which seems to have been consistent for the last decade.[40] Despite the legislative intent for routine (generalist and specialist) use of money laundering powers, CPS policy and practice is an inhibitor. According to the CPS, money laundering should only be considered as an additional charge for significant attempts to transfer or conceal proceeds of crime.[41] Where an offender has laundered his own proceeds, the advice is that the court may consider a consecutive sentence where there are significant efforts to conceal the proceeds of crime. It appears that money laundering offences considered by a CPS lawyer to be less than "significant" will not be charged, irrespective of whether law enforcement apply a robust approach per government policy.[42]

There appears to be a lack of research which provides reliable empirical data for the use of money laundering powers and the prosecution of them across law enforcement (not just in policing) at all levels (strategic, tactical and practice). Although proper that prosecutors retain impartiality as evidential reviewers, there does appear to be need for a step change in the behaviours of all agencies and a more cohesive approach to the money laundering problem. Whether money laundering offences are considered by law enforcement at the strategic and tactical level, or an unwillingness to use the powers, a lack of money laundering training at all levels, the reluctance to prosecute or antipathy by the courts, the consistent theme is a lack of reliable empirical data concerning such matters.[43]

In the absence of law enforcement and prosecutors developing an integrated approach, it is difficult to see how the UK can enhance its domestic or international reach.[44] The intention to do so seems clear particularly in respect of serious and organised crime and under the auspices of the NCA.[45] Multiple pledges are made including, attempting to influence citizens of countries which feed crime syndicates in the UK and which create illicit financial flows in and out of its borders. Success will be measured[46]:

> through baseline assessments of the current situation and ongoing evaluation, using both quantitative measures (including disruptions data, and independent third-party indices) and qualitative assessments.

Whether current UK policy can address international money laundering issues within the digital environment (cyber) seems to be unknown and elusive. Financial investigation skills do not seem embedded in traditional law enforcement investigations[47] and there is evidence suggesting that money laundering applied to the digital environment is perceived as complex, time-consuming and the remit of specialist financial investigators.[48]

3 Conclusion

This chapter provided a discussion of money laundering as it currently appears to be applied at all levels of UK law enforcement, how it is perceived and prosecuted and whether government policy translates into effective practice and measurable outcomes in traditional (real-world) or digital environments (internet). Consideration was given to current anti-money laundering measures such as SARs and whether existing legislation and investigative techniques can be used to penetrate the increasing threat from the digital environment and result in real-world outcomes (interventions, arrests and prosecutions). Efforts against serious and organised criminality may be one area of good practice, but in general terms this chapter must endorse the observation that the UK approach to money laundering at all levels appears to remain incohesive.[49] Policy, investigation and prosecution do not appear to exert efforts in the same direction and the intention that money laundering powers be routinely used appears usurped by legal practice advice. Lack of clarity regarding the number of money laundering offences investigated, charged, prosecuted or discarded is not helpful in understanding the nature of money laundering practice at all levels of law enforcement, nor is the position helped by limited (if any) training in proceeds of crime legislation at routine level.[50] International policies are in place[51] but their translation into UK investigation and prosecution results remains opaque. The real challenge identified by all of these points is how to provide reliable empirical data to ensure that policy drives practice and practice is able to robustly address money laundering in all its forms from investigation and prosecution perspectives within traditional and digital environments.[52]

Notes

1 Proceeds of Crime Act 2002, c. 29. London: The Stationery Office.
2 Financial Action Task Force (FATF), *2021 FATF Standards*. Available at: https://www.fatf-gafi.org/home/.
3 E Fell, J Owen, H Dienes, N Shah, and J Grimshaw, *Understanding Organised Crime 2015/16: Estimating the Scale and the Social and Economic Costs* (2nd edn, Home Office 2019). Available at: https://assets.publishing.service.gov.uk/government/uploads/system/uploads/attachment_data/file/782656/understanding-organised-crime-mar16-horr103-2nd.pdf, accessed 09 October 2023; Law Commission, *Anti-Money Laundering: The SARs Regime Consultation Paper* (no. 236) (Law Commission 2018). Available at: https://webarchive.nationalarchives.gov.uk/ukgwa/20250109130835mp_/https://cloud-platform-e218f50a4812967ba1215eaecede923f.s3.amazonaws.com/uploads/sites/30/2018/07/Anti-Money-Laundering-the-SARS-Regime-Consultation-paper.pdf, accessed 26 June 2025; A Moiseienko and T Keatinge, *The Scale of Money Laundering in the UK. Too Big to Measure?* (Royal United Services Institute 2019).
4 House of Commons, *Proceeds of Crime: Fifth Report of Session 2016–2017* (House of Commons 2016). Available at: https://www.publications.parliament.uk/pa/cm201617/cmselect/cmhaff/25/25.pdf, accessed 09 October 2023.
5 HM Government, *Serious and Organised Crime Strategy 2017-2022* (HM Government 2018). Available at: https://assets.publishing.service.gov.uk/government/uploads/system/uploads/attachment_data/file/752850/SOC-2018-web.pdf, accessed 09 October 2023.

6 E Fell and others (n 3).
7 H Mills, S Skodbo, and P Blyth, *Understanding Organised Crime: Estimating the Scale and the Social and Economic Costs* (Home Office 2013). Available at https://assets.publishing.service.gov.uk/media/5a7c74e8e5274a5255bcec63/horr73.pdf, accessed 09 October 2023.
8 House of Commons (2016) (n 4).
9 Home Office and HM Treasury, *Action Plan for Anti-Money Laundering and Counter-Terrorist Finance* (Home Office 2016). Available at: https://assets.publishing.service.gov.uk/government/uploads/system/uploads/attachment_data/file/517992/6-2118-Action_Plan_for_Anti-Money_Laundering__web_.pdf, accessed 09 October 2023.
10 Law Commission (2018) (n 3).
11 HM Treasury and Home Office, *National Risk Assessment of Money Laundering and Terrorist Financing* (HM Treasury 2020). Available at: https://assets.publishing.service.gov.uk/government/uploads/system/uploads/attachment_data/file/945411/NRA_2020_v1.2_FOR_PUBLICATION.pdf, accessed 09 October 2023.
House of Commons (2016) (n 4).
12 C Howell, T Horton, and M Gill, *Financial Investigation: Identifying the Value* (Perpetuity Research and Consultancy International 2013).
13 J Madinger, *Money Laundering: A Guide for Criminal Investigators* (3rd edn, CRC Press 2012); B Milosevic, 'Money Laundering as a Form of Economic Crime in the Role of Financing Terrorism' (2016) 14(4) *Law and Politics* 549–560. Available at: casopisi.junis.ni.ac.rs/index.php/FULawPol/article/download/2423/1581, accessed 09 October 2023; M Levi and P Reuter, 'Money Laundering', in M Tonry (ed.), *Crime and Justice: A Review of Research* (University of Chicago Press 2006) 1; S Platt, *Criminal Capital* (Palgrave Macmillan 2015); J Robinson, *The Laundrymen* (Pocket Books 1998).
14 I Davidson, R Walker, and I Dayman, *Money Laundering in England and Wales: A Response to Academic Research* (Unpublished report 2014).
15 House of Commons (2016) (n 4).
16 D Chave, 'Proceeds of Crime Training: Bringing It Up to Date' (2017) 24(3) *Journal of Financial Crime* 437.
17 D Hicks and A Graycar, 'Money Laundering', in M Natarajan (ed.), *International and Transnational Crime and Justice* (Cambridge University Press 2019) 80–85.
18 Proceeds of Crime Act 2002 s340.
19 Proceeds of Crime Act 2002 s340, 11 (d).
20 Criminal Finances Act 2017 s362B 2-4.
21 HM Government, UK Anti-Corruption Plan (HM Government 2014). Available at: https://assets.publishing.service.gov.uk/government/uploads/system/uploads/attachment_data/file/388894/UKantiCorruptionPlan.pdf, accessed 09 October 2023.
22 N Maxwell and M Race, *Empowering the UK to Recover Corrupt Assets* (Transparency International 2016). Available at https://archive.transparency.org.uk/sites/default/files/pdf/publications/March2016_UWO.pdf, accessed 26 June 2025.
23 Home Office and HM Treasury, *Action Plan for Anti-Money Laundering and Counter-Terrorist Finance* (Home Office 2016) 3. Available at: https://assets.publishing.service.gov.uk/government/uploads/system/uploads/attachment_data/file/517992/6-2118-Action_Plan_for_Anti-Money_Laundering__web_.pdf, accessed 09 October 2023.
24 Home Office and HM Treasury (n 9).
25 HM Government, *National Cyber Security Strategy 2016-2021* (HM Government 2016). Available at: https://assets.publishing.service.gov.uk/government/uploads/system/uploads/attachment_data/file/567242/national_cyber_security_strategy_2016.pdf, accessed 09 October 2023; HM Government, *United Kingdom Anti-Corruption Strategy 2017-2022* (HM Government 2017). Available at: https://assets.publishing.service.gov.uk/government/uploads/system/uploads/attachment_data/file/667221/6_3323_Anti-Corruption_Strategy_WEB.pdf, accessed 09 October 2023; HM Government, *Serious and Organised Crime Strategy 2017-2022* (HM Government 2018). Available at: https://assets.publishing.service.gov.uk/government/uploads/system/uploads/attachment_data/file/752850/SOC-2018-web.pdf, accessed 09 October 2023; Home Office and HM Treasury (n 23).
26 HM Government (2018); House of Commons (2016) (n 4); National Crime Agency, *Money Laundering and Illicit Finance* (National Crime Agency 2021). Available at: https://www.nationalcrimeagency.gov.uk/what-we-do/crime-threats/money-laundering-and-illicit-finance, accessed 09 October 2023.

27 Europol, *From Suspicion to Action* (Europol 2017). Available at: https://www.europol.europa.eu/cms/sites/default/files/documents/ql-01-17-932-en-c_pf_final.pdf, accessed 09 October 2023.
28 National Crime Agency, *Suspicious Activity Reports* (National Crime Agency 2021). Available at: https://www.nationalcrimeagency.gov.uk/what-we-do/crime-threats/money-laundering-and-illicit-finance/suspicious-activity-reports, accessed 09 October 2023.
29 Law Commission (2018) (n 3); National Crime Agency, *Guidance on Submitting Better Quality Suspicious Activity Reports (SARs)* (National Crime Agency 2020).
30 Law Commission (2018) (n 3).
31 Law Commission (2018) (n 3).
32 National Crime Agency, *SARs in Action*, Issue No. 8 (National Crime Agency 2020). Available at: https://www.nationalcrimeagency.gov.uk/who-we-are/publications/482-sars-in-action-november-2020/file, accessed 09 October 2023.
33 C Hughes, *Financial Investigation: Establishing the Principles of a Generic and Effective Philosophy* (PhD Thesis, University of Derby 2021).
34 EU Directive 2018/843 of the European Parliament and of the Council of 30 May 2018. Available at: https://www.legislation.gov.uk/eudr/2018/843/introduction.
35 HM Government (n 5); N8 Policing and Research Partnership, *Policing Bitcoin: Investigating, Evidencing and Prosecuting Crimes Involving Cryptocurrency* (N8 Policing and Research Partnership 2018). Available at: https://www.n8prp.org.uk/home/library/small-grants/policing-bitcoin/, accessed 09 October 2023.
36 Home Office and HM Treasury (n 9).
37 House of Commons (2016) (n 4).
38 HM Treasury and Home Office (n 11); C Lawson and M Gill, *Money Laundering: Generating Evidence to Inform Practice* (Perpetuity Research and Consultancy International 2011).
39 HM Treasury and Home Office (n 11).
40 Crown Prosecution Service (CPS), *Proceeds of Crime Act 2002 Part 7 - Money Laundering Offences* (CPS 2010); Crown Prosecution Service (CPS), *Proceeds of Crime Act 2002 Part 7 - Money Laundering Offences* (CPS 2018).
41 CPS, Money Laundering Offences (2024). Available at: https://www.cps.gov.uk/legal-guidance/money-laundering-offences.
42 CPS (2024).
43 House of Commons (2016) (n 4).
44 Home Office and HM Treasury (n 9).
45 HM Government (n 5).
46 HM Government (n 5) 60.
47 D Chave (n 16).
48 National Crime Agency (n 32).
49 D Chave (n 16).
50 D Chave (n 16); National Crime Agency (n 32); House of Commons (2016) (n 4).
51 HM Government (n 25).
52 C Hughes, and D Hicks, *Financial Investigation and Financial Intelligence: A Critical Analysis* (Routledge 2025). https://doi.org/10.4324/9781003438649

Bibliography

Chave D, 'Proceeds of Crime Training: Bringing it up to Date' (2017) 24(3) *Journal of Financial Crime* 437.

Crown Prosecution Service (CPS), *Proceeds of Crime Act 2002 Part 7 - Money Laundering Offences* (CPS 2010).

Crown Prosecution Service (CPS), *Proceeds of Crime Act 2002 Part 7 - Money Laundering Offences* (CPS 2018).

Davidson I, Walker R, and Dayman I, *Money Laundering in England and Wales: A Response to Academic Research* (Unpublished report 2014).

European Parliament, Directive (EU) 2018/843 of the European Parliament and of the Council (2018). Available at: https://www.legislation.gov.uk/eudr/2018/843/contents, accessed 09 October 2023.

Europol, *From Suspicion to Action* (Europol 2017). Available at: https://www.europol.europa.eu/cms/sites/default/files/documents/ql-01-17-932-en-c_pf_final.pdf, accessed 09 October 2023.

Fell E, Owen J, Dienes H, Shah N, and Grimshaw J, *Understanding Organised Crime 2015/16: Estimating the Scale and the Social and Economic Costs* (2nd edn, Home Office 2019). Available at: https://assets.publishing.service.gov.uk/government/uploads/system/uploads/attachment_data/file/782656/understanding-organised-crime-mar16-horr103-2nd.pdf, accessed 09 October 2023.

Financial Action Task Force (FATF), *2021 FATF Standards*. Available at: https://www.fatf-gafi.org/home/.

Hicks D, and Graycar A, 'Money Laundering' In M Natarajan (ed.), *International and Transnational Crime and Justice* (Cambridge University Press 2019) 80–85.

HM Government, *UK Anti-Corruption Plan* (HM Government 2014). Available at: https://assets.publishing.service.gov.uk/government/uploads/system/uploads/attachment_data/file/388894/UKantiCorruptionPlan.pdf, accessed 09 October 2023.

HM Government, *National Cyber Security Strategy 2016-2021* (HM Government 2016). Available at: https://assets.publishing.service.gov.uk/government/uploads/system/uploads/attachment_data/file/567242/national_cyber_security_strategy_2016.pdf, accessed 09 October 2023.

HM Government, *United Kingdom Anti-Corruption Strategy 2017-2022* (HM Government 2017). Available at: https://assets.publishing.service.gov.uk/government/uploads/system/uploads/attachment_data/file/667221/6_3323_Anti-Corruption_Strategy_WEB.pdf, accessed 09 October 2023.

HM Government, *Serious and Organised Crime Strategy 2017-2022* (HM Government 2018). Available at: https://assets.publishing.service.gov.uk/government/uploads/system/uploads/attachment_data/file/752850/SOC-2018-web.pdf, accessed 09 October 2023.

HM Treasury and Home Office, *National Risk Assessment of Money Laundering and Terrorist Financing* (HM Treasury 2020). Available at: https://assets.publishing.service.gov.uk/government/uploads/system/uploads/attachment_data/file/945411/NRA_2020_v1.2_FOR_PUBLICATION.pdf, accessed 09 October 2023.

Home Office and HM Treasury, *Action Plan for Anti-Money Laundering and Counter-Terrorist Finance* (Home Office 2016). Available at: https://assets.publishing.service.gov.uk/government/uploads/system/uploads/attachment_data/file/517992/6-2118-Action_Plan_for_Anti-Money_Laundering__web_.pdf, accessed 09 October 2023.

House of Commons, *Proceeds of Crime: Fifth Report of Session 2016–2017* (House of Commons 2016). Available at: https://www.publications.parliament.uk/pa/cm201617/cmselect/cmhaff/25/25.pdf, accessed 09 October 2023.

Howell C, Horton T, and Gill M, *Financial Investigation: Identifying the Value* (Perpetuity Research and Consultancy International 2013).

Hughes C, *Financial Investigation: Establishing the Principles of a Generic and Effective Philosophy* (PhD Thesis, University of Derby 2021).

Hughes C, and Hicks D, *Financial Investigation and Financial Intelligence: A Critical Analysis* (Routledge 2025). https://doi.org/10.4324/9781003438649

Law Commission, *Anti-Money Laundering: The SARs Regime Consultation Paper* (no. 236) (Law Commission 2018). Available at: https://webarchive.nationalarchives.gov.uk/ukgwa/20250109130835mp_/https://cloud-platform-e218f50a4812967ba1215eaecede923f.s3.amazonaws.com/uploads/sites/30/2018/07/Anti-Money-Laundering-the-SARS-Regime-Consultation-paper.pdf, accessed 26 June 2025.

Lawson C, and Gill M, *Money Laundering: Generating Evidence to Inform Practice* (Perpetuity Research and Consultancy International 2011).

Levi M, and Reuter P, 'Money Laundering', in M Tonry (ed.), *Crime and Justice: A Review of Research* (University of Chicago Press 2006) 1.

Madinger J, *Money Laundering: A Guide for Criminal Investigators* (3rd edn, CRC Press 2012).

Maxwell N, and Race M, *Empowering the UK to Recover Corrupt Assets* (Transparency International, 2016). Available at: https://archive.transparency.org.uk/sites/default/files/pdf/publications/March2016_UWO.pdf, accessed 26 June 2025.

Mills H, Skodbo S, and Blyth P, *Understanding Organised Crime: Estimating the Scale and the Social and Economic Costs* (Home Office 2013). Available at: https://assets.publishing.service.gov.uk/media/5a7c74e8e5274a5255bcec63/horr73.pdf, accessed 09 October 2023.

Milosevic B, 'Money Laundering as a Form of Economic Crime in the Role of Financing Terrorism' (2016) 14(4) *Law and Politics* 549–560. Available at: casopisi.junis.ni.ac.rs/index.php/FULawPol/article/download/2423/1581, accessed 09 October 2023.

Moiseienko A, and Keatinge T, *The Scale of Money Laundering in the UK. Too Big to Measure?* (Royal United Services Institute 2019).

National Crime Agency, *Guidance on Submitting Better Quality Suspicious Activity Reports (SARs)* (National Crime Agency 2020).

National Crime Agency, *SARs in Action*, Issue No. 8 (National Crime Agency 2020). Available at: https://www.nationalcrimeagency.gov.uk/who-we-are/publications/482-sars-in-action-november-2020/file, accessed 09 October 2023.

National Crime Agency, *Money Laundering and Illicit Finance* (National Crime Agency 2021). Available at: https://www.nationalcrimeagency.gov.uk/what-we-do/crime-threats/money-laundering-and-illicit-finance, accessed 09 October 2023.

National Crime Agency, *Suspicious Activity Reports* (National Crime Agency 2021). Available at: https://www.nationalcrimeagency.gov.uk/what-we-do/crime-threats/money-laundering-and-illicit-finance/suspicious-activity-reports, accessed 09 October 2023.

N8 Policing and Research Partnership, *Policing Bitcoin: Investigating, Evidencing and Prosecuting Crimes Involving Cryptocurrency* (N8 Policing and Research Partnership 2018). Available at: https://www.n8prp.org.uk/home/library/small-grants/policing-bitcoin/, accessed 09 October 2023.

Platt S, *Criminal Capital* (Palgrave Macmillan 2015).

Robinson J, *The Laundrymen* (Pocket Books 1998).

3 Illicit Offshore Finance

Examining the Measures Adopted by the United Kingdom to Enhance Corporate Transparency

Paul Gilmour and Branislav Hock

1 Introduction

The United Kingdom (UK) and its dominions have often been viewed as 'safe havens' for criminals, oligarchs, and kleptocrats to hide their ill-gotten gains behind secretive offshore entities.[1] It is well known that since the collapse of the Soviet Union in the 1990s, the City of London has welcomed an increasing amount of funds from post-Soviet kleptocracies attracted to the UK's prosperous financial- and professional-services sectors.[2] While measuring the extent of money laundering is difficult, some estimate that £90 billion is laundered through the UK per year, amounting to around 5% of the UK's gross domestic product.[3] Approximately a quarter of the global market for offshore financial services is controlled by the UK, alongside its Crown Dependencies and Overseas Territories. They achieve this through intricate offshore corporate structures that enable illicit money flows directed towards London's financial centre.[4]

Concerns surrounding the UK's role as a global money laundering hub have focused public attention on the source of suspicious wealth, including official efforts to identify the real beneficial ownership behind dubious corporate entities and structures.[5] These concerns have been further amplified by a deteriorating global security situation, including the impact of the Russo-Ukrainian War. In response, the UK and other allies have urgently enacted new laws and regulations to combat economic crime.[6] Within this context, this chapter aims to explore the legal and practical measures adopted by the UK in its effort to enhance corporate transparency.

The remainder of this chapter is structured as follows. This chapter starts by highlighting the link between money laundering and corporate secrecy. This chapter then reviews key developments of the UK's legal and policy measures brought in to address corporate secrecy, before providing a critical analysis of key gaps and challenges for the future.

2 The Intersection between Money Laundering and Corporate Secrecy

Money laundering has been conventionally defined as a process of converting criminal profit to apparently legitimate income so as to not alert policing authorities. The process has been extensively debated by the anti-money laundering (AML) community, with most consensus centred on the three-stage cycle of placement, layering, and integration.[7] First, the criminal profit—the so-called 'dirty' money—is placed into the legitimate financial system through a bank account deposit or similar. Second, funds are layered via discrete transactions (typically via multiple smaller amounts mixed with legally obtained money) to mask their real origin. Third, the funds will undergo further processing to 'clean' and

DOI: 10.4324/9781003324843-5

integrate them into ostensibly legitimate income, like real estate, business investment, or luxury goods.[8] In reality, there are many other money laundering methods, which do not involve the traditional financial system and the three-stage cycle. For example, funds can be transferred through false trade transactions (i.e. trade-based money laundering) or avoid the traditional economy completely, as is the case with informal value transfer systems (such as Hawala) and cryptocurrencies.[9]

Leaving the terminological and conceptual complexity aside, important enablers of money laundering are corporate secrecy techniques allowing for a smooth transfer of illicit funds. The facilitation of money laundering through corporate secrecy involves, for example, employing anonymous shell companies, trust arrangements, or other business dealings to obscure the true origins of dirty money from law enforcement, tax authorities, or other officials. Concealing beneficial ownership aims to distance the legally registered owner (i.e. the director or some other company entity) and the real person(s) who ultimately owns or controls company assets, known as the beneficial owner.[10] In doing so, criminals often use anonymous shell companies—legal entities that conduct little to no actual commercial endeavours and exist only on paper to protect the real identity of the beneficial owner.[11] Although shell companies have legitimate business uses (such as company mergers or protecting legitimate business interests within competitive markets) they can be exploited for illicit purposes.[12] Criminals might name nominee shareholders, trustees, or even professional intermediaries (e.g. lawyers, accountants, and trust and company service providers) across multiple corporations registered offshore as beneficial owners to layer company ownership and obscure their criminal assets further.[13] However, governments recognise the link between corporate secrecy and money laundering, so have focused their AML efforts towards enhancing beneficial ownership transparency.

3 The Need for Beneficial Ownership Transparency

Beneficial ownership transparency has become a key tool for governments in combating illicit financial flows and money laundering. Knowing the identity of beneficial owners of companies is important for policing authorities because it helps them to identify illicit wealth, overcome evidentiary issues, and recover illicit assets tied to corporate entities. In other words, an increase in beneficial ownership transparency creates an extra hurdle for criminals using secretive offshore practices (e.g. concealing the identity of a beneficial owner through an offshore company) in an attempt to avoid scrutiny from law enforcement and tax authorities.

Recent exposés have further heightened the need for more transparency in offshore corporate dealings. The 2016 Panama Papers and other offshore leaks have pressured international governments to restrict immoral or even criminal acts that abuse the financial system and erode public trust in the rule of law.[14] Although many of these schemes are situated within a realm of legal ambiguity, global transparency campaigners understandably condemn abusive tax schemes that benefit large multinational companies, the wealthy or political elite.

Despite an existing trade-off between corporate transparency and some legitimate values associated with secrecy and freedom of capital flows, many governments and civil-society representatives argue that having stronger AML measures and/or tighter regulations focusing on ensuring beneficial ownership transparency is necessary to curb economic crime effectively. Perhaps the most important manifestation of this view comes via governments adhering to global standards set by the Financial Action Task Force (FATF) on beneficial ownership transparency. The FATF standards aspire that financial institutions have effective, robust customer due diligence procedures in place to identify suspicious transactions, manage high-risk entities, and understand their customers' financial dealings. Where appropriate, the automatic exchange of information on beneficial owners between tax authorities and financial institutions allows various authorities to receive, collate, and share information from other countries about residents with bank accounts and investments overseas. The automatic exchange of such information also ensures that intergovernmental cooperative efforts operate smoothly.[15] As such, an effective beneficial ownership regime relies on a robust system involving accurate disclosure and verification of beneficial ownership, strong monitoring, and supervision of financial transactions.[16]

4 Key Developments of the UK's Legal and Policy Measures against Corporate Secrecy

In recent years, the UK has been undergoing significant transformations in its legal and policy landscape with regard to enhancing transparency and accountability within the commercial sector. Such developments have primarily involved establishing central registers of beneficial owners, reforming the powers and function of Companies House (the UK's executive agency responsible for company registrations), and tightening the rules on corporate disclosure.

Central registers of beneficial owners were first established in the UK through the Small Business, Enterprise and Employment Act 2015. The Persons of Significant Control (PSC) register, launched in April 2016, holds publicly available data on most UK companies (including, e.g. their beneficial owners' name, date of birth, home address, and the nature of their control over the company).[17] A PSC is an individual holding more than 25% of shares or voting rights in the company or having the right to appoint or remove the majority of the board of directors of the company.[18] This arbitrary threshold has raised concerns because individuals can layer company ownership (through multiple entities or other complex corporate structures) to ensure ownership falls below the threshold; thus, avoiding disclosing the true beneficiary of illicit company assets. Indeed, countries like India and Kenya use a lower 10% threshold, while in Burkina Faso, and Ghana, no such threshold exists, meaning each individual involved in company ownership, irrespective of the extent of their ownership or control, must be included on the register.[19] While ensuring that all individuals involved in company ownership are disclosed may help to trace beneficial owners and associated assets, this is not a guarantee, and disclosure must function in conjunction with a broader set of tools and mechanisms.

The UK's register of beneficial owners of trusts is managed by His Majesty's Revenue and Customs (HMRC).[20] This register, accessible only to those with a 'legitimate interest' (e.g. government authorities and the UK Financial Intelligence Unit) extends only to express trust arrangements, testamentary trusts, and foundation trusts. This limitation is associated with the competence of the HMRC, which in this area has been to collect UK taxes from trustees liable to pay tax in the UK. Therefore, until a recent legislative change, an overseas trust without any such liability did not have to be disclosed even if the overseas trust owned UK property.[21] This is notable considering that it is well known that trusts, especially overseas trusts, can be abused to obscure company ownership and facilitate money laundering.[22]

New rules introduced on 6 October 2020 mean that express trusts registered overseas that acquire land or property from this date, or have at least one UK resident trustee and enter a new business relationship with a UK 'relevant person', are now required to register. Furthermore, more trust types must be registered, including:

UK trusts without UK tax liabilities;
The vast majority of bare trusts[23];
Taxable trusts; and
Trusts holding UK land despite not having UK resident trustees.[24]

Furthermore, the UK has also introduced a register of overseas entities through the Economic Crime (Transparency and Enforcement) Act 2022, which requires "anonymous foreign owners of UK property to reveal their real identities".[25] Effective from 1 August 2022, this register lists the beneficial owner of any overseas entity that buys, sells, or transfers property or land in the UK.[26] The aim of the register is:

Enhancing the transparency of beneficial ownership of overseas corporations linked to the purchase and sale of UK housing stocks;
Boosting confidence in the UK property market; and
Supporting official investigations into related money laundering and tax evasion cases.

Yet, a recent study assessing data within the new register of overseas entities found that beneficial ownership information was missing or was publicly unavailable in 87% of cases.[27] This may be due to overseas entities falling outside the jurisdictional scope of the UK law.[28] Furthermore, critics argue that it is still quite possible for individuals to list a nominee company or split ownership between other associates to circumvent disclosure rules[29]—similar concerns shared with the more established PSC register. These issues demonstrate that individuals can still exploit legal loopholes in the UK's beneficial ownership regime, which undermines new efforts to strengthen beneficial ownership transparency.

Recent reforms to Companies House under the Economic Crime and Corporate Transparency Act (2023) should, nonetheless, help to strengthen beneficial ownership transparency by ensuring more robust verification procedures around the disclosure of beneficial owners' information. Companies House has historically acted as a repository for data on company incorporation; its role has been to simply accept company ownership data on face value and add company details to the register. The new reforms oblige Companies House to verify company information supplied to it, and query information already on the register, ensuring beneficial ownership data is more accurate and reliable.[30] It now has broader powers to investigate and enforce disclosure rules and share beneficial ownership information, while safeguarding sensitive personal information from potential fraud and other harms. Companies House's increased role as an active gatekeeper of ownership information should strengthen regulatory oversight, improve the accuracy of company data, and limit opportunities for tax abuse and money laundering.

5 The State of Corporate Transparency in the UK

Despite efforts by the UK government to clamp down on illicit financial flows following the Panama Papers' revelations, the UK remains a global hub for financial secrecy.[31] According to the Tax Justice Network, the UK and its British network of overseas tax havens contribute an estimated US$189 billion of global tax revenue losses every year.[32] The UK is ranked top of a global Financial Secrecy Index,[33] which positions jurisdictions based on how secretive they are to international financial flows—contradicting the common perception that successful tax havens relate to those idyllic tropical island microstates located in far-flung reaches of the globe.[34] Arguably, the UK has been able to position itself as a conduit to a global network of corporate secrecy quite successfully through a strong financial-services sector welcoming to foreign investment and fiscal policies based on deregulation.[35] It is understandable that such a stance has attracted corrupt wealth and controversy with transparency campaigners arguing that the UK is not doing enough to tackle economic crime.

One modest step in enhancing beneficial ownership transparency is having a more substantive approach to beneficial ownership disclosures. This means a more qualitative criteria of control are needed, rather than the set 25% threshold at which companies are required to disclose beneficial ownership. The current arbitrary threshold is easily avoided by layering company ownership to hide the real beneficial owner of the companies involved.[36] This threshold was only ever a mere suggestion in the FATF's 2012 Recommendations[37] without having any evidential basis for its existence, and its adoption by the UK and other jurisdictions may have been ill-advised. Arguably, the level of beneficiary interest of each person associated with a company should be verified to avoid false or fraudulent disclosure of company information.

Stronger and more robust verification mechanisms should also be developed to improve the reliability and accuracy of data held on all three of the UK's registers of beneficial owners. Although reforms to Companies House strengthening checks around the identity of beneficial owners of UK companies are welcome, it is equally important that robust checks are made to verify the *nature* and *extent* of the interest of a beneficial owner. Enhanced verification should focus on evidencing to what extent each person owns or controls the company on the register.[38] This will help to evidence that the person disclosed to the register as the beneficial owner *actually* has direct or indirect interest in the company. It may also highlight details concerning wider corporate structures disclosed on various registers of other jurisdictions, which should ensure more consistent data and cohesive automatic exchange of information on beneficial ownership.

In practice, stronger verification of beneficial ownership would likely require extensive cross-checking of data with various other centralised public databases or implementing decentralised digital-ledger technologies, such as blockchain.[39] For example, in the Republic of Ireland, the identity of beneficial owners is compared with personal data (e.g. date of birth and personal public service numbers) held on the Department of Social Protection (DSP) database.[40] Checks should involve real-time data exchange between all of the following: various government databases (e.g. land registries and tax systems); systems held by law firms and accountants; and banking systems used for onboarding clients and recording 'Know Your Customer' information and bank account opening details. Similarly, adopting blockchain technology may help to integrate beneficial ownership data without disturbing existing systems and corporate processes.[41] Blockchain's use of computer cryptography and consensus protocols that encrypt and verify transactional data electronically may provide for better interoperability between various systems and improve the consistency of beneficial ownership data.[42] Having a more joined-up approach supported through new digital technologies should, therefore, help to verify the nature and extent of company ownership.

6 Conclusion

This chapter has examined the legal and practical measures adopted by the UK to enhance corporate transparency. In doing so, it has offered new insight into illicit offshore finance and the challenges facing governments in tackling money laundering through offshore jurisdictions. Corporate secrecy has been exposed through successive financial scandals as a significant problem for the UK in its efforts to tackle illicit offshore finance.[43] The UK's policy response to the controversy of the 2016 Panama Papers and subsequent leaks has involved introducing new company disclosure requirements through central registers of beneficial owners to enhance corporate transparency.[44] However, scholars and transparency campaigners have questioned the usefulness of these registers due to concerns over inadequate verification mechanisms, unreliable beneficial ownership data, and incompetence of Companies House to manage accurate company records.[45] Recent geopolitical tensions have renewed the UK's resolve to clamp down on bad actors using overseas entities and other means of corporate secrecy through which to abuse the financial system.[46]

Although new corporate transparency laws and reforms in Companies House should improve the UK's beneficial ownership regime, more work is needed to ensure criminals cannot exploit existing loopholes in AML law or related policy to launder money and evade taxes. The UK must ensure that every person associated with a company irrespective of their beneficial interest or level of company ownership is verified and recorded to strengthen corporate transparency. Stronger verification of company records must also ensue through better integration of personal data held within various databases of government and regulated sectors. Such measures will provide a more meaningful contribution to the UK's AML response to strengthen beneficial ownership transparency and disrupt illicit offshore flows.

Bibliography

Table of Legislation: UK

Economic Crime and Corporate Transparency Act 2023.
Economic Crime (Transparency and Enforcement) Act 2022.
Small Business, Enterprise and Employment Act 2015.

Table of Legislation: Other Legislation

Article 3(6) of Council Directive (EU) 2015/849/EU of 20 May 2015 on the prevention of the use of the financial system for the purposes of money laundering or terrorist financing, amending Regulation (EU) 2012/648 of the European Parliament and of the Council, and repealing Directive 2005/60/EC of the European Parliament and of the Council and Commission Directive 2006/70/EC [2015] OJ L141, 73–117

List of Secondary Sources

Advani A, Poux C, Powell-Smith A and Summers A, 'Catch me if you can: Gaps in the Register of Overseas Entities' (September 2023), https://warwick.ac.uk/fac/soc/economics/research/centres/cage/publications/workingpapers/2023/catch_me_if_you_can_gaps_in_the_register_of_overseas_entities/, accessed 2 December 2023.

Azrilyant J, 'Shell game: How the Corporate Transparency Act aims to end the illicit use of shell companies, where it fails, and what to do about it' (2021) 51(1) *Pub Cont L J* 1.

Bieler SA, 'Peeking into the house of cards: Money laundering, luxury real estate, and the necessity of data verification for the Corporate Transparency Act's beneficial ownership registry' (2022) 27(1) *Fordham J Corp & Fin L* 193.

Blakeley G, 'On borrowed time: Finance and the UK's current account deficit' (*The IPPR Commission on Economic Justice*, 2018), https://www.ippr.org/files/2018-07/1531217614_cej-on-borrowed-time-june18-.pdf, accessed 8 January 2024.

Button M, Hock B and Shepherd D, *Economic crime: From conception to response* (Routledge, 2022).

Central Bank of Ireland, 'Beneficial ownership register FAQ' (2024), https://www.centralbank.ie/regulation/anti-money-laundering-and-countering-the-financing-of-terrorism/beneficial-ownership-register/about-the-register-and-faqs, accessed 12 January 2024.

Christensen J, 'Can we afford the City of London?' (2018) 25 *IPPR Progress Rev* 47.

Cobham A, Janský P and Meinzer M, 'The Financial Secrecy Index: Shedding new light on the geography of secrecy', (2015) 91(3) *Econ Geogr* 281.

Companies House, 'Register an overseas entity and its beneficial owners' (25 July 2022), https://www.gov.uk/guidance/register-an-overseas-entity, accessed 2 December 2023.

Companies House, 'Economic Crime and Corporate Transparency Act: Outline transition plan for Companies House' (*Companies House*, 16 October 2024), https://www.gov.uk/government/publications/economic-crime-and-corporate-transparency-act-outline-transition-plan-for-companies-house, accessed 7 November 2024.

FATF, 'The misuse of corporate vehicles, include Trust and Company Service Providers' (*FATF*, 13 October 2006), https://www.fatf-gafi.org/content/dam/fatf-gafi/reports/Misuse%20of%20Corporate%20Vehicles%20including%20Trusts%20and%20Company%20Services%20Providers.pdf, accessed 25 November 2023.

FATF, 'Guidance on beneficial ownership of legal persons' *(FATF*, March 2023), https://www.fatf-gafi.org/en/publications/Fatfrecommendations/Guidance-Beneficial-Ownership-Legal-Persons.html, accessed 7 November 2024.

FATF, 'International standards on combating money laundering and the financing of terrorism & proliferation the FATF recommendations' (*FATF*, November 2023), https://www.fatf-gafi.org/en/publications/Fatfrecommendations/Fatf-recommendations.html, accessed 06 January 2024.

Gillis M, 'Shell companies and exposing beneficial ownership: Testing the boundaries of the international commitment to fight corruption' (2019) 20(2) *Melb J Int Law* 378.

Gilmour N, 'Illustrating the incentivised steps criminals take to launder cash while avoiding government anti-laundering measures' (2020) 23(2) *J Money Laund Control* 515.

Gilmour PM, 'Lifting the veil on beneficial ownership: Challenges of implementing the UK's registers of beneficial owners' (2020) 23(4) *J Money Laund Control* 717.

Gilmour PM, 'Decentralized blockchain technology: Towards a trusted and transparent beneficial ownership regime' in Doron Goldbarsht and Louis de Koker (eds) *Financial technology and the law: Combating financial crime* (Springer, 2022) 185–209.

Gilmour PM, 'Reexamining the anti-money-laundering framework: A legal critique and new approach to combating money laundering' (2023) 30(1) *J Financ Crime* 35.

Gilmour PM, 'Understanding beneficial ownership disclosure' (2023) 57 *J Financ Transformation* 70.

Heathershaw J, Cooley A, Mayne T, Michel C, Prelec T, Sharman J and Soares de Oliveira R, 'The UK's kleptocracy problem' (*Chatham House*, 8 December 2021), https://www.chathamhouse.org/2021/12/uks-kleptocracy-problem/03-global-money-laundering-capital, accessed 24 September 2023.

HMRC, 'Understanding risks and taking action for Trust or Company Service Providers' (*HMRC*, 8 October 2021), https://www.gov.uk/government/publications/understanding-risks-and-taking-action-for-trust-or-company-service-providers/understanding-risks-and-taking-action-for-trust-or-company-service-providers, accessed 25 November 2023.

HMRC, 'HMRC internal manual: Trusts, settlements and estates manual' (HMRC, 22 December 2023), https://www.gov.uk/hmrc-internal-manuals/trusts-settlements-and-estates-manual/tsem1563, accessed 10 January 2024.

Hock B, 'Policing fiscal corruption: Tax crime and legally corrupt institutions in the United Kingdom' (2023) 85 *Law Contemp Probl* 159, https://scholarship.law.duke.edu/lcp/vol85/iss4/7, accessed 17 December 2023.

Hock B, Button M, Shepherd D and Gilmour P, 'What works in policing money laundering?' (2024) 27 *J Money Laund Control* 5.

Home Office, Department for Business and Trade, HM Treasury, Ministry of Justice, Serious Fraud Office and Department for Business, Energy & Industrial Strategy, 'Policy paper Factsheet: Economic Crime and Corporate Transparency Bill overarching' (26 October 2023), https://www.gov.uk/government/publications/economic-crime-and-corporate-transparency-bill-2022-factsheets/fact-sheet-economic-crime-and-corporate-transparency-bill-overarching, accessed 09 January 2024.

Kemsley D, Kemsley SA and Morgan FT, 'Tax evasion and money laundering: A complete framework' (2022) 29(2) *J Financ Crime* 589.

Knobel A, 'The Achilles heel of effective beneficial ownership registration: Why is everyone fixed on 25%?' (*Tax Justice Network*, 11 May 2017), https://taxjustice.net/2017/05/11/achilles-heel-effective-beneficial-ownership-registration-everyone-fixed-25, accessed 25 November 2023.

Knobel A and Lorenzo F, 'Beneficial ownership registration around the world 2022' (December 2022), https://taxjustice.net/wp-content/uploads/2022/12/State-of-Play-of-Beneficial-Ownership-2022-Tax-Justice-Network.pdf, accessed 19 December 2023.

Konovalova M, Tuck P and Pérez RO, 'In search of the owner: Regulating through transparency' (2022) 91(102421) *Crit Perspect Account* 1–17.

Mansour MB, 'King Charles urged to address British tax havens in public letter' (*Tax Justice Network*, 30 April 2023), https://taxjustice.net/press/king-charles-urged-to-address-british-tax-havens-in-public-letter, accessed 8 January 2024.

Mourant, 'The UK register of beneficial ownership of trusts' (*Mourant*, August 2017), https://www.mourant.com/file-library/media---2017/2017-guides/the-uk-register-of-beneficial-ownership-of-trusts.pdf, accessed 25 November 2023.

Neate R, 'New register of overseas owners of UK properties 'riddled with flaws'' (*The Guardian*, 1 August 2022), https://www.theguardian.com/business/2022/aug/01/new-register-of-overseas-owners-of-uk-properties-riddled-with-flaws, accessed 7 December 2023.

Organisation for Economic Co-operation and Development (OECD) and the Inter-American Development Bank (IDB), 'Building effective beneficial ownership frameworks: A joint global forum and IDB toolkit' (2021), https://www.oecd.org/tax/transparency/documents/effective-beneficial-ownership-frameworks-toolkit_en.pdf, accessed 09 January 2024.

Pontes R, Lewis N, McFarlane P and Craig, P, 'Anti-money laundering in the United Kingdom: New directions for a more effective regime' (2021) 25 *J Money Laund Control* 401.

Raphael M, 'The money laundering capital of the world' (2016) 32 *Int Enforcement L Rep* 302.

Sabbagh D, 'New bill vows to stop kleptocrats 'treating UK as their safe deposit box'' (*Guardian*, 22 September 2022), https://www.theguardian.com/world/2022/sep/22/new-bill-vows-to-toughen-stance-on-kleptocrats-fraudulent-uk-claims, accessed 24 September 2023.

Shahaab A, Khan IA, Maude R, Hewage C and Wang Y, 'Public service operational efficiency and blockchain: A case study of Companies House, UK' (2023) 40(1) *Gov Inf Q* 101759.

Sharman JC, 'Shopping for anonymous shell companies: An audit study of anonymity and crime in the international financial system' (2010) 24(4) *J Econ Perspect* 127.

Soudijn MRJ, 'Rethinking money laundering and drug trafficking: Some implications for investigators, policy makers and researchers' (2016) 19(3) *J Money Laund Control* 298.

Tax Justice Network, 'Financial Secrecy Index 2022' (*Tax Justice Network*, 2022), https://fsi.taxjustice.net, accessed 7 November 2024.

The London School of Economics and Political Science, 'Over two thirds of properties held by overseas shell companies remain anonymous' (*LSE*, 3 September 2023), https://www.lse.ac.uk/News/Latest-news-from-LSE/2023/i-September-2023/Over-two-thirds-of-properties-held-by-overseas-shell-companies-remain-anonymous, accessed 2 December 2023.

Thorpe C, *Implied trusts and beneficial ownership in Modern UK tax law* (Spiramus Press, 2021).

Tiwari M, Ferrill J, Gepp A and Kumar K, 'Factors influencing the choice of technique to launder funds: The APPT framework' (2023) 1(100006) *J Econ Criminol* 1–11.

Tiwari M, Gepp A and Kumar K, 'A review of money laundering literature: The state of research in key areas' (2020) 32(2) *Pacific Account Rev* 271.

Transparency International UK, 'Hiding in plain sight: How UK companies are used to launder corrupt wealth' (*Transparency International UK*, 2017), https://www.transparency.org.uk/news/hiding-plain-sight, accessed 25 September 2023.

UK Government, 'Policy paper, Fact sheet: The Register of Overseas Entities (web accessible)' (26 October 2023), https://www.gov.uk/government/publications/economic-crime-transparency-and-enforcement-bill-2022-overarching-documents/factsheet-the-register-of-overseas-entities-web-accessible, accessed 7 December 2023.

Waitzman E, 'Deregulation: Government policy since 1997' (*House of Lords*, 10 July 2017), https://lordslibrary.parliament.uk/research-briefings/lln-2017-0041, accessed 06 January 2024.

Wells N, 'New HMRC Trust Registration Service (TRS)' (*Azets*, 12 July 2022), https://www.azets.co.uk/news-insights/articles/new-hmrc-trust-registration-service-trs/, accessed 25 November 2023.

Notes

1 Dan Sabbagh, 'New bill vows to stop kleptocrats 'treating UK as their safe deposit box'' (*Guardian*, 22 September 2022), https://www.theguardian.com/world/2022/sep/22/new-bill-vows-to-toughen-stance-on-kleptocrats-fraudulent-uk-claims, accessed 24 September 2023.

2 John Heathershaw, Alexander Cooley, Thomas Mayne, Casey Michel, Tena Prelec, Jason Sharman, Ricardo Soares de Oliveira, 'The UK's kleptocracy problem' (*Chatham House*, 8 December 2021), https://www.chathamhouse.org/2021/12/uks-kleptocracy-problem/03-global-money-laundering-capital, accessed 24 September 2023.

3 Rafael Pontes, Nick Lewis, Paul McFarlane, Patrick Craig, 'Anti-money laundering in the United Kingdom: New directions for a more effective regime' (2021) 25 *J Money Laund Control* 401, 402; John Christensen, 'Can we afford the City of London?' (2018) 25 *IPPR Progress Rev* 47, 49; For discussion about challenges associated with money laundering see Branislav Hock, Mark Button, David Shepherd, Paul Gilmour, 'What works in policing money laundering?' (2024) 27 *J Money Laund Control* 5.

4 John Christensen (n 3) 49.

5 Paul Michael Gilmour, 'Understanding beneficial ownership disclosure' (2023) 57 *J Financ Transformation* 70; The source of suspicious wealth in the UK's property market has led some to declare the City of London as 'The Money Laundering Capital of the World', see, for example, Monty Raphael, 'The money laundering capital of the world' (2016) 32 *Int Enforcement L Rep*, 302; Transparency International UK 'Hiding in plain sight: How UK companies are used to launder corrupt wealth' (*Transparency International UK*, 2017), https://www.transparency.org.uk/news/hiding-plain-sight, accessed 25 September 2023.

6 Notably, the Economic Crime (Transparency and Enforcement) Act 2022; see Home Office, Department for Business and Trade, HM Treasury, Ministry of Justice, Serious Fraud Office, and Department for Business, Energy & Industrial Strategy, 'Policy paper Factsheet: Economic Crime and Corporate Transparency Bill overarching' (26 October 2023), https://www.gov.uk/government/publications/economic-crime-and-corporate-transparency-bill-2022-factsheets/fact-sheet-economic-crime-and-corporate-transparency-bill-overarching, accessed 09 January 2024.

7 See, for example, Milind Tiwari, Jamie Ferrill, Adrian Gepp, Kuldeep Kumar, 'Factors influencing the choice of technique to launder funds: The APPT framework' (2023) 1(100006) *J Econ Criminol* 1–11; Nicholas Gilmour, 'Illustrating the incentivised steps criminals take to launder cash while avoiding government anti-laundering measures' (2020) 23(2) *J Money Laund Control* 515; Paul Michael Gilmour, 'Reexamining the anti-money-laundering framework: A legal critique and new approach to combating money laundering' (2023) 30(1) *J Financ Crime* 35; Melvin R J Soudijn, 'Rethinking money laundering and drug trafficking: Some implications for investigators, policy makers and researchers' (2016) 19(3) *J Money Laund Control* 298.

8 Deen Kemsley, Sean A Kemsley, Frank T Morgan, 'Tax evasion and money laundering: A complete framework' (2022) 29(2) *J Financ Crime* 589, 592; Mark Button, Branislav Hock, David Shepherd, *Economic crime: From conception to response* (Routledge, 2022) 164–165.

9 Paul Michael Gilmour (n 7).

10 Article 3(6) of Council Directive (EU) 2015/849/EU of 20 May 2015 on the prevention of the use of the financial system for the purposes of money laundering or terrorist financing, amending Regulation (EU) 2012/648 of the European Parliament and of the Council, and repealing

Directive 2005/60/EC of the European Parliament and of the Council and Commission Directive 2006/70/EC [2015] OJ L141, 73–117; see also, FATF, 'Guidance on beneficial ownership of legal persons' (*FATF*, March 2023) 15, https://www.fatf-gafi.org/en/publications/Fatfrecommendations/Guidance-Beneficial-Ownership-Legal-Persons.html, accessed 7 November 2024; The beneficial owner is the individual who stands to benefit or enjoy an asset—not necessarily the same person listed as the legal or official owner the asset. Beneficial ownership recognises the fundamental separation of the legal and rightful owner of assets or other property. As a concept historically derived from trust law, beneficial ownership determines the equitable interest in property through the principle of equity, a remedial measure that seeks to overcome injustice caused by the strict application of common law rules; see Chris Thorpe, *Implied trusts and beneficial ownership in Modern UK tax law* (Spiramus Press, 2021).

11 For further insights into the illicit uses of shell companies, see Milind Tiwari, Adrian Gepp and Kuldeep Kumar, 'A review of money laundering literature: the state of research in key areas' (2020) 32(2) *Pacific Account Rev* 271; see also Jason C Sharman, 'Shopping for anonymous shell companies: An audit study of anonymity and crime in the international financial system' (2010) 24(4) *J Econ Perspect* 127.

12 Jacob Azrilyant, 'Shell game: How the Corporate Transparency Act aims to end the illicit use of shell companies, where it fails, and what to do about it' (2021) 51(1) *Pub Cont L J* 1; Matilda Gillis, 'Shell companies and exposing beneficial ownership: Testing the boundaries of the international commitment to fight corruption' (2019) 20(2) *Melb J Int Law* 378, 381.

13 Paul Michael Gilmour (n 5); S Alexandra Bieler, 'Peeking into the house of cards: Money laundering, luxury real estate, and the necessity of data verification for the Corporate Transparency Act's beneficial ownership registry' (2022) 27(1) *Fordham J Corp & Fin L* 193.

14 Paul Michael Gilmour (n 5).

15 The FATF standards (FATF Recommendations) were initially adopted on 16 February 2012 with regular updates since, see FATF, 'International standards on combating money laundering and the financing of terrorism & proliferation the FATF recommendations' (*FATF*, November 2023), https://www.fatf-gafi.org/en/publications/Fatfrecommendations/Fatf-recommendations.html, accessed 06 January 2024; Mayya Konovalova, Penelope Tuck, Rodrigo Ormeño Pérez, 'In search of the owner: Regulating through transparency' (2022) 91(102421) *Crit Perspect Account* 1–17.

16 Organisation for Economic Co-operation and Development (OECD) and the Inter-American Development Bank (IDB), 'Building effective beneficial ownership frameworks: A joint global forum and IDB toolkit' (2021), https://www.oecd.org/tax/transparency/documents/effective-beneficial-ownership-frameworks-toolkit_en.pdf, accessed 09 January 2024.

17 The PSC register includes private companies limited by shares, and those by guarantee, limited liability partnerships (LLPs) and Societates Europaeae (SEs) and most public limited companies, amongst others. However, it does not hold data on sole traders, companies operating within the UK but registered elsewhere, and limited partnerships (LPs).

18 The PSC also includes, in limited circumstances, an individual who has the right to exercise, or actually exercises, significant influence or control over the company, or (where a trust or firm would satisfy one of the first four conditions if it were an individual) any individual holding the right to exercise, or actually exercising, significant influence or control over the activities of that trust or firm.

19 Paul Michael Gilmour, 'Lifting the veil on beneficial ownership: Challenges of implementing the UK's registers of beneficial owners' (2020) 23(4) *J Money Laund Control* 717; Andres Knobel, 'The Achilles heel of effective beneficial ownership registration: Why is everyone fixed on 25%?' (*Tax Justice Network*, 11 May 2017), https://taxjustice.net/2017/05/11/achilles-heel-effective-beneficial-ownership-registration-everyone-fixed-25, accessed 25 November 2023.

20 A trust is an arrangement, in which a 'settlor' divides the ownership of a company asset between a 'trustee', who commands legal title over the asset and, thus, controls it; and a 'beneficiary', who stands to benefit from the asset.

21 Mourant, 'The UK register of beneficial ownership of trusts' (*Mourant*, August 2017), https://www.mourant.com/file-library/media---2017/2017-guides/the-uk-register-of-beneficial-ownership-of-trusts.pdf, accessed 25 November 2023.

22 FATF, 'The misuse of corporate vehicles, include Trust and Company Service Providers' (*FATF*, 13 October 2006), https://www.fatf-gafi.org/content/dam/fatf-gafi/reports/Misuse%20of%20Corporate%20Vehicles%20including%20Trusts%20and%20Company%20Services%20

Providers.pdf, accessed 25 November 2023; HMRC, 'Understanding risks and taking action for Trust or Company Service Providers' (*HMRC*, 8 October 2021), https://www.gov.uk/government/publications/understanding-risks-and-taking-action-for-trust-or-company-service-providers/understanding-risks-and-taking-action-for-trust-or-company-service-providers, accessed 25 November 2023.

23 A bare trust is a legal arrangement that provides beneficiaries with immediate and absolute ownership to both capital and income. Bare trusts are often used where assets are held for minors. The beneficiary of the trust does not hold legal title; see HMRC, 'HMRC internal manual: Trusts, settlements and estates manual' (HMRC, 22 December 2023), https://www.gov.uk/hmrc-internal-manuals/trusts-settlements-and-estates-manual/tsem1563, accessed 10 January 2024.

24 Naomi Wells, 'New HMRC Trust Registration Service (TRS)' (*Azets*, 12 July 2022), https://www.azets.co.uk/news-insights/articles/new-hmrc-trust-registration-service-trs/, accessed 25 November 2023.

25 UK Government, 'Policy paper, Fact Sheet: The Register of Overseas Entities (web accessible)' (26 October 2023), https://www.gov.uk/government/publications/economic-crime-transparency-and-enforcement-bill-2022-overarching-documents/factsheet-the-register-of-overseas-entities-web-accessible, accessed 7 December 2023.

26 The register also lists any overseas entities that that have bought property or land on or after the 1 January 1999 in England and Wales or 8 December 2014 in Scotland; see Companies House, 'Register an overseas entity and its beneficial owners' (25 July 2022), https://www.gov.uk/guidance/register-an-overseas-entity, accessed 2 December 2023.

27 See Arun Advani, Cesar Poux, Anna Powell-Smith, Andy Summers, 'Catch me if you can: Gaps in the Register of Overseas Entities' (September 2023), https://warwick.ac.uk/fac/soc/economics/research/centres/cage/publications/workingpapers/2023/catch_me_if_you_can_gaps_in_the_register_of_overseas_entities/, accessed 2 December 2023; The London School of Economics and Political Science, 'Over two thirds of properties held by overseas shell companies remain anonymous' (*LSE*, 3 September 2023), https://www.lse.ac.uk/News/Latest-news-from-LSE/2023/i-September-2023/Over-two-thirds-of-properties-held-by-overseas-shell-companies-remain-anonymous, accessed 2 December 2023.

28 Arun Advani and others (n 27).

29 Rupert Neate, 'New register of overseas owners of UK properties 'riddled with flaws'' (*The Guardian*, 1 August 2022), https://www.theguardian.com/business/2022/aug/01/new-register-of-overseas-owners-of-uk-properties-riddled-with-flaws, accessed 7 December 2023.

30 See Companies House, 'Economic Crime and Corporate Transparency Act: Outline transition plan for Companies House' (*Companies House*, 16 October 2024), https://www.gov.uk/government/publications/economic-crime-and-corporate-transparency-act-outline-transition-plan-for-companies-house, accessed 7 November 2024.

31 Branislav Hock, 'Policing fiscal corruption: Tax crime and legally corrupt institutions in the United Kingdom' (2023) 85 *Law Contemp Probl* 159, https://scholarship.law.duke.edu/lcp/vol85/iss4/7, accessed 17 December 2023.

32 Mark Bou Mansour, 'King Charles urged to address British tax havens in public letter' (*Tax Justice Network*, 30 April 2023), https://taxjustice.net/press/king-charles-urged-to-address-british-tax-havens-in-public-letter, accessed 8 January 2024.

33 The Financial Secrecy Index ranks jurisdictions based on their involvement in enabling individuals to conceal their financial activities from legal oversight, see Tax Justice Network, 'Financial Secrecy Index 2022' (*Tax Justice Network*, 2022), https://fsi.taxjustice.net, accessed 7 November 2024.

34 Alex Cobham, Petr Janský, Markus Meinzer, 'The Financial Secrecy Index: Shedding new light on the geography of secrecy', (2015) 91(3) *Econ Geogr* 281, https://doi.org/10.1111/ecge.12094.

35 Grace Blakeley, 'On borrowed time: Finance and the UK's current account deficit' (*The IPPR Commission on Economic Justice*, 2018), https://www.ippr.org/files/2018-07/1531217614_cej-on-borrowed-time-june18-.pdf, accessed 8 January 2024; Eren Waitzman, 'Deregulation: Government policy since 1997' (*House of Lords*, 10 July 2017), https://lordslibrary.parliament.uk/research-briefings/lln-2017-0041, accessed 06 January 2024.

36 Paul Michael Gilmour (n 19).

37 The FATF's 2012 Recommendations were last updated in 2023, but the same 25% threshold remains, see FATF (n 15).

38 Andres Knobel, Florencia Lorenzo, 'Beneficial ownership registration around the world 2022' (December 2022), https://taxjustice.net/wp-content/uploads/2022/12/State-of-Play-of-Beneficial-Ownership-2022-Tax-Justice-Network.pdf, accessed 19 December 2023.
39 For further insights on the role of blockchain in registers of beneficial owners, see Paul Michael Gilmour, 'Decentralized blockchain technology: Towards a trusted and transparent beneficial ownership regime' in Doron Goldbarsht, Louis de Koker (eds) *Financial technology and the law: Combating financial crime* (Springer, 2022) 185–209.
40 Central Bank of Ireland, 'Beneficial ownership register FAQ' (2024), https://www.centralbank.ie/regulation/anti-money-laundering-and-countering-the-financing-of-terrorism/beneficial-ownership-register/about-the-register-and-faqs, accessed 12 January 2024.
41 For example, using public-private hybrid blockchain architecture was reported to enhance cross organisation data interoperability, traceability and integrity of Companies House records, see Ali Shahaab, Imtiaz A Khan, Ross Maude, Chaminda Hewage, Yingli Wang, 'Public service operational efficiency and blockchain: A case study of Companies House, UK' (2023) 40(1) *Gov Inf Q* 101759, https://doi.org/10.1016/j.giq.2022.101759.
42 Ali Shahaab and others (n 41).
43 Grace Blakeley (n 35).
44 Paul Michael Gilmour (n 5).
45 For example, Open Ownership, Transparency International, and Tax Justice Network; see also Andres Knobel (n 38).
46 Home Office, Department for Business and Trade, HM Treasury, Ministry of Justice, Serious Fraud Office, and Department for Business, Energy & Industrial Strategy (n 6).

Part Two

Corruption

4 'Help at Any Cost' – Impacts and Enablers of Corruption in Humanitarian Sector

Dolapo Fakuade

1 Introduction

Corruption is no new concept. It is often motivated by different factors with potential to generate a range of adverse effects. It exists in societies in varied forms, on local and global scales across the world,[1] enabled when unaddressed. Corruption is a multifaceted and complex phenomenon that may threaten systems and create risks in affected sectors.[2] This and perhaps the lack of a singular authoritative definition creates further confusion about what exactly corruption is.[3]

Research indicates that governments tend to be more interested in investigating the causes of corruption, while less keen on investigating charities, voluntary and community groups, perhaps because they are non-profit making.[4] This may be because corruption can be motivated by different factors and exhibited in varied forms with unpleasant connotations of theft.

Castro, Phillips and Ansari[5] discuss the motivations behind corruption, detailing that this phenomenon tends to occur when officials decide the gain from engaging in activities outweighs the cost of being caught and typically involves a party that provides improper incentives, i.e., bribery. This description links well with a more popular and well-used definition of corruption, posed by Lee and Muh[6] – '[t]he abuse of entrusted power for private benefit or gain' – as well as Castro, Phillips and Ansari's[7] definition, which explains corruption as the abuse of authority by people in positions of power. Castro, Phillips and Ansari's explanation of corruption portray it as a practice by those in positions of power, a suggestion that only those in power are perpetuators of corruption and therefore cannot be perpetuated by those who are not powerful or in positions of authority. However, when one unpacks the definition by Lee and Muh, it may be more wide-reaching, yet subjective in context and interpretation. Against this backdrop that presents corruption as a complex phenomenon, this chapter adopts a non-complex approach to examine corruption in the humanitarian sector.

This chapter provides background to forms of corruption and its impacts when unaddressed (part 2). This second section unravels how the subtle sources or forms of corruption may have eluded the conventional definition of corruption in the humanitarian sector. An overview of the humanitarian sector is provided to determine the enablers and implications of corruption in the sector (part 3) which helps to make a case for further scrutiny of humanitarian assistance (part 4). This chapter concludes by suggesting that the risk of corruption ought to be mitigated through policy tailored to the mode of humanitarian operations, a reminder that humanitarian assistance should not be provided at any cost.

DOI: 10.4324/9781003324843-7

2 Impacts of Corruption

Corruption can take place anywhere and in different forms. This ubiquitous nature highlights the importance of understanding how corruption is perceived, forms in which it may occur and the impacts they cause so that institutions are clear on what constitutes corrupt behaviour. Corruption may emerge from governmental, institutional and corporate sectors. The way society is governed at times creates an enabling environment for corruption to occur. For example, public resources are misallocated to those offering highest bribes and ignores those who offer the best value for money for society.[8] Such misallocation of resources can prevent those in need from getting the necessary benefits or aid, especially after an emergency or a disaster.[9] Causes of corruption and forms in which corruption takes place differ. Studies on causes of corruption indicate that corruption may be caused by political, economic, ecological and social factors.[10] For instance, in terms of economic corruption, businesses may engage in bribery,[11] tax evasion[12] and extortion[13] to maintain a competitive edge over their competitors if and when not properly regulated. Regardless of the causes, be it political, economic, social or ecological, the impacts of corruption are not as covert as their causes.

The theory of institutional corruption draws attention to the 'impact of policy incentives and regulation on organisational culture' and the need to investigate how corruption causes organisations to diverge from its purpose.[14] Deduction from theory of institutional corruption indicates that the organisation itself is also a victim of its corrupt acts. An example of institutional corruption as described by Fotaki may include the health sector engaging in activities, legal or not, that prioritise its reputation and its protection above the fidelity to the truth. While activities of this nature may not include bribery, it is a departure from the very core mission of the health sector which is to prioritise and protect lives. A justification for referencing theory of institutional corruption is its relevance to the mode of operation of the humanitarian sector. The humanitarian sector prioritises the humanitarian principles as foundation for humanitarian action.[15] The four principles, humanity, neutrality, impartiality and independence, are used to establish and maintain access to affected communities or people who require aid or assistance due to the impact of an adverse event, such as an emergency, war or other types of disasters. While debate remains on the challenges associated with complying with the humanitarian principles and violations of international humanitarian law,[16] such debates are not held through the lens of corruption but human rights.

Acknowledgement that corruption can be harmful is not denied, but consensus on impacts of its forms remains subjective. Perhaps rightly so, beyond the immediate financial loss resulting from corruption,[17] corruption may also lead to medium- and long-term effects.[18] For instance, humanitarian aid is observed to facilitate corruption in Central America and the Caribbean where assistance from international donors may not reach affected people.[19] Corruption as mentioned here may be endemic occurring in the form of aid diversion or misappropriation of funds leading to poverty and economic inequality in the aforementioned regions and in Afghanistan.[20] In Afghanistan, where social corruption further leads to an environment that fosters the violation of human rights, violence and subsequently, social unrest, the situation is further aggravated by political corruption. Studies have shown that the political form of corruption,[21] such as excluding citizen representation from political decision,[22] may generate obstacles to democracy and subsequently may impact on leadership and legitimacy of institution or government. Such dual or multiple dimensions in which corruption may affect a society, institution and organisation make it an important, yet challenging problem to tackle in the humanitarian sector.

3 Enablers in Humanitarian Sector

Humanitarian sector has always been relevant amidst continued conflict, crises, disasters and disruptive events that impact people, which subsequently result in need for assistance to alleviate suffering. While allowing for transparency and integrity in both private and public sectors is essential, the third sector (i.e. non-profit, charitable, voluntary) tends to prioritise the humanitarian principles as the fundamental premise for their operations and desperation to provide aid.[23] Common operations in this sector involve camp coordination, food security, education, emergency shelter, health, water, sanitation and hygiene and logistics[24] which may alleviate people's sufferings as well as provide opportunities for corruption. Walter[25] suggests that the humanitarian sector and effective humanitarian aid create a desire in people to take part in social change. Walter's explanation portrays the sector as one that prioritises care for the people, and the community those in need live in, which may explain the "help at any cost" mindset.[26] The unusual environment in which humanitarian assistance is provided suggests that the difficulty of adhering to humanitarianism may provide an enabling environment for corruption. The resultant outcome of such compromise is often evidenced by reduced quality of aid, reduced quantity or no aid reaching the beneficiaries for whom assistance is intended. While such a scenario creates further crises that require humanitarian assistance, one may argue that this cycle masks and facilitates corruption in the sector.

For corruption to occur, there must be some incentive in place that motivates people or organisations to engage in the practice. The factors that contribute to the occurrence of corruption can be referred to as 'enablers' that persuade those involved that there would be some benefit to these acts. Enablers can include economic incentives, political stability,[27] a lack of transparency or even weak rule of law.[28] Lack of transparency appears to be one of the major enablers of corruption in the humanitarian sector as observed over the last two decades.[29] Lack of transparency led to fraud, resources mismanagement and diversion of funds in Liberia which subsequently affected the Red Cross' Ebola response and recovery in the country.[30] Further evaluation of the case indicates that corruption significantly limited the effectiveness of the pandemic response, and the efficacy of the humanitarian work in Liberia, due to lack of trust from the community, and the withdrawal of funds from donors. While lack of communication may have contributed to the corruption witnessed, the enablers were a lack of transparency, the ability to capitalise on the weak enforcement and the lack of a corruption control mechanism throughout the period.[31] This scenario highlights weak or limited enforcement of compliance and lack of a corruption control mechanism as other enablers of corruption in the humanitarian sector.

Corruption is not only prevalent in emerging economies, but also in developed countries among donors of aid or among the parent organisations of charities offering aid in emerging countries. Reports show that charitable organisations abuse the system due to limited enforcement or weak enforcement of fraud control mechanism instituted by government. For instance, the report by the Centre for Tax Policy and Administration reveals that charitable organisations in Belgium, Canada, Italy, Norway, Spain, the UK and the USA have been involved in tax offences, tax evasion, money laundering and tax crimes.[32] The OECD report released in 2009 reveals that overpayment of refund claims and fraudulent claims cost the Canadian treasury millions of dollars due to insufficient preventive measures or insufficient regulatory policy.[33] Thus, corruption appears to be an institutional phenomenon at operational level where aid is administered to affected people or communities and at strategic level among those who make decisions to provide aid or donation. Within the humanitarian sector, corruption in its varied forms and levels appears to be enabled and a driver of help at any cost. Should this continue unaddressed when other sectors are tightly regulated and monitored?

4 Help at Any Cost?

Patterns of corruption in humanitarian aid are not without their risks.[34] Though not always overt and may be facilitated through the humanitarian supply chain, humanitarian assistance from organisations to a crisis is always the focus and useful measure of the impact and benefits of humanitarian assistance.[35] For example, the needs and vulnerabilities in communities are often identified by humanitarian workers within conflict areas. From this, a pattern of needs may evolve with how an organisation chooses to respond to a specific type of emergency; this idea was discussed by Mena and Hilhorst as they explained the pattern of path dependency in humanitarian aid.[36] Such pattern of needs resulting from crisis or disaster impacts often times create an enabling environment for corrupt practices to thrive.

Lebanon is known for several unresolved crises. Political and community leaders in the country are seen to conspire to abuse public resources, and with weak enforcement, funds for humanitarian assistance are at the crossroads of misappropriation and fraud. While the political leaders divert funds from beneficiaries, non-governmental organisations (NGOs) accept bribes and use education funds to train rebels.[37] Forms of corruption, such as fraud, bribes, bid rigging, kickbacks, to mention a few, are the possible practices in pursuit of humanitarian assistance in the country. While it is important not to neglect those in need of aid, the pattern described in Lebanon is an example of how the cycle of crises may fuel corrupt practices in a country, though enablers may vary.

Pattern of humanitarian work to address socio-economic issues in countries have also created systematic institutional corruption. In Democratic Republic of Congo (DRC), corruption is affecting those with lower economic status.[38] Women experience the impact of corruption more severely than men due to their weaker socio-economic status in the country. Women in this country are seen to suffer sexual exploitation or abuse by those influencing provision of humanitarian aid.[39] A similar scenario is observed in Haiti with Oxfam as the charitable organisation involved in such fraudulent acts of sexual exploitation of victims.[40] Evidence suggests aid organisations have a hard time resolving legal matters due to corruption in the system and the misapplication of laws for their own good.[41] Such self-regulating within the humanitarian sector facilitates continued corrupt practices that may later adversely impact the humanitarian organisation itself as seen in the case of Oxfam[42] or a country like Haiti where there is systematic withdrawal of aid.[43]

Scenarios that reflect corrupt practices in the humanitarian sector appear to be one of intricate interdependencies between forms, impacts and patterns leading to a motion of cascading effects of corruption. Such interdependencies make a case for scrutiny in the humanitarian sector and policy tailored to address institutional corruption. The forms and impacts of corruption as well as enablers are realities within the sector that can be challenging to manage without scrutiny of the drivers of practices that encourage corruption. Schultz and Søreide provide an extensive review of the drivers of corruption within humanitarian assistance and note that these drivers are also attributable to aid receivers, not just relief personnel.[44] Therefore, policy should be formulated to address institutional corruption aimed at regulating the donations received by humanitarian organisations and their activities, including monitoring of impacts and needs that triggered the humanitarian response. Policy should be tailored to address both the enablers and impacts of corrupt practices in countries receiving humanitarian assistance and those providing it. While it is possible that corruption may still persist in some forms, regardless of the need for humanitarian assistance, the mission of humanitarian workers should not be one that is undertaken at any cost, whether economic, ecological, political or social cost.

5 Conclusion

Cases of corruption examined in this chapter indicate that corruption is a phenomenon that undermines trust in humanitarian organisations, donors and perpetuators of corruption.[45] Institutional corruption appears to be the most prominent in the sector based on analysis of different cases in Central America, Europe, Asia, Africa and the USA referenced in this chapter. Whilst government corruption is the most studied, institutional corruption especially in the humanitarian sector is also present in most countries throughout the world, using similar methods for personal gain. Many common aid activities, such as food aid and community resettlement can be influenced by political, social or economic motivations to engage in corruption. From the discussion in this chapter, it can be seen that resource misallocation and embezzlement are among the main types of corruption that organisations and governments partake in, with a lack of transparency and weak or limited enforcement within the humanitarian sector being the main enablers in most, if not all, cases.

Corruption within the humanitarian sector can affect aid delivery and donation in several ways. Corrupt governments and humanitarian organisation can impact aid or assistance through the diversion of funds and aid, which can alter the number of available resources for an area. However, humanitarian organisations can also be the source of the corruption. As unravelled in this chapter, there is a case for the mitigation of corruption risks through the implementation of better policies and better transparency between governments, humanitarian organisations and affected communities in need of assistance. Not only does this increase trust among the actors and stakeholders, but it also facilitates a smoother response and recovery implementation. Corruption in this sector is still very much evident in both emerging and developed countries, thereby providing a rationale for further research into drivers and enablers in country or regional context to inform policy and practice in the hope of preventing and reducing corrupt practices in the humanitarian sector.

Notes

1 Chang-Qing Song, Chun-Ping Chang and Qiang Gong, 'Economic Growth, Corruption, and Financial Development: Global Evidence' (2021) 94 *Economic Modelling* 822.
2 Issa Luna-Pla and José R Nicolás-Carlock, 'Corruption and Complexity: A Scientific Framework for the Analysis of Corruption Networks' (2020) 5 *Applied Network Science* 13.
3 Jonathan Rose, 'The Meaning of Corruption: Testing the Coherence and Adequacy of Corruption Definitions' (2018) 20 *Public Integrity* 220.
4 Armando Castro, Nelson Phillips and Shaz Ansari, 'Corporate Corruption: A Review and an Agenda for Future Research' (2020) 14 *Academy of Management Annals* 935.
5 Castro, Phillips and Ansari 2020.

6 Cheng-Wen Lee and Muh Irfandy Azis, 'Determinants of Transparency, Accountability, and Corruption in Sub-Saharan African Countries' (2024) 13 *Review of Integrative Business and Economics Research* 71.
7 Castro, Phillips and Ansari 2020.
8 Huong Vu, Tuyen Quang Tran, Tuan Nguyen and Steven Lim, 'Corruption, Types of Corruption and Firm Financial Performance: New Evidence from a Transitional Economy' (2018) 148(4) *Journal of Business Ethics* 847.
9 James Lewis, 'Social Impacts of Corruption upon Community Resilience and Poverty' (2017) 9 *Jàmbá: Journal of Disaster Risk Studies* 1.
10 Luna-Pla and Nicolás-Carlock 2020.
11 Vu et al. 2018.
12 Halyna Halyna Samiilenko, Nataliia Ivanova, Iryna Shaposhnykova, Lidiia Vasylchenko, Iryna Solomakha and Svitlana Povna, 'Corruption as a Threat to Economic Security of the Country' (2021) 21(12) *International Journal of Computer Science and Network Security* 316.
13 Stephen D Morris, 'Forms of Corruption' (2011) 9(2) *CESifo DICE Report* 10. Available at https://www.econstor.eu/bitstream/10419/167031/1/ifo-dice-report-v09-y2011-i2-p10-14.pdf (accessed 27 March 2025).
14 Marianna Fotaki, 'Why We Must Talk about Institutional Corruption to Understand Wrongdoing in the Health Sector: Comment on "We Need to Talk about Corruption in Health Systems"' (2020) 9 *International Journal of Health Policy and Management* 206.
15 Grant Grant Broussard, Leonard S Rubenstein, Courtland Robinson, Wasim Maziak, Sappho Z Gilbert and Matthew DeCamp, 'Challenges to Ethical Obligations and Humanitarian Principles in Conflict Settings: A Systematic Review' (2019) 15(4) *Journal of International Humanitarian Action* 1.
16 Noam Noam Lubell, Jelena Pejic and Claire Simmons, 'Guidelines on Investigating Violations of International Humanitarian Law' (Geneva Academy of International Humanitarian Law and Human Rights 2019). Available at https://www.icrc.org/sites/default/files/document/file_list/guidelines_on_investigating_violations_of_ihl_final.pdf (accessed 27 March 2025).
17 Jonatas Dutra Sallaberry, Liz Spinello Quaesner, Mayla Cristina Costa and Leonard Flach, 'Measurement of Damage from Corruption in Brazil' (2020) 27 *Journal of Financial Crime* 1239.
18 Joseph Keneck-Massil, Clery Nomo-Beyala and Ferdinand Owoundi, 'The Corruption and Income Inequality Puzzle: Does Political Power Distribution Matter?' (2021) 103 *Economic Modelling* 105610.
19 Simisola O Fasehun, 'Impact of Humanitarian Aid on Facilitating Corruption: A Look at Nations in Central America and the Caribbean' (2021) Doctoral dissertation, George Mason University.
20 Jelena Bjelica and T Rutting, 'The State of Aid and Poverty in 2018. A New Look at Aid Effectiveness in Afghanistan' (2018) 17 *Afghanistan Analyst Network*. Available at: https://www.afghanistan-analysts.org/en/reports/economy-development-environment/the-state-of-aid-and-poverty-in-2018-a-new-look-at-aid-effectiveness-in-afghanistan/ (accessed 27 March 2025).
21 Kristen Kao, Ellen Lust and Lise Rakner, 'Vote-Buying, Anti-Corruption Campaigns, and Identity in African Elections' (2022) 160 *World Development* 106064.
22 Daniel Nyberg, 'Corporations, Politics, and Democracy: Corporate Political Activities as Political Corruption' (2021) 2(1) *Organization Theory* 1–24. https://doi.org/10.1177/2631787720982618
23 Broussard et al. 2019.
24 Mizan Bustanul Fuady Bisri, 'Comparative Study on Inter-Organizational Cooperation in Disaster Situations and Impact on Humanitarian Aid Operations' (2016) 1 *Journal of International Humanitarian Action* 8.
25 C Corelia Walther, *Development, Humanitarian Aid, and Social Welfare* (Springer 2020).
26 Robert M Kelly, 'Corruption in Africa: Cultural, Economic and Political Factors Which Impact Corruption and Potential Solutions' (2014) Doctoral dissertation, Rutgers University-Camden Graduate School.
27 Kelly 2014.
28 Cornelius Dudzai and Robert Chigangaidze, 'The Conundrum of Corruption during a Coronavirus Lockdown in Zimbabwe: Lessons for Social Work' (2023) 17(3) *Ethics and Social Welfare* 312–326.

29 Kevin Savage, Lorenzo Delesgues, Ellen Martin and Gul Pacha Ulfat, 'Corruption Perceptions and Risks in Humanitarian Assistance: An Afghanistan Case Study' (2007) HPG Working Paper. Available at https://www.files.ethz.ch/isn/91181/2007-07_Corruption%20Perceptions.pdf (accessed 27 March 2025); Sarah Bailey, 'Perceptions of Corruption in Humanitarian Assistance among Internally Displaced Persons in Northern Uganda' (2008) HPG Working Paper. Available at https://www.files.ethz.ch/isn/98998/2008-07_Uganda.pdf (accessed 27 March 2025).

30 Jenise R DePinto, 'Corruption and the 2014 EVD Crisis in Sierra Leone: Ebola as "Total Disease"' (2016) *Democratization and Human Security in Postwar Sierra Leone* 217.

31 Bouchabke Soha and Gloria Haddad, 'The Influence of Human Resources' Practices on Corruption Behaviour in Humanitarian Aid', in Andrea Bonomi Savignon, Luca Gnan, Alessandro Hinna and Fabio Monteduro (eds), *Hybridity in the Governance and Delivery of Public Services*, Volume 7 (Emerald Publishing Limited 2018) 89–122.

32 Organisation for Economic Cooperation and Development, *Report on Abuse of Charities for Money Laundering and Tax Evasion* (OECD Centre for Tax Policy and Administration 2009).

33 Organisation for Economic Cooperation and Development, *Report on Abuse of Charities for Money Laundering and Tax Evasion* (OECD Centre for Tax Policy and Administration 2009).

34 Pete Ewins, Paul Harvey, Kevin Savage and Alex Jacobs, 'Mapping the Risks of Corruption in Humanitarian Action' (2006) Report for Transparency International and the U4 Anti-Corruption Resource Centre. Available at https://interagencystandingcommittee.org/sites/default/files/migrated/2014-11/Mapping%20the%20Risk%20of%20Corruption%20in%20Humanitarian%20Assistance%2C%20July%202006.pdf (accessed 27 March 2025).

35 Charles Keely, Holly Reed and Ronald Waldman, 'Understanding Mortality Patterns in Complex Humanitarian Emergencies' (2001) Forced Migration and Mortality, National Academies Press, Washington, DC.

36 R Mena and D Hilhorst, 'Path Dependency When Prioritising Disaster and Humanitarian Response under High Levels of Conflict: A Qualitative Case Study in South Sudan' (2022) 7(1) *Journal of International Humanitarian Action* 5.

37 Soha et al. 2021.

38 Nicole Henze, François Grünewald and Sharanjeet Parmar, 'Operational Review of Exposure to Corrupt Practices in Humanitarian Aid Implementation Mechanisms in the DRC' (2020) 28 ReliefWeb. Available at https://reliefweb.int/report/democratic-republic-congo/operational-review-exposure-corrupt-practices-humanitarian-aid (accessed 27 March 2025).

39 Henze et al. 2020.

40 Mishal S Khan, 'Oxfam: Sex Scandal or Governance Failure?' (2018) 391 *The Lancet* 1019.

41 Henze et al. 2020.

42 Monika Bauhr, Nicholas Charron and Naghmeh Nasiritousi, 'Does Corruption Cause Aid Fatigue? Public Opinion and the Aid-Corruption Paradox' (2013) 57(3) *International Studies Quarterly* 568.

43 Claire Antone Claire Antone Payton, 'Building Corruption in Haiti: In Haiti, Illicit Income Extraction Is a Constantly Constructed Mode of Governance, Helping to Explain Popular Outrage Surrounding the Recent PetroCaribe Scandal' (2019) 51 *NACLA Report on the Americas* 182; Vijaya Ramachandran and Julie Walz, 'Haiti: Where Has All the Money Gone?' (2015) 21 *Journal of Haitian Studies* 26; Scott M Anderson, 'Development Assistance in Haiti: Where Has the Money Gone?' (2014) Doctoral dissertation, Naval Postgraduate School, Monterey, CA.

44 Jessica Schultz and Tina Søreide, 'Corruption in Emergency Procurement' (2008) 32 *Disasters* 516.

45 Graham Heaslip, Ira Haavisto and Gyöngyi Kovács, 'Cash as a Form of Relief' (2016) 59 *Advances in Managing Humanitarian Operations* 235.

Bibliography

Sarah Bailey, 'Perceptions of Corruption in Humanitarian Assistance among Internally Displaced Persons in Northern Uganda' (2008) HPG Working Paper.

Monika Bauhr, Nicholas Charron and Naghmeh Nasiritousi, 'Does Corruption Cause Aid Fatigue? Public Opinion and the Aid-Corruption Paradox' (2013) 57(3) *International Studies Quarterly* 568.

Mizan Bustanul Fuady Bisri, 'Comparative Study on Inter-Organizational Cooperation in Disaster Situations and Impact on Humanitarian Aid Operations' (2016) 1 *Journal of International Humanitarian Action* 8.

Jelena Bjelica and T Rutting, 'The State of Aid and Poverty in 2018. A New Look at Aid Effectiveness in Afghanistan' (2018) 17 *Afghanistan Analyst Network*. Available at: https://www.afghanistan-analysts.org/en/reports/economy-development-environment/the-state-of-aid-and-poverty-in-2018-a-new-look-at-aid-effectiveness-in-afghanistan/ (accessed 27 March 2025)

Grant Broussard, Leonard S Rubenstein, Courtland Robinson, Wasim Maziak, Sappho Z Gilbert and Matthew DeCamp, 'Challenges to Ethical Obligations and Humanitarian Principles in Conflict Settings: A Systematic Review' (2019) 15(4) *Journal of International Humanitarian Action* 1.

Armando Castro, Nelson Phillips and Shaz Ansari, 'Corporate Corruption: A Review and an Agenda for Future Research' (2020) 14 *Academy of Management Annals* 935.

Jenise R DePinto, 'Corruption and the 2014 EVD Crisis in Sierra Leone: Ebola as "Total Disease"' (2016) *Democratization and Human Security in Postwar Sierra Leone* 217.

Cornelius Dudzai and Robert Chigangaidze, 'The Conundrum of Corruption during a Coronavirus Lockdown in Zimbabwe: Lessons for Social Work' (2023) 17(3) *Ethics and Social Welfare* 312–326.

Pete Ewins, Paul Harvey, Kevin Savage and Alex Jacobs, 'Mapping the Risks of Corruption in Humanitarian Action' (2006) Report for Transparency International and the U4 Anti-Corruption Resource Centre.

Marianna Fotaki, 'Why We Must Talk about Institutional Corruption to Understand Wrongdoing in the Health Sector: Comment on "We Need to Talk about Corruption in Health Systems"' (2020) 9 *International Journal of Health Policy and Management* 206.

Michal Givoni, 'Reluctant Cosmopolitanism: Perceptions Management and the Performance of Humanitarian Principles' (2016) 7(2) Humanity*:* An International Journal of Human Rights, Humanitarianism, and Development 255.

Graham Heaslip, Ira Haavisto and Gyöngyi Kovács, 'Cash as a Form of Relief' (2016) 59 *Advances in Managing Humanitarian Operations* 59–78.

Nicole Henze, François Grünewald and Sharanjeet Parmar, 'Operational Review of Exposure to Corrupt Practices in Humanitarian Aid Implementation Mechanisms in the DRC' (2020) 28 ReliefWeb.

Kristen Kao, Ellen Lust and Lise Rakner, 'Vote-Buying, Anti-Corruption Campaigns, and Identity in African Elections' (2022) 160 *World Development* 106064.

Joseph Keneck-Massil, Clery Nomo-Beyala and Ferdinand Owoundi, 'The Corruption and Income Inequality Puzzle: Does Political Power Distribution Matter?' (2021) 103 *Economic Modelling* 105610.

Mishal S Khan, 'Oxfam: Sex Scandal or Governance Failure?' (2018) 391 *The Lancet* 1019.

Cheng-Wen Lee and Muh Irfandy Azis, 'Determinants of Transparency, Accountability, and Corruption in Sub-Saharan African Countries' (2024) 13 *Review of Integrative Business and Economics Research* 71.

James Lewis, 'Social Impacts of Corruption upon Community Resilience and Poverty' (2017) 9 *Jàmbá: Journal of Disaster Risk Studies* 1.

Noam Lubell, Jelena Pejic and Claire Simmons, 'Guidelines on Investigating Violations of International Humanitarian Law' (Geneva Academy of International Humanitarian Law and Human Rights 2019).

Issa Luna-Pla and José R Nicolás-Carlock, 'Corruption and Complexity: A Scientific Framework for the Analysis of Corruption Networks' (2020) 5 *Applied Network Science* 13.

Stephen D Morris, 'Forms of Corruption' (2011) 9 *CESifo DICE Report* 10.

National Research Council (United States), *Forced Migration & Mortality: Roundtable on the Demography of Forced Migration*, HE Reed and CB Keely (eds) (National Academies Press (US) 2001).

Daniel Nyberg, 'Corporations, Politics, and Democracy: Corporate Political Activities as Political Corruption' (2021) 2(1) *Organization Theory* 1–24.

Organisation for Economic Cooperation and Development, *Report on Abuse of Charities for Money Laundering and Tax Evasion* (OECD Centre for Tax Policy and Administration 2019).

Claire Antone Payton, 'Building Corruption in Haiti: In Haiti, Illicit Income Extraction Is a Constantly Constructed Mode of Governance, Helping to Explain Popular Outrage Surrounding the Recent PetroCaribe Scandal' (2019) 51 *NACLA Report on the Americas* 182.

Vijaya Ramachandran and Julie Walz, 'Haiti: Where Has All the Money Gone?' (2015) 21 *Journal of Haitian Studies* 26.

Jonathan Rose, 'The Meaning of Corruption: Testing the Coherence and Adequacy of Corruption Definitions' (2018) 20(3) *Public Integrity* 220.

Jonatas Dutra Sallaberry, Liz Spinello Quaesner, Mayla Cristina Costa and Leonard Flach, 'Measurement of Damage from Corruption in Brazil' (2020) 27 *Journal of Financial Crime* 1239.

Halyna Samiilenko, Nataliia Ivanova, Iryna Shaposhnykova, Lidiia Vasylchenko, Iryna Solomakha and Svitlana Povna, 'Corruption as a Threat to Economic Security of the Country' (2021) 21(12) *International Journal of Computer Science and Network Security* 316.

Kevin Savage, Lorenzo Delesgues, Ellen Martin and Gul Pacha Ulfat, 'Corruption Perceptions and Risks in Humanitarian Assistance: An Afghanistan Case Study' (2007) HPG Working Paper.

Jessica Schultz and Tina Søreide, 'Corruption in Emergency Procurement' (2008) 32 *Disasters* 516.

Bouchabke Soha and Gloria Haddad, "The Influence of Human Resources' Practices on Corruption Behaviour in Humanitarian Aid', in Andrea Bonomi Savignon, Luca Gnan, Alessandro Hinna and Fabio Monteduro (eds), *Hybridity in the Governance and Delivery of Public Services*, Volume 7 (Emerald Publishing Limited 2018) 1–5.

Bouchabke Soha and Gloria Haddad, 'Ineffectiveness, Poor Coordination, and Corruption in Humanitarian Aid: The Syrian Refugee Crisis in Lebanon' (2021) 32 *VOLUNTAS: International Journal of Voluntary and Nonprofit Organizations* 894.

Chang-Qing Song, Chun-Ping Chang and Qiang Gong, 'Economic Growth, Corruption, and Financial Development: Global Evidence' (2021) 94 *Economic Modelling* 822.

Huong Vu, Tuyen Quang Tran, Tuan Nguyen and Steven Lim, 'Corruption, Types of Corruption and Firm Financial Performance: New Evidence from a Transitional Economy' (2018) 148(4) *Journal of Business Ethics* 847.

Corelia Walther, *Development, Humanitarian Aid, and Social Welfare* (Springer 2020).

Doctoral Dissertations

Scott M Anderson, 'Development Assistance in Haiti: Where Has the Money Gone?' (2014) Doctoral dissertation, Naval Postgraduate School, Monterey, CA.

Simisola O Fasehun, 'Impact of Humanitarian Aid on Facilitating Corruption: A Look at Nations in Central America and the Caribbean' (2021) Doctoral dissertation, George Mason University.

Robert M Kelly, 'Corruption in Africa: Cultural, Economic and Political Factors Which Impact Corruption and Potential Solutions' (2014) Doctoral dissertation, Rutgers University-Camden Graduate School.

5 Critical Analysis of the Legal Framework for Corporate Anti-Bribery Policies

The United Kingdom and Colombian Approaches

Yudy Paola Pinzon Fernandez

Introduction

Scandals associated with corruption and bribery seem to be a generalised international phenomenon.[1] For that reason, society increasingly demands from corporations the performance of their activities responsibly, and preventing bribery and corruption certainly is part of it.[2] Corporations tend to argue that bribes in some countries are part of the culture (e.g. exchanging favours is considered a normal practice), thus they must act equally or they will lose contracts against corporations that are willing to bribe.[3] This cannot be considered an excuse, conversely, corporations are expected to adopt measures that prevent irregular business practices and transform the business culture.[4]

On this matter, international organisations believe that corporate self-regulation is an important tool to produce corporate behavioural changes.[5] For instance, Transparency International (TI) considers as a business principle to tackle bribery, the enterprises' commitment to prohibit bribery and the implementation of a programme to counter bribery within the organisation.[6] Similarly, the Organisation for Economic Co-operation and Development (OECD) recommends that corporations should implement corporate anti-bribery policies (CAB-policies) based on their circumstances and review internal procedures periodically.[7]

This chapter compares the legal frameworks of the United Kingdom (UK) and Colombia on CAB-policies. Despite differences in their legal systems – UK common law and Colombia civil law – both countries have adopted international standards in the fight against bribery, among other things, by integrating corporate anti-bribery self-regulation measures into their domestic laws. Nevertheless, international reports on anti-bribery efforts reveal a stark contrast: the UK consistently ranks among the top performers, while Colombia is positioned near the bottom.[8] This chapter examines case studies from both countries, highlighting the importance of understanding corporate anti-bribery self-regulation as a complement to formal regulations, and explores some of the challenges corporations face in developing and implementing CAB-policies. This chapter concludes that both countries share similar approaches towards CAB-policies and identifies areas where their legal frameworks could complement each other. Additionally, it proposes a strategy that, despite certain limitations, would enable governments to adopt a more proactive approach towards this self-regulation tool.

DOI: 10.4324/9781003324843-8

1 *The UK and Colombian Legal Frameworks on CAB-Policies*

1.1 *International Standards*

UNITED KINGDOM

The OECD Anti-Bribery Convention established legally binding standards for the UK to actively tackle bribery since 1997.[9] Some argue that despite warnings from the OECD, the UK's compliance with the Convention was overdue.[10] Nonetheless, as expressed by TI, the UK Bribery Act (UKBA) '(...) is now among the strictest legislation internationally on bribery'.[11] Moreover, the 2018 TI report on the OECD Convention progress classified the UK within the category of active enforcement.[12] Additionally, the UK seems to have understood the intention of the OECD regarding the legally binding standards established to criminalise bribery[13] since the UKBA also enforced '(...) the effectiveness of internal controls, ethics and compliance programmes or measures for preventing and detecting bribery (...)'.[14]

The United Nations (UN) Convention against Corruption[15] is considered a more detailed and global legally binding instrument that has been replicated by the UK and "(...) requires the States Parties to implement numerous and detailed anti-bribery and corruption measures impacting upon their laws, institutions and practices".[16] For example, the UKBA includes private sector activities and establishes a wider range of offences. Nonetheless, it is worth mentioning that for the European Union (EU) member states, bribery in the private sector has been considered a crime since 1999.[17]

COLOMBIA

The Organisation of American States (OEA) Inter-American Convention against Corruption[18] was the first international anti-corruption instrument adopted by Colombia in 1996. Nonetheless, between 1996 and 2012,[19] the fight against corruption seems to have been deficient; a fact confirmed in the TI reports from this period, which note that Colombia is one of the countries with little or no enforcement.[20] The TI reports have highlighted important developments to establish the liability of legal persons and increase the fines for corruption-related crimes.[21] However, the TI has also recommended the implementation by Colombia of further initiatives, in a bid to strengthen corporate sector awareness about compliance with the business principles for countering bribery.[22] TI is right in making this observation because before the anti-corruption statute was enacted in 2011,[23] the expression bribery was understood in Colombia to apply *only* to conducts involving the public sector. In this regard, it is important to highlight that Colombia made reforms to ensure alignment with the OECD standards.[24] For instance, it included in the legislation "(...) the recommendations from the OECD on corporate responsibility and effective prosecution against legal entities, leniency programmes and the obligation to adopt compliance programmes (...)".[25] This author considers that corporate consciousness about bribery is still far from the desired but recognises the Secretariat of Transparency's efforts to promote the creation of compliance programmes, cooperative codes of ethics, self-regulation pacts between corporations operating within the same sector,[26] and particularly the initiative called 'Private Companies Active in Compliance with Anti-Corruption Measures (EACA)' that was launched in 2015 with EU support.[27]

COMPARISON

Table 5.1 Comparison of the United Kingdom and Colombia's Compliance with International Standards

General			
Instrument	*UK*	*Colombia*	*Nature*
OECD			
- Convention on Combating Bribery of Foreign Public Officials in International Business Transactions (1997).	✓	✓	Legally binding
UN			
- Convention against Transnational Organised Crime (2000).	✓	✓	Legally binding
- Convention against Corruption (2003).	✓	✓	Legally binding
- Sustainable Goals (2015): 16.5. 'Substantially reduce corruption and bribery in all their forms'.	✓	✓	Non-binding
EU			
- Convention on the fight against Corruption involving Officials of the European Communities or Officials of Member States of the EU (1997).	✓		Legally binding
- Council of Europe Criminal Law Convention on Corruption (1999).	✓		Legally binding
OEA			
Inter-American Convention against Corruption (1996).		✓	Legally binding
Corporate Landscape against Corruption			
- Recommendations for responsible business conduct incorporated in the OECD 'Declaration on International Investment and Multinational Enterprises (MNEs)' and its annexes 'Guidelines for MNEs'.	✓	✓	Legally binding
- International Organisation of Standardisation (ISO) – 'Anti-bribery management systems'.	✓	✓	Non-binding
- UN Global Compact (UNGC) – Principle: 'Businesses should work against corruption in all its forms, including extortion and bribery'.	✓	✓	Non-binding

National laws

United Kingdom

Table 5.2 United Kingdom National Laws

UKBA (into force 1 July 2011)	*Section 7*. Offence: Failure of commercial organisations to prevent bribery *(2)* Defence for Corporations: Prove that had in place adequate procedures to prevent bribery. *Section 9*. Guidance for Corporations about procedures to prevent bribes. *Section 12*. Territorial application.
UK Crime and Courts Act 2013 (UKCCA)	*Schedule 17*. Deferred Prosecution Agreements (DPAs) and Code of Practice for prosecutors.

COLOMBIA

Table 5.3 Colombia's National Laws

Law 599/2000 (Criminal Code)	Article 250A Private corruption offence. Articles 405, 406, 407 Passive and active bribery offences (Public Sector). Article 433 Transnational bribery offence.
Law 1474/2011 (Anti-corruption Statute) Amended by Law 1778/2016 (on the liability of legal persons for acts of transnational corruption) and Law 2195/2022 (on transparency and prevention against corruption)	Article 16 Creation of a new offence called 'Private corruption'. Article 34-2 Administrative sanctions for corporations. Article 34-3 Gradation of administrative sanctions for corporations. Article 34-7 Transparency and business ethics programs. Legal entities (...) shall adopt transparency and business ethics programs that include internal auditing mechanisms and standards. The respective superintendencies or inspection, surveillance or control authorities will determine the content of the transparency and business ethics programs considering criteria such as the sector, its risks, the amount of assets, income, the number of employees and corporate purpose. (...) Paragraph 2. The superintendencies or inspection, surveillance or control authorities of the executive branch in coordination with the Transparency Secretariat of the Presidency of the Republic, will determine the minimum guidelines that must be provided for in the transparency and business ethics programs to standardise the actions, policies, methods, procedures, prevention, control, evaluation and continuous improvement mechanisms. These guidelines will be evaluated and updated, in accordance with international standards and new practices that strengthen transparency and business ethics programs, at least every four (4) years. Paragraph 3.Those responsible for auditing or internal control of legal entities subject to the obligation must include in their annual audit plan the verification of compliance and effectiveness of transparency and business ethics programs (...). Article 66 Creation of the National Citizen Commission for the Fight against Corruption. Article 68 Functions of the National Citizen Commission for the Fight against Corruption (d) Promotion of codes of conduct for the private sector. Article 72 Functions of the Secretariat of Transparency of the Presidency (f) Duty to promote strategies to fight against corruption in public and private sectors.
Decree 1023/2012 Structure of the Superintendency of Companies	Article 7 (22) Fines for breaking the law.
Law 1778/2016 Amended by Law 2195/2022	*Article* 2 Administrative liability of legal persons *(Administrative investigation). Article 5* Sanctions imposed by the Colombian Superintendence of Companies (CSOC). *Article 7* Criteria for the imposition of sanctions *(7)* Existence, implementation and effectiveness of anti-corruption programs. *Article 23* Promotion of Business Ethics Programs (Colombian Superintendence of Companies (CSOC)).

COMPARISON

Table 5.4 Comparison of the United Kingdom and Colombia's National Laws

Criterion	*United Kingdom (UK)*	*Colombia*
Basic Concepts		
National authorities involved in the promotion of Anti-bribery Self-regulation (AB-Self-regulation)	The Secretary of State (United Kingdom Bribery Act (UKBA) s 9).	a National Citizen Commission for the Fight against Corruption (Law 1474/2011 articles 66, 68 (d). b Secretariat of Transparency of the Presidency (Law 1474/2011 paragraph 1 article 34-7). c Colombian Superintendence of Companies (CSOC) (Law 1778/16 art 23). d Other Superintendencies (Depending on the economic sector of the company. Law 1474/2011 article 34-7).
Which corporations must implement anti-bribery procedures?	All relevant commercial organisations(UKBA s 7).	Legal entities subject to inspection, surveillance, or control by superintendencies (Law 1474/2011 article 34-7).
Is there any *government organisation* that provides personalised assistance to corporations for the creation, implementation, and monitoring of the policies?	No, only the document known as the UKBA Guidance.	Yes, the Integrity Team of the Secretariat of Transparency and Superintendencies (Depending on the economic sector of the company. Law 1474/2011 article 34-7). However, it is not clear how this support is given and if there is any cost for this service.
Responsibility placed on corporations for the creation, implementation, and monitoring of the policies	100%	95% National authorities dictate minimum requirements and content of the Corporate anti-bribery policies (CAB-Policies) (Law 1474/2011 article 34-7 and the Secretariat of Transparency Guide for the development and implementation of Transparency and Business Ethics Programs).
Enforcement (CAB-Policies)		
Regulatory bodies	UKBA s 10: a Director of the Serious Fraud Office (SFO). b Director of Public Prosecutions.	CSOC or other superintendence depending on the economic sector of the company (Law 1474/2011 article 34-7, Law 1778 article 23).

(*Continued*)

Table 5.4 (Continued)

Criterion	*United Kingdom (UK)*	*Colombia*
Monitoring by governments	No, only if a case of bribery occurs (UKBA s 7 (1) (2)).	CSOC or other superintendence depending on the economic sector of the company. These national authorities impose sanctions for the failure to comply with the instructions and orders given to companies regarding AB-Policies (Law 1474/2011 article 34-7).
Is the 'failure of commercial organisations to prevent bribery' considered an offence?	Yes (UKBA s 7 (1)).	No Nevertheless, national corporations and foreign company branches involved in bribery cases could face administrative liability sanctions (Law 1474/2011 article 34-2, 34-3).
Is it a defence for commercial organisations to have "had in place adequate procedures"?	Yes "Adequate procedures" (UKBA s 7 (2)).	It is not a defence but is a key criterion for the CSOC to reduce fines in transnational bribery cases (Law 1778 2016, article 7). Furthermore, the amended version of Law 1474/2011 introduced a related mitigation factor for sanctions in bribery cases. This factor involves the implementation of measures and actions that evaluated by the authority, reasonably contribute to preventing future acts of corruption (Law 1474/2011, letter f, article 34-3).

Outcomes of the UK and Colombian legal frameworks comparative analysis

Table 5.5 Outcomes of the United Kingdom and Colombian Legal Frameworks Comparative Analysis

United Kingdom (UK)	+	–	*Colombia*	+	–
All situations related to bribery are condensed into just one piece of legislation.	+		Colombia has different legal instruments referring to bribery. This multiplicity of laws can be confusing for corporations, especially for Multinational Enterprises (MNEs) with subsidiaries in Colombia.		–
'The failure to prevent bribery' is considered as an offence.	+		The 'failure to prevent bribery' is not typified as an offence. This is considered a weakness because it is a means to compel corporations to self-regulate. Nevertheless, it is worth mentioning that domestic corporations and foreign company branches involved in bribery cases could face administrative liability sanctions.	+	–

(*Continued*)

Table 5.5 (Continued)

United Kingdom (UK)	+	–	*Colombia*	+	–
Having 'adequate' procedures to prevent bribery is a defence for the offence of failure to prevent it. Good attempt to promote self-regulation.	+		It is not a defence but is a key criterion for the CSOC to reduce fines in transnational bribery cases. Furthermore, the amended Law 1474/2011 introduced a related mitigation factor for sanction gradation in bribery cases. This factor involves the implementation of measures and actions that evaluated by the authority, reasonably contribute to preventing future acts of corruption.	+	
The promotion of CAB-Policies is just on one authority.		–	Colombia seems to have a more proactive stance towards the promotion of CAB-Policies because different bodies and authorities are involved.	+	
EU member states consider bribery in the private sector since 1999.	+		Regarding bribery laws for the private sector, Colombia has been far behind the UK because only since 2011 the Colombian legislation included bribery for the private sector.		–
Both legal frameworks have broadened the territorial application of the law. However, the UK went further because it contemplates not only bribery of foreign public officials but also any bribe performed by a person associated with the UK; this means extraterritorial application of the law even for the private sector.	+		In this regard, comparing to the UK, the Colombian legislation fell short by limiting the extraterritorial element of bribery to bribes of foreign public officials, leaving behind transactions exclusively performed in the private sector.		–
The UKBA only establishes unlimited fines as penalty for relevant commercial organisations for the failure to prevent bribery.		–	Similarly, national authorities impose sanctions for the failure to comply with the instructions and orders given to companies regarding CAB-Policies. However, it applies to all legal entities subject to inspection, surveillance, or control by superintendencies. Additionally, Colombian legislation outlines broader procedures for corporations involved in bribery offences. These include administrative investigations to impose fines, a ten-year prohibition on receiving government incentives, and mandatory publication of the sanction in national newspapers and the company's website for up to a year to highlight	+	

(*Continued*)

Table 5.5 (Continued)

United Kingdom (UK)	+	–	*Colombia*	+	–
			reputational damage. For bribery involving government officials, further measures may include suspension or cancellation of the company's license if there is evidence of criminal activity, particularly when bribery of a government official is involved, as this constitutes an offence against public administration.		

The UK and Colombia have adhered to international legally binding instruments. Nonetheless, adjustment of the national laws in both countries was belated, wasting valuable years to transform business culture. The UK approach to self-regulation involves a criminal prosecution since the UKBA considers an offence, the 'failure of commercial organisations to prevent bribery' but having in place 'adequate' procedures to prevent it could be alleged as a defence.[28] Similarly, in the Colombian legal framework, the importance of CAB-policies arises within criminal prosecutions, not as an offence or defence but as part of the criteria to mitigate sanctions in bribery cases, for instance, the amended version of Law 1474/2011 introduced a related mitigating factor in the sanction's gradation in bribery cases. This factor involves implementing measures and actions that, as determined by the relevant administrative authority conducting the investigation, reasonably contribute to preventing future acts of corruption,[29] and Law 1778/2016 includes the existence, execution, and effectiveness of corporate codes of ethics as one of the criteria to impose a lower fine for transnational bribery cases.[30] Consequently, these two countries' frameworks towards CAB-policies are relatively similar. However, some important issues surrounding their self-regulation approach remain unclear. For instance, what kind of regulation is expected from corporations? Within the UK setting, what does 'adequate' mean? How does the Colombian authority assess 'the effectiveness' of the CAB-policies to impose a lower fine? Because it seems contradictory to assess 'the effectiveness' of the CAB-policies when the bribery has been proven. To clarify 'adequate' procedures, the UKBA Guidance seems to equate it with six principles (proportionate procedures, top-level commitment, risk assessment, due diligence, communication and training, and monitoring and review).[31] Principles seem well explained in the guidance but someone could argue that even after reading the guidance, corporations could need assistance to materialise those principles according to their size and business, especially small corporations due to the lack of budget limits for this. Similarly, the Colombian Guide for the Development and Implementation of Transparency and Business Ethics Programs[32] explains the minimum content to consider CAB-policies effective but still described theoretically, leaving the challenge for corporations to materialise them in practice according to their size and business.

The Colombian approach seems more proactive towards CAB-policies because national laws establish duties in this regard for some government institutions, aiming to assist corporations in creating, implementing, and monitoring these policies. However, despite the Colombian government's initiatives, and the more passive stance of the UK, the truth is that Colombia still occupies one of the last positions in the fight against corruption while the UK is one of the best.[33] As argued before, this situation is the result of cultural differences, and sadly, corruption is still very entrenched in Colombian culture.[34] Unfortunately, corporations are still not conscious of the value of CAB-policies and governments have not found the best strategy to use self-regulation to change business culture rather than an incentive to avoid prosecutions or reduce fines.[35]

2 *Impact of Bribery Scandals on CAB-Policies (Case Studies)*

This segment briefly describes cases from the UK and Colombia to highlight the impact of bribery scandals on CAB-policies. The analysis of these cases is further explored in the author's master's dissertation,[36] providing additional context and in-depth insights.

2.1 *United Kingdom*

STANDARD BANK[37]

The Serious Fraud Office (SFO) investigated Standard Bank (SB) for a bribery case involving its subsidiary and the Tanzanian Government.[38] The subsidiary signed an agreement with a third party, failing to recognise that two of its directors were government officials.[39] SB lacked adequate CAB-policies, relying on the subsidiary's judgement to subscribe to the agreement and set the commission for the third party.[40] Suspicious transactions led to a report, prompting an investigation.[41] The SFO found SB's policies unclear and insufficiently communicated.[42] This case was significant as it tested the offence of failing to prevent bribery and the defence of having adequate procedures, resulting in the first Deferred Prosecution Agreement (DPA)[43] under Section 7 of the UKBA.[44] The DPA required SB to independently review its anti-bribery controls, policies, and procedures.[45] Price Waterhouse Coopers (PWC) LLP was appointed to review SB's anti-bribery policies, providing recommendations that were implemented within a year, including clearer language and detailed procedures for reporting suspicious activities.[46]

SWEETT GROUP[47]

Sweett Group (SG) pleaded guilty to failing to prevent bribery in securing a contract for hotel construction in Dubai.[48] The offence, committed over 18 months, was marked by a wilful disregard for the auditor's concerns.[49] A DPA was not offered, and the company was rebranded as Currie & Brown, which means no further monitoring of the policies.[50] SG, now Currie & Brown, includes UKBA principles but with insufficient detail.[51] The zero-tolerance statement is vague, and unclear employee procedures may fail to prevent future bribery.[52]

ROLLS ROYCE[53]

In 2012, Rolls Royce (RR) was investigated for bribery by its subsidiaries across several countries.[54] Despite having anti-bribery policies, RR's procedures were ineffective, leading to bribes for over 24 years.[55] The company voluntarily reported the issue, and a DPA was reached.[56] As part of the DPA, RR was required to improve its compliance programme and make independent reviews on them.[57] Significant changes included clearer policies, enhanced employee training, and a stronger focus on risk assessment, adopting a cultural shift towards compliance.[58]

SKANSEN INTERIORS[59]

Skansen Interiors (SI), a small UK-based company, lacked a formal anti-bribery policy and relied on general instructions.[60] The company's failure to prevent bribery led to the first contested conviction under the UKBA. The case highlighted key steps for companies to implement adequate anti-bribery procedures, including senior-level responsibility, staff training, reporting systems, legal updates, and documentation of actions taken.[61]

2.2 *Colombia*

INTER-AMERICAN SOCIETY OF WATER AND SERVICES S.A.[62]

Inter-American Society of Water and Services S.A., (Inassa), a Colombian subsidiary of Canal Extensia S.A., pleaded guilty to transnational bribery charges related to securing public contracts in Latin America.[63] Following the investigation, Inassa collaborated by providing vital evidence, leading to a 50% fine reduction.[64] The company implemented a business ethics programme and transparency measures, though it lacked anti-bribery policies before the investigation.[65]

UNKNOWN COMPANY[66]

An unknown company (UC) obstructed a CSOC investigation into potential transnational bribery in Venezuela by refusing access to information, claiming confidentiality concerns.[67] The CSOC imposed a fine for obstructing preliminary procedures under Law 1778/2016, and the company's appeal was rejected, confirming the decision.[68] This case is relevant because it highlights not only the lack of corporations' commitment but also the legal tools available to address attempts by corporations to obstruct investigations.

ODEBRECHT[69]

This case involved bribes paid across Latin America for public contracts, including in Colombia, from 2009 to 2014.[70] Despite the competition, Odebrecht secured contracts through bribery, which later led to economic setbacks and investigations in multiple countries.[71] The company has signed an agreement with the U.S. Department of Justice.[72] The Odebrecht case has involved criminal investigation, with no evidence of discussed anti-bribery policies.[73] However, the company now has compliance policies focused on prevention, detection, and remediation.[74] These include employee guidance, whistle-blower protection, and training.[75] However, the real commitment will be proved if they apply them and avoid being part of bribery scandals in the future.

3 *Corporate Policies – A Complement to Formal Regulation*

Corporate policies, as a form of self-regulation, involve the adoption of a culture of corporate legality.[76] This raises questions about whether self-regulation complements state regulation or replaces formal legislation. Some argue that in countries with weak formal regulation, self-regulation fills the gap and can gradually influence new legislation,[77] while others contend that self-regulation may shift responsibility from the public to the private sector, potentially weakening overall regulatory effectiveness.[78] Self-regulation seems positive because it has been argued that fighting against corruption should involve private sector efforts.[79] Additionally, governments are not able to constantly monitor legislation and react to a fast-changing business environment, whereas corporations can fill this gap by adjusting and monitoring their policies as required since they have the resources and know the specific line of business.[80] However, someone could say that a key disadvantage is that governments may not monitor corporate policies, leaving self-regulation largely in the hands of corporations, and as previously discussed in the literature, the verification of compliance with the self-regulatory measures cannot continue in the hands of society as before.[81] Therefore, for self-regulation to complement legislation, government involvement is essential, ensuring compliance with corporate policies and promoting both government and corporate regulation.[82] Scholars suggest that regulating corporate behaviour requires not only a strong interventionist attitude towards self-regulation by governments[83] but also the adoption of mixed regulation models to include both government regulation and corporate self-regulation measures.[84] Furthermore, governments are expected to enforce self-regulation by ensuring that measures adopted by corporations are enforceable[85] and having specialised trained staff within organisations to monitor compliance.[86]

4 *Importance of Corporate Anti-Bribery Self-Regulation*

The capitalist model places corporations in a position where they can play a significant role in promoting transparency and ethical behaviour.[87] Therefore, it is important to make corporations aware of the fact that by implementing CAB-policies they also 'create value for the population of the regions and countries where they have a presence (and most importantly) contribute to fair market conditions without corruption'.[88] Moreover, as explained by the Colombian Secretariat of Transparency, corporations need to understand that they are also beneficiaries of self-regulation since the implementation of compliance programmes, among other things, minimises the possibility of reputational losses that may even cause the closure and disappearance of the company or its brands.[89]

Self-regulation can be used by governments as an instrument to gradually change business culture. For instance, there is an extraordinary public-private initiative that invests in the worldwide training of corporations, including Small and Medium-sized Enterprises (SMEs), that surely are the Multinational Enterprises (MNEs) of the future.[90] The Alliance for Integrity initiative seems to believe that assisting SMEs to grow with strong corporate values will make a significant impact on the future business culture.[91] The initiative reaches different business sectors and different company sizes, thus it is good to support SMEs that usually lack the budget to hire specialised services to implement CAB-policies.[92]

5 *Challenges for Corporations during the Implementation of CAB-Policies*

Businesses face significant challenges in implementing CAB-policies across large, complex, geographically dispersed operations.[93] These challenges are amplified by company size, limited resources, and cultural differences.[94] For instance, previous studies suggest that collectivist cultures may tolerate bribery more than individualistic ones, as relationships are highly valued.[95] However, the challenge is not the culture itself but to identify (depending on the country) appropriate mechanisms to successfully communicate policies to stakeholders both at headquarters and foreign subsidiaries.[96] Conversely, other studies suggest that companies often cite cultural differences while the real issue is organisational culture and values that tacitly support bribery as a business survival strategy.[97]

Challenges related to company size affect compliance with CAB-policies.[98] SMEs struggle with limited resources, while MNEs face difficulties ensuring that policies reach employees worldwide and address industry-specific risks.[99] Standardised CAB-policies, created by compliance specialists, are affordable for large companies but often fail to address specific risks.[100] Hence, it has been argued that governments should be aware that SMEs could be the MNEs in the future, therefore it is necessary to invest in their values because '(…) as they grow and expand it becomes increasingly difficult to change or alter entrenched perceptions and expectations'.[101]

6 *Conclusion and Recommendations*

The analysis suggests that the legal frameworks of the UK and Colombia regarding CAB-policies are similar. For instance, both countries have adhered to international standards, incorporated them into their national laws, and published guidelines for creating CAB-policies.

However, there are areas where they could complement each other, as outlined below:

1 Colombia could benefit from adopting the UK approach by consolidating its bribery laws into a single piece of legislation. The current use of multiple legal instruments can create confusion for corporations, making compliance more complex and challenging to navigate.
2 Bribery is a crime in Colombia, however, failing to prevent bribery is not. Currently, corporations may face administrative sanctions but elevating the failure to prevent bribery to a criminal offence could enforce anti-bribery self-regulation, as in the UK.
3 The UK could evaluate a more personalised and proactive approach to promoting CAB-policies, by involving additional authorities, as seen in Colombia.
4 Colombia could consider expanding the extraterritorial application of the law to cover not only bribery involving government officials but also any bribe committed in the private sector by a person associated with Colombia, like the UK approach. This would certainly impact CAB-policies.
5 The UK could expand the law to cover all legal entities (subject to inspection, surveillance, or control by superintendencies), as in Colombia. The term "relevant" is unclear and limits the broader impact of CAB-policies, as imposing unlimited fines solely on "relevant commercial organisations" diminishes their influence on business culture overall.
6 The UK could consider adopting procedures like those in Colombian legislation for corporations involved in bribery offences. These could include banning companies from receiving government benefits, publishing sanctions in national newspapers and on company websites to highlight reputational damage, and allowing the suspension or cancellation of a company's license if there is evidence of criminal activity.

Furthermore, case studies from both countries lead to the conclusion that CAB-policies are assessed only during bribery investigations, leaving corporations to define by themselves what 'adequate' or 'effective' means. Both governments have made efforts to enforce anti-bribery self-regulation; however, there remains a need to promote CAB-policies as a preventive measure rather than a reactionary strategy to avoid prosecutions or reduce fines. This need urges governments to explore new regulatory approaches such as the one discussed in the literature to enforce both the implementation and compliance of CAB-policies selected by corporations. Such a mechanism would encourage corporations to adopt feasible procedures rather than impractical self-regulation difficult to materialise. Therefore, governments must invest in strategies to support corporations in creating and monitoring CAB-policies.

Considering the above, this research proposes a government model for a more proactive approach towards corporate anti-bribery self-regulation. However, it is acknowledged that this proposal may seem idealistic or may not be implemented soon due to budget constraints or a lack of interest in making CAB-policies enforceable. This model involves the creation of two government organisations as follows (Figure 5.1):

This model should include the following features:

1 Compulsory Assistance from Organisation No. 1 for all corporations.
2 Compulsory collaboration between Organisation No. 1 and corporations to select appropriate CAB-policies.
3 Organisations No. 1 and No. 2 must remain independent to ensure impartial monitoring.

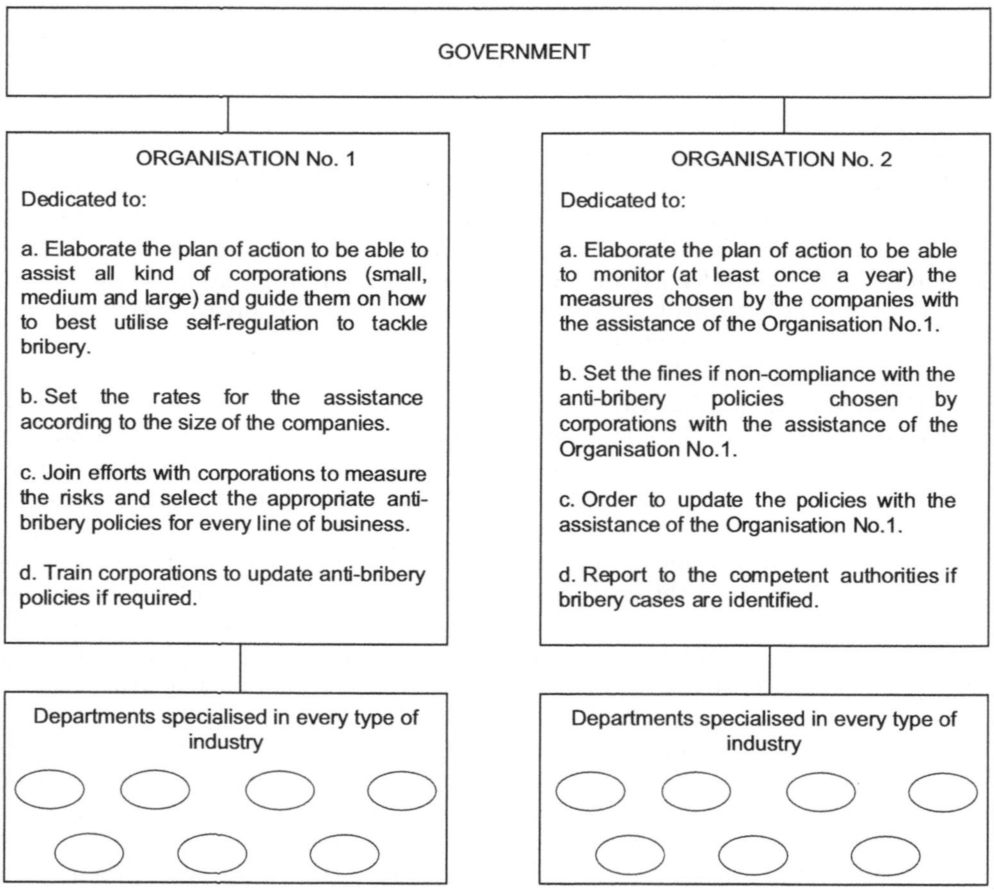

Figure 5.1 Proposal for a government-led model promoting corporate anti-bribery self-regulation.

4 Both organisations must have specialised departments with technical expertise in each economic sector.
5 Both organisations should be incentivised with a larger annual budget as bribery charges decrease.
6 The rates for assistance from Organisation No. 1 should be affordable based on a corporation's size.
7 Strategies to ensure the integrity must be developed to prevent bribery attempts.

This model promotes self-regulation as a complement to the law, acknowledging that both humans and government institutions are susceptible to corruption. Issues related to structure, operation, and possible bureaucracy are not addressed here but could be explored in future research.

Notes

1 Transparency International, 'Four Ways the G20 Can Take the Lead on Anti-Corruption' (2019), https://www.transparency.org/news/feature/four_ways_the_g20_can_take_the_lead_on_anti_corruption. Accessed 5 June 2019.
2 Nick Kochan and Robin Goodyear, *Corruption: The New Corporate Challenge* (Palgrave Macmillan 2011) 243.
3 Kochan and Goodyear, *Corruption*, 13, 14.
4 Kochan and Goodyear, *Corruption.*
5 Iris Chiu, 'An Institutional Theory of Corporate Regulation' (2018) 71 *Current Legal Problems* 279, 281.
6 Transparency International, *Business Principles for Countering Bribery: A Multi-Stakeholder Initiative* (Transparency International 2013) 8.
7 Organisation for Economic Co-operation and Development (OECD), *OECD Guidelines for Multinational Enterprises* (OECD Publishing 2011).
8 Transparency International, 'Exporting Corruption Progress report 2018: Assessing enforcement of the OECD Anti-Bribery Convention' (2018), https://images.transparencycdn.org/images/2018_Report_ExportingCorruption_English_200402_075046.pdf. Accessed 1 October 2019.
9 OECD Convention on Combating Bribery of Foreign Public Officials in International Business Transactions 1997.
10 Cecily Rose, 'The UK Bribery Act 2010 and Accompanying Guidance: Belated Implementation of the OECD Anti-Bribery Convention' (2012) 61 *The International and Comparative Law Quarterly* 485.
11 Transparency International, 'Exporting Corruption 2018' (n 8).
12 Transparency International, 'Exporting Corruption 2018' (n 8).
13 Axel Palmer, *Countering Economic Crime* (Routledge 2018) 94.
14 OECD Convention on Combating Bribery of Foreign Public Officials in International Business Transactions 1997 (n 9).
15 United Nations Convention against Corruption 2003.
16 Nicholas Lord, 'Responding to Transnational Corporate Bribery Using International Frameworks for Enforcement: Anti-Bribery and Corruption in the UK and Germany' (2014) 14 *Criminology & Criminal Justice* 100, 104.
17 Council of Europe Criminal Law Convention on Corruption 1999.
18 Organisation of American States Inter-American Convention against Corruption 1996.
19 Colombia Adhered to the OECD Anti-Bribery Convention on the 20 November 2012.
20 Transparency International, 'Exporting Corruption 2018' (n 8).
21 Transparency International, 'Exporting Corruption 2018' (n 8).
22 Transparency International, 'Exporting Corruption 2018' (n 8).
23 Law on the anti-corruption statute 1474 2011.
24 Colombia joined the OECD on 28 April 2020.
25 Maria Carolina Pardo and Luis Alberto Castell, 'Colombia' in Mark Mendelsohn (ed), *The Anti-Bribery and Anti-Corruption Review* (10th ed, Law Business Research Ltd 2021) 96.

26 El gremio de la protección contra incendios (ANRACI), 'Reunión Con La Secretaría de Transparencia de Presidencia de La República' (2019), http://anraci.org/asociacion/reunion-con-la-secretaria-de-transparencia-de-presidencia-de-la-republica/. Accessed 10 October 2019.
27 EUROSOCIAL, 'Taller de Lanzamiento de La Iniciativa Empresas Activas En Cumplimiento Anticorrupción (Registros Proética)' (2019), http://www.sia.eurosocial-ii.eu/actividad.php?id=2461. Accessed 10 October 2019.
28 UK Bribery Act 2010 s 7 (1) (2).
29 Law on the anti-corruption statute 1474 2011, article 34 (3) (n 23).
30 Law on the liability of legal persons for acts of transnational corruption 1778 2016, article 7 (7).
31 UK Ministry of Justice, 'The Bribery Act 2010 - Guidance' (2010).
32 Secretaría de Transparencia de la República de Colombia, 'Guía Propositiva de la Secretaría de Transparencia para la elaboración e implementación de los Programas de Transparencia y Ética Empresarial -PTEE' (2024).
33 Transparency International, 'Exporting Corruption 2018' (n 8).
34 Javier Sanclemente-Arciniegas, 'Transparency and Business Ethics Programs in Colombia: Lights and Shadows' (2023) 20 *Juridicas* 163.
35 Sanclemente-Arciniegas, 'Transparency and Business Ethics Programs in Colombia'.
36 Yudy Paola Pinzon Fernandez, 'Critical Analysis of the Legal Framework on Corporate Anti-Bribery Policies: The United Kingdom and Colombian Approaches' (Master's thesis, University of the West of England 2019).
37 *Serious Fraud Office v Standard Bank Plc* [2015] 11 WLUK 804; Lauren Sales, 'Important Lessons for Corporates: Standard Bank PLC DPA and Sweet Group PLC Sentence' (2016) 4 *International Banking and Financial Law* 243.
38 Serious Fraud Office, 'Standard Bank PLC Case' (2015), https://www.sfo.gov.uk/cases/standard-bank-plc/. Accessed 10 November 2019.
39 Serious Fraud Office, 'Standard Bank PLC Case'.
40 *Serious Fraud Office v Standard Bank PLC* (n 37).
41 *Serious Fraud Office v Standard Bank PLC* (n 37).
42 *Serious Fraud Office v Standard Bank PLC* (n 37).
43 UK Crime Courts Act 2013, Schedule 17. A DPA is an agreement between the prosecutor and an individual under investigation, where the individual agrees to comply with specific conditions, and the prosecutor suspends proceedings upon court approval.
44 Nicholas Ryder and Axel Palmer, 'Is Justice Deferred, Justice Denied? Not Necessarily' (January 2016) *Financial Regulation International* 6–11.
45 *Serious Fraud Office v Standard Bank PLC* (n 37).
46 Serious Fraud Office, 'Standard Bank - Details of Compliance' (2015), https://www.sfo.gov.uk/cases/standard-bank-plc/. Accessed 10 November 2019.
47 *Serious Fraud Office v Sweet Group* Southwark Crown Court 19 February 2016.
48 Serious Fraud Office, 'Sweett Group Case' (2015), https://www.sfo.gov.uk/cases/sweett-group/. Accessed 10 November 2019.
49 Sales (n 37).
50 *Serious Fraud Office v Sweet Group* Southwark Crown (n 47).
51 Currie & Brown, 'Anti-Bribery and Corruption Group Policy Statement' (2019), https://www.curriebrown.com/media/ombbskle/anti-bribery-and-corruption-group-policy-statement-en.pdf. Accessed 10 November 2019.
52 Currie & Brown, 'Anti-Bribery and Corruption Group Policy Statement'.
53 *Serious Fraud Office v Rolls Royce* [2017] 1 WLUK 189; Serious Fraud Office, 'Rolls-Royce PLC Case' (2017), https://www.sfo.gov.uk/cases/rolls-royce-plc/. Accessed 10 November 2019.
54 *Serious Fraud Office v Rolls Royce* (n 53).
55 *Serious Fraud Office v Rolls Royce* (n 53).
56 *Serious Fraud Office v Rolls Royce* (n 53).
57 *Serious Fraud Office v Rolls Royce* (n 53).
58 *Serious Fraud Office v Rolls Royce* (n 53).
59 *R v Skansen Interiors Limited* (unreported).
60 Eoin O'shea, 'The Bribery Act: Beyond Adequate?' (2019) 169 *New Law Journal* 11.
61 Brodies, 'R V Skansen Interiors Limited: Anti-Bribery And Corruption Compliance – It's Alive…!' (2018), https://brodies.com/binformed/legal-updates/r-v-skansen-interiors-limited-anti-bribery-and-corruption-compliance. Accessed 10 November 2019.

62 Superintendencia de Sociedades, 'Decisiones En Firme' (2018), https://www.supersociedades.gov.co/delegatura_aec/Paginas/Decisiones_en_firme.aspx. Accessed 11 November 2019.
63 Superintendencia de Sociedades, 'Decisiones En Firme'.
64 Superintendencia de Sociedades, 'Decisiones En Firme'.
65 Grupo Inassa, 'Código de Ética' (2018), https://www.grupoinassa.com/?page_id=428. Accessed 27 November 2019.
66 Superintendencia de Sociedades, 'Decisiones En Firme' (n 62).
67 Superintendencia de Sociedades, 'Decisiones En Firme' (n 62).
68 Superintendencia de Sociedades, 'Decisiones En Firme' (n 62).
69 Liam Timmons, 'Odebrecht Scandal Threatens Peruvian Infrastructure' (2017) 37 14 *Washington Report on the Hemisphere* 7.
70 Revista Semana, 'El Tsunami Por Los Sobornos de Odebrecht' (2017), https://www.semana.com/economia/articulo/caso-de-sobornos-de-odebrecht-en-colombia/512077. Accessed 11 November 2019.
71 Revista Semana, 'El Tsunami Por Los Sobornos de Odebrecht'.
72 Mitch Rogers, 'After Plea Bargain, Brazil's Odebrecht Giant Pays Up' (2017) 37 *Washington Report on the Hemisphere* 14.
73 Fiscalía General de la Nación, 'Odebrecht', https://www.fiscalia.gov.co/colombia/page/2/?s=odebrecht. Accessed 11 November 2019.
74 Odebrecht, 'Compliance Policy' (2019), https://www.odebrecht.com/en/compliance. Accessed 12 November 2019.
75 Odebrecht, 'Código de Conduta Do Fornecedor' (2019), https://www.odebrecht.com/sites/default/files/codigocondutafornecedorptbr.pdf. Accessed 12 November 2019.
76 Paula Andrea Ramirez Barbosa and Juan Carlos Ferre Olive, *Compliance, Derecho Penal Y Corporativo Y Buena Gobernanza Empresarial* (2nd edn, Tirant lo Blanch 2024) 18.
77 Soili Nysten-Haarala, Elena Klyuchnikova and Heidi Helenius, 'Law and Self-Regulation – Substitutes or Complements in Gaining Social Acceptance?' (2015) 45 *Resources Policy* 52.
78 W Cragg, Ethics Codes, *Corporations and the Challenge of Globalization* (Edward Elgar 2005) 15.
79 Theodore Kahn and Víctor Saavedra, 'La corrupción en Colombia: diagnóstico y recomendaciones para controlarla. Documento elaborado en el marco de la Comisión de Expertos Anticorrupción de Fedesarrollo' (2021) 51 *Coyuntura Económica: Investigación Económica y Social* 115, 172.
80 Wayne Norman, 'Business Ethics as Self-Regulation: Why Principles That Ground Regulations Should Be Used to Ground Beyond-Compliance Norms as Well' (2011) 102 *Journal of Business Ethics* 43, 50.
81 Gustavo Adolfo Yepes Lopez, 'Corporate Social Responsibility, Transparency and Prevention of Business Bribery in Colombia' (2011) 8 *US-China Law Review* 188.
82 David Graham and Ngaire Woods, 'Making Corporate Self-Regulation Effective in Developing Countries' (2006) 34 *World Development* 868, 869.
83 Anna Beckers, 'Towards a Regulatory Private Law Approach for CSR Sel-Regulation? The Effect of Private Law on Corporate CSR Strategies' (2019) 27 *European Review of Private Law* 221.
84 Ans Kolk and Rob Van, 'The Effectiveness of Selfregulation: Corporate Codes of Conduct and Child Labour' (2002) 20 *European Management Journal* 260.
85 Graham and Woods (n 82).
86 John Braithwaite, 'Enforced Self-Regulation: A New Strategy for Corporate Crime Control' (1982) 80 *Michigan Law Review* 1466, 1468.
87 David Levi-Faur, 'The Global Diffusion of Regulatory Capitalism' (2005) 598 *The Annals of the American Academy of Political and Social Science* 27.
88 Transparencia por Colombia, *Segunda Encuesta Nacional sobre Prácticas contra el Soborno en Empresas Colombianas* (Noviembre 2010) https://transparenciacolombia.org.co/segunda-encuesta-soborno/. Accessed 6 November 2019.
89 Secretaría de Transparencia de la Presidencia de la República, 'Guía Para Empresas En Colombia: ¿Cómo y Por Qué Implementar Un Programa Empresarial de Cumplimiento Anticorrupción?' (2016).
90 Alliance for Integrity (2019), https://www.allianceforintegrity.org/en/alliance-for-integrity/about-us/. Accessed 6 November 2019.
91 Alliance for Integrity (2019).

92 Alliance for Integrity (2019).
93 Kathryn Gordon and Maiko Miyake, 'Business Approaches to Combating Bribery: A Study of Codes of Conduct' (2001) 34 *Journal of Business Ethics* 166.
94 Juan I Sanchez, Carolina Gomez and Guillermo Wated, 'A Value-Based Framework for Understanding Managerial Tolerance of Bribery in Latin America' (2008) 83 *Journal of Business Ethics* 341.
95 Juanita Pizano, 'Colombian Anti-Corruption Law: A Comparative Analysis with the United States' Foreign Corrupt Practices Act (FCPA) on the Public Official Bribery Elements and Penalties' (Bachelor's thesis, University of Cincinnati 2023) 5.
96 Vijay Sampath and Noushi Rahman, 'Bribery in MNEs: The Dynamics of Corruption Culture Distance and Organizational Distance to Core Values' (2019) 159 *Journal of Business Ethics* 817.
97 Julian Klinkhammer, 'On the Dark Side of the Code: Organizational Challenges to an Effective Anti-Corruption Strategy' (2013) 60 *Crime, Law and Social Change* 191.
98 Klinkhammer, 'On the Dark Side of the Code'.
99 Mollie Painter-Morland, *Business Ethics as Practice: Ethics as the Everyday Business of Business* (Cambridge University Press 2008).
100 Painter-Morland, *Business Ethics as Practice.*
101 Painter-Morland, *Business Ethics as Practice.*

Bibliography

Primary Sources

United Kingdom

STATUTES

UK Bribery Act 2010.
UK Crime Courts Act 2013.

CASES

R v Skansen Interiors Limited (unreported).
Serious Fraud Office v Rolls Royce [2017] 1 WLUK 189.
Serious Fraud Office v Standard Bank Plc [2015] 11 WLUK 804.
Serious Fraud Office v Sweet Group Southwark Crown Court 19 February 2016.

European Union

Convention on the fight against Corruption involving Officials of the European Communities or Officials of Member States of the EU (1997).
Council of Europe Criminal Law Convention on Corruption 1999.

International

Organisation of American States Inter-American Convention Against Corruption 1996.
United Nations Convention against Transnational Organised Crime (2000).
OECD Convention on Combating Bribery of Foreign Public Officials in International Business Transactions 1997.
United Nations Convention against Corruption 2003.

Colombia

STATUTES

Criminal Code Law 599 2000.

Decree on the Structure of the Superintendency of Companies 1023 2012.
Law on the anti-corruption statute 1474 2011.
Law on the liability of legal persons for acts of transnational corruption 1778 2016.
Law on transparency and prevention against corruption 2195 2022.

Cases

Fiscalía General de la Nacion v Odebrecht (In process).
*Superintendencia de Sociedades v Inassa (*2018).
Superintendencia de Sociedades v Unknown Company (Unknown date).

Secondary Sources

Beckers A, 'Towards a Regulatory Private Law Approach for CSR Self-Regulation? The Effect of Private Law on Corporate CSR Strategies' (2019) 27 *European Review of Private Law* 221.
Braithwaite J, 'Enforced Self-Regulation: A New Strategy for Corporate Crime Control' (1982) 80 *Michigan Law Review* 1466, 1468.
Chiu I, 'An Institutional Theory of Corporate Regulation' (2018) 71 *Current Legal Problems* 279, 281.
Cragg W, Ethics Codes, *Corporations and the Challenge of Globalization* (Edward Elgar 2005).
Gordon K and Miyake M, 'Business Approaches to Combating Bribery: A Study of Codes of Conduct' (2001) 34 *Journal of Business Ethics* 166.
Graham D and Woods N, 'Making Corporate Self-Regulation Effective in Developing Countries' (2006) 34 *World Development* 868, 869.
Kahn T and Saavedra V, 'La corrupción en Colombia: diagnóstico y recomendaciones para controlarla. Documento elaborado en el marco de la Comisión de Expertos Anticorrupción de Fedesarrollo' (2021) 51 *Coyuntura Económica: Investigación Económica y Social* 115, 172.
Klinkhammer J, 'On the Dark Side of the Code: Organizational Challenges to an Effective Anti-Corruption Strategy' (2013) 60 *Crime, Law and Social Change* 191.
Kochan N and Goodyear R, *Corruption: The New Corporate Challenge* (Palgrave Macmillan 2011).
Kolk A and Van R, 'The Effectiveness of Selfregulation: Corporate Codes of Conduct and Child Labour' (2002) 20 *European Management Journal* 260.
Levi-Faur D, 'The Global Diffusion of Regulatory Capitalism' (2005) 598 *The Annals of the American Academy of Political and Social Science* 27.
Lord N, 'Responding to Transnational Corporate Bribery Using International Frameworks for Enforcement: Anti-Bribery and Corruption in the UK and Germany' (2014) 14 *Criminology & Criminal Justice* 100, 104.
Norman W, 'Business Ethics as Self-Regulation: Why Principles That Ground Regulations Should Be Used to Ground Beyond-Compliance Norms as Well' (2011) 102 *Journal of Business Ethics* 43, 50.
Nysten-Haarala S, Klyuchnikova, E and Helenius, H, 'Law and Self-Regulation – Substitutes or Complements in Gaining Social Acceptance?' (2015) 45 *Resources Policy* 52.
Organisation for Economic Co-operation and Development (OECD), *OECD Guidelines for Multinational Enterprises* (OECD Publishing 2011).
O'Shea E, 'The Bribery Act: Beyond Adequate?' (2019) 169 *New Law Journal* 11.
Painter-Morland M, *Business Ethics as Practice: Ethics as the Everyday Business of Business* (Cambridge University Press 2008).
Palmer A, *Countering Economic Crime* (Routledge 2018).
Pardo M and Castell L, 'Colombia' in M Mendelsohn (ed), *The Anti-Bribery and Anti-Corruption Review* (10th edn, Law Business Research Ltd 2021) 96.
Ramirez P and Ferre J, *Compliance, Derecho Penal Y Corporativo Y Buena Gobernanza Empresarial* (2nd edn, Tirant lo Blanch 2024).
Rogers M, 'After Plea Bargain, Brazil's Odebrecht Giant Pays Up' (2017) 37 *Washington Report on the Hemisphere* 14.

Rose C, 'The UK Bribery Act 2010 and Accompanying Guidance: Belated Implementation of the OECD Anti-Bribery Convention' (2012) 61 *The International and Comparative Law Quarterly* 485.

Ryder N and Palmer A, 'Is Justice Deferred, Justice Denied? Not Necessarily' (January 2016) *Financial Regulation International* 6, 9.

Sales L, 'Important Lessons for Corporates: Standard Bank PLC DPA and Sweet Group PLC Sentence' (2016) 4 *International Banking and Financial Law* 243.

Sampath V and Rahman N, 'Bribery in MNEs: The Dynamics of Corruption Culture Distance and Organizational Distance to Core Values' (2019) 159 *Journal of Business Ethics* 817.

Sanchez J, Gomez C and Wated G, 'A Value-Based Framework for Understanding Managerial Tolerance of Bribery in Latin America' (2008) 83 *Journal of Business Ethics* 341.

Sanclemente-Arciniegas J, 'Transparency and Business Ethics Programs in Colombia: Lights and Shadows' (2023) 20 *Juridicas* 163.

Secretaría de Transparencia de la República de Colombia, 'Guía Propositiva de la Secretaría de Transparencia para la elaboración e implementación de los Programas de Transparencia y Ética Empresarial - PTEE' (2024).

Secretaría de Transparencia de la Presidencia de la República, 'Guía Para Empresas En Colombia: ¿Cómo y Por Qué Implementar Un Programa Empresarial de Cumplimiento Anticorrupción?' (2016).

Timmons L, 'Odebrecht Scandal Threatens Peruvian Infrastructure' (2017) 37 14 *Washington Report on the Hemisphere* 7.

Transparencia por Colombia, 'Segunda Encuesta Nacional sobre Prácticas contra el Soborno en Empresas Colombianas' (Noviembre 2010) https://transparenciacolombia.org.co/segunda-encuesta-soborno/. Accessed 6 November 2019.

Transparency International, *Business Principles for Countering Bribery: A Multi-Stakeholder Initiative* (Transparency International 2013).

UK Ministry of Justice, 'The Bribery Act 2010 - Guidance'.

Yepes Lopez G, 'Corporate Social Responsibility, Transparency and Prevention of Business Bribery in Colombia' (2011) 8 *US-China Law Review* 188.

Thesis

Pizano J, 'Colombian Anti-Corruption Law: A Comparative Analysis with the United States' Foreign Corrupt Practices Act (FCPA) on the Public Official Bribery Elements and Penalties' (Bachelor's thesis, University of Cincinnati 2023).

Pinzon Y, 'Critical Analysis of the Legal Framework on Corporate Anti-Bribery Policies: The United Kingdom and Colombian Approaches' (Master's thesis, University of the West of England 2019).

Websites

Alliance for Integrity (2019), https://www.allianceforintegrity.org/en/alliance-for-integrity/about-us/. Accessed 6 November 2019.

Brodies, 'R V Skansen Interiors Limited: Anti-Bribery And Corruption Compliance – It's Alive…!' (2018), https://brodies.com/binformed/legal-updates/r-v-skansen-interiors-limited-anti-bribery-and-corruption-compliance. Accessed 10 November 2019.

Currie & Brown, 'Anti-Bribery and Corruption Group Policy Statement' (2019) https://www.curriebrown.com/media/ombbskle/anti-bribery-and-corruption-group-policy-statement-en.pdf. Accessed 10 November 2019.

El gremio de la protección contra incendios (ANRACI), 'Reunión Con La Secretaría De Transparencia de Presidencia de La República' (2019), https://anraci.org/asociacion/reunion-con-la-secretaria-de-transparencia-de-presidencia-de-la-republica/. Accessed 10 October 2019.

EUROSOCIAL, 'Taller de Lanzamiento de La Iniciativa Empresas Activas En Cumplimiento Anticorrupción (Registros Proética)' (2019), https://www.sia.eurosocial-ii.eu/actividad.php?id=2461. Accessed 10 October 2019.

Fiscalía General de la Nación, 'Odebrecht', https://www.fiscalia.gov.co/colombia/page/2/?s=odebrecht. Accessed 11 November 2019.

Grupo Inassa, 'Código de Ética' (2018), https://www.grupoinassa.com/?page_id=428. Accessed 27 November 2019.

Odebrecht, 'Código de Conduta Do Fornecedor' (2019), https://www.odebrecht.com/sites/default/files/codigocondutafornecedorptbr.pdf. Accessed 12 November 2019.

Odebrecht, 'Compliance Policy' (2019), https://www.odebrecht.com/en/compliance. Accessed 12 November 2019.

Revista Semana, 'El Tsunami Por Los Sobornos de Odebrecht' (2017), https://www.semana.com/economia/articulo/caso-de-sobornos-de-odebrecht-en-colombia/512077. Accessed 11 November 2019.

Serious Fraud Office, 'Standard Bank - Details of Compliance' (2015), https://www.sfo.gov.uk/cases/standard-bank-plc/. Accessed 10 November 2019.

Serious Fraud Office, 'Standard Bank PLC Case' (2015), https://www.sfo.gov.uk/cases/standard-bank-plc/. Accessed 10 November 2019.

Serious Fraud Office, 'Sweett Group Case' (2015), https://www.sfo.gov.uk/cases/sweett-group/. Accessed 10 November 2019.

Serious Fraud Office, 'Rolls-Royce PLC Case' (2017), https://www.sfo.gov.uk/cases/rolls-royce-plc/. Accessed 10 November 2019.

Superintendencia de Sociedades, 'Decisiones En Firme' (2018), https://www.supersociedades.gov.co/delegatura_aec/Paginas/Decisiones_en_firme.aspx. Accessed 11 November 2019.

Transparency International, 'Exporting Corruption 2018' (2018), https://www.transparency.org/exporting_corruption. Accessed 1 October 2019.

Transparency International, 'Four Ways the G20 Can Take the Lead on Anti-Corruption' (2019), https://www.transparency.org/news/feature/four_ways_the_g20_can_take_the_lead_on_anti_corruption. Accessed 5 June 2019.

6 The End of a Corruption-Free Era? The Story of Hong Kong

Horace Yeung and Flora Huang

1 Introduction

Hong Kong's Independent Commission Against Corruption (ICAC) is one of the most acclaimed anti-corruption commissions in Asia (and indeed perhaps the whole world), often seen and studied as a role model in combating corruption. Incidentally, Hong Kong is among the most affluent in the region, to a large extent, illustrating the importance of fighting corruption. The concern about corruption lies in the related costs in economic, political, and social development.[1] In Hong Kong, the ICAC was set up in 1974 to tackle corruption, marking a milestone in Hong Kong's anti-corruption history. Before its establishment, corruption was rampant in the public sector. The Prevention of Bribery Ordinance (POBO) is the primary anti-corruption legislation in Hong Kong, regulating offences in both public and private sectors. By having an effective regulatory infrastructure, Hong Kong has managed to control corruption successfully.

This success can be reflected in the fact that the city has done well in the Corruption Perception Index (CPI) throughout the years. However, at the same time, there may be worrying signs, especially after the city's reunification with China in 1997. There have been several high-profile cases involving senior officials in the government. For example, the former Financial Secretary of Hong Kong, Rafael Hui, was convicted of five counts of misconduct in public office and was sentenced to 7.5 years in prison. Former Chief Executive, Donald Tsang, was guilty on one charge of misconduct in public office and was sentenced to a 20-month imprisonment (but later cleared of any wrongdoings). This chapter seeks to conduct an up-to-date appraisal of the anti-corruption regime in Hong Kong. The changing perception of the degree of corruption will be discussed, drawing on various indicators and recent high-profile cases. Also, an analysis of local anti-corruption legislations will be given. Furthermore, the intensity of enforcement is to be evaluated with a focus on input and output, concerning whether adequate resources are given to the regulator and whether there are robust enforcement actions as deterrence.

2 The Perception of Corruption in Hong Kong

There is not a universal definition of corruption. In general, it can be referred to as 'acts in which the power of public office is used for personal gain in a manner that contravenes the rules of the game'.[2] It involves the use of public power. Also, it involves people who are regarded as public officials and politicians. Before proceeding to the problems caused by corruption, some actually believe that there may be benefits from corruption.[3] Most notably, it is regarded as a way to overcome bureaucracy.

DOI: 10.4324/9781003324843-9

Shleifer and Vishny believed that 'corruption is both pervasive and significant around the world'.[4] In their research, they showed that corruption may be costly to economic development.[5] First, it can hamper investment and growth around the world, especially in countries with weak governments. Foreign investors will choose not to invest in countries with widespread corruption. Second, it prevents the most efficient allocation of social resources, in which useless projects may be financed instead of projects of value, such as health and education. The linkage between corruption and development has also been examined by Mauro and Bardhan.[6] Mauro used a cross-country dataset consisting of subjective indices of bureaucratic honesty and efficiency to provide empirical evidence on the effects of corruption on economic growth. In his study, he found a negative association between corruption and investment, as well as growth (i.e. corruption does not promote investment/growth). Similarly, Bardhan believed that the historical relationship between economic growth and corruption is likely to have been negative in general (i.e. corruption does not promote growth), but there may be variations in different countries. He cited the lesson of transitional economies such as Eastern Europe, China, and Vietnam where there were some special factors increasing corruption even as income grew.

Despite the difficulties in measuring corruption, there have been several notable attempts to do so.[7] Among these, Transparency International's CPI is perhaps one of the most widely reported ones. Transparency International is a non-partisan, non-profit, and non-governmental organisation founded in Berlin in 1993. The CPI was first published in 1995, and the most recent one in 2024. In its most recent 2023 Index (published in 2024), it ranks 180 countries and territories around the world by their perceived levels of public sector corruption, scoring on a scale of 0 (highly corrupt) to 100 (very clean). The Index aggregates data from a number of different sources that provide perceptions by businesspeople and country experts of the level of corruption in the public sector.[8] In the past decade, the global average has largely remained at around 43 out of 100. In 2023, the top performers were in the order of Denmark, Finland, New Zealand, Norway, Singapore (joint sixth), Sweden (joint sixth), Switzerland, the Netherlands, Germany (joint ninth), and Luxembourg (joint ninth). Hong Kong was not far behind, sitting at joint 12th (with Australia). It can be seen that Hong Kong stands out as one of the most corruption-free territories in Asia, while almost all other top performers (except Singapore) are mostly located in Europe. Meanwhile, as a comparison, China was in the 76th place, demonstrating a notable but narrowing gap between the two jurisdictions. The performances of both Hong Kong and China in the past decade in the CPI are given in Figure 6.1. It can be seen from the chart that in most of the years Hong Kong has been lingering between a score of 76 and 77, whilst there has been a general upward trend in the case of China. Although not readily shown in the CPI, a worrying downward trend (see Figure 6.2) has been witnessed in Hong Kong, according to a public opinion poll conducted by the Hong Kong Public Opinion Research Institute (formerly the Public Opinion Programme of the University of Hong Kong).[9] This somewhat coincided with Transparency International's observation that '[most countries] have made no significant progress against corruption or have declined since 2012'.[10]

Quah conducted a comparative study of Hong Kong and Singapore in combating corruption.[11] In his view, Hong Kong's and Singapore's approaches may be most relevant to those countries with similar features, that is, small countries with strategic locations, well-developed infrastructure, high degree of urbanisation, and an increasingly diversified

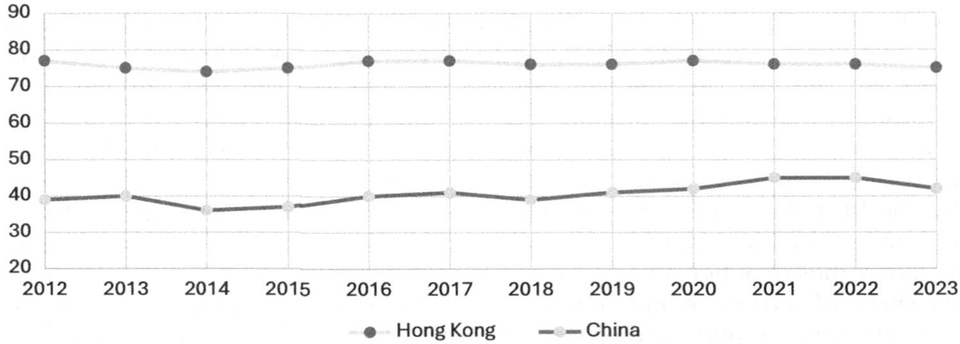

Figure 6.1 Comparative Performance of Hong Kong and China in CPI (Score Changes 2012–2023).

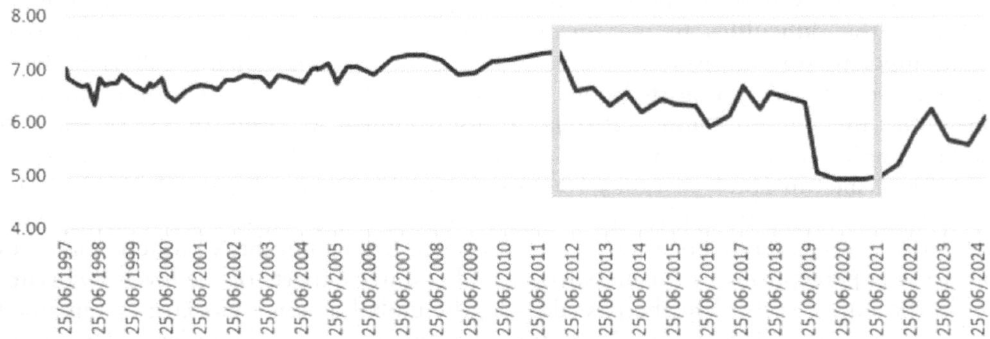

Figure 6.2 Performance of Hong Kong in Local Public Opinion Poll throughout the Years.

economy. By drawing on the two city-states' successful experiences, he identified six lessons that other aspiring countries can learn from

Lesson No. 1: The political leadership must be sincerely committed to the eradication of corruption.

Lesson No. 2: It is futile to combat corruption using incremental or piecemeal measures. Comprehensive anti-corruption measures are required to minimise corrupt behaviour among civil servants and the population.

Lesson No. 3: The anti-corruption agency must itself be incorruptible.

Lesson No. 4: The anti-corruption agency must be removed from the police.

Lesson No. 5: It is necessary to reduce the opportunities for corruption, especially in those government departments which are usually vulnerable to corrupt activities (viz., customs, immigration, internal revenue, and traffic police).

Lesson No. 6: It is important to reduce the incentive for corruption among civil servants and political leaders by ensuring that their salaries and fringe benefits are competitive with the private sector.[12]

Overall, Quah attributed the most important reason for both Hong Kong's and Singapore's success to their strong political will to curb corruption. Abdulai shares Quah's view by stating the reason why Hong Kong and Singapore have often been studied as successful examples in fighting corruption is largely thanks to the 'genuine commitment on the part of political leaders'.[13] According to him, the four main indicators that can be used to assess the extent of political will include the: (1) independence and freedom of anti-corruption institutions in executing their mandates; (2) provision of adequate budgets and staff for anti-corruption agencies; (3) prevalence of incentives and sanctions to deter corrupt behaviour; and (4) extent of encouraging citizen participation in anti-corruption crusades.[14] These indicators can in turn be reflected by the relevant anti-corruption law and its enforcement in a country. This will form the focus of the following section, in which the successful experience of Hong Kong is to be examined in more detail.

3 How Hong Kong Has Established Itself as an Asian Leader in Anti-Corruption

It is widely believed that Hong Kong's success has been largely owed to the ICAC. The ICAC was set up in 1974 to tackle corruption, marking a milestone in Hong Kong's anti-corruption history.[15] Before its establishment, corruption was rampant in the public sector. A landmark case during the dark era was that of Peter Godber.[16] Controlling assets of over HKD 4.3 million (which was believed to be six times the total official income in his entire spanning around two decades), Peter Godber, a Chief Police Superintendent, was under investigation in 1973. It was suspected that his unearned wealth had been obtained from corrupt means. At that point, a prima facie case was established, but the Police were still unable to prove that Godber's wealth was amassed through illegal means. After relentless efforts by the ICAC and with the assistance of the UK police, as he had escaped from Hong Kong earlier, Godber was arrested on 29 April 1974. In the end, Godber was charged and convicted with one count of conspiracy and one count of accepting a bribe. He was sentenced to four years' imprisonment and the HKD 25,000 he took as a bribe was ordered to be confiscated. Furthermore, the ICAC subsequently filed a writ to try to recover, through civil proceedings, the HKD 4 million in assets suspected to be corrupt income, but unfortunately without much success owing to Godber's use of offshore accounts spreading across several continents to hide its assets. As Yang Ti-Liang, who was the presiding judge in the Godber case (and much later rising to the rank of Chief Justice of Hong Kong), remarked, 'This case was not only an important milestone for the Commission, but also was instrumental in restoring public confidence in the Government and the justice system'.[17]

The ICAC is independent of the civil service and its chief, known as the Commissioner, is answerable directly to the Chief Executive of the Hong Kong government. The ICAC is committed to fighting corruption through a three-pronged strategy of law enforcement, education, and prevention to maintain Hong Kong as a fair and just society. Law enforcement is the responsibility of the Operations Department which receives, considers, and investigates reports of alleged offences under the POBO, the Independent Commission Against Corruption Ordinance, and the Elections (Corrupt and Illegal Conduct) Ordinance. However, it is worth noting that the legal efforts to combat corruption had started far earlier than in 1974.[18]

As early as 1898, bribery was made an offence with the enactment of the Misdemeanours Punishment Ordinance. Replaced by the Prevention of Corruption Ordinance in 1948, the legislation was enforced by the Anti-Corruption Office of the Police Force. In May 1971, the Ordinance was further strengthened with new offences, heavier penalties, and stronger investigative powers to become the POBO of today. Apart from law enforcement, the Commission has a statutory duty to examine the practices and procedures of government departments and public bodies and to secure the revision of methods of work or procedures which may be conducive to corrupt practices. The Commissioner is also required by law to provide corruption prevention assistance on request to any member of the public. These duties are discharged by the Corruption Prevention Department. Finally, the Community Relations Department is responsible for educating the public against the evils of corruption and enlisting community support in the fight against graft. In addition to its role in fighting corruption, the ICAC has closely co-operated with the Securities and Futures Commission to combat financial market misconduct by regularly reviewing the work of the financial regulator as well as exchanging cases and information with its counterpart.[19]

The Independent Commission Against Corruption Ordinance mainly vests the regulator with law enforcement powers such as: (i) power of arrest, detention, and granting bail; (ii) power of search and seizure; and (iii) power of handling any other offence disclosed during the corruption investigation process.[20] Meanwhile, the main law in prescribing various offences and penalties related to corruption is the POBO. The law tries to distinguish between 'prescribed officer' and also any 'employee of a public body', with the former liable to a broader spectrum of possible corruption-related offences. A prescribed officer is defined broadly as 'any person holding an office of emolument, whether permanent or temporary, under the Government'.[21] Meanwhile, public bodies can include companies with significant government ownership, such as utilities companies, public transportation companies, hospitals, and so on. A full list of these public bodies is given by Schedules 1 and 2 of the Ordinance. The four main types of offences as prescribed by the law are:

Section 3: No prescribed officer is allowed to solicit or accept any advantage without the general or special permission of the Chief Executive.

Section 4: Any public servant who solicits or accepts any advantage as an inducement to or reward for performing duties shall be guilty of an offence; the offeror of the advantage shall also be guilty of an offence.

Section 5: Any public servant who solicits or accepts any advantage as an inducement to or reward for giving assistance or using influence in matters relating to a contract shall be guilty of an offence; the offeror of the advantage shall also be guilty of an offence.

Section 10: Any prescribed officer who maintains a standard of living or has assets not commensurate with his official emoluments shall be guilty of an offence.

Under the law, 'advantage' includes money, gifts, loans, commissions, offices, contracts, services, favours, and discharge of liability in whole or in part but does not include entertainment.[22] The distinction between 'prescribed officers' and 'employees of public bodies' is crucial in the sense that the former are subject to Sections 3, 4, 5, and 10 of POBO while the latter are subject to Sections 4 and 5 only. For corruption within the private sector, Section 9 can apply.[23] For election-related corruption, it will be covered by the Elections (Corrupt and Illegal Conduct) Ordinance.

Hui praises the fact that Hong Kong has comprehensive legislations to deal with corruption.[24] Jackson describes Section 4 of POBO as 'the workhorse' of the POBO in relation to public sector bribery and observes that remaining public sector offences are rarely prosecuted.[25] For example, Section 10 has often been described as 'draconian' due to the burden of proof it places on the accused.[26] Indeed, it was this particular Section which was used to bring Peter Godber to justice in the 1970s. However, as indicated by Jackson, he found no record of a prosecution under Section 10 since 1994 (until 2013).[27] As observed by Scott, the Ordinance had been drafted at a time when the most common form of corruption was bribery and when an immediate advantage would be received by the person providing the service.[28] One way to get around the law would be to defer the advantage offered. In this case, the prosecutor may need to resort to the common law offence of misconduct in public office, as opposed to the POBO.[29]

4 Enforcement and International Cooperation

The ICAC employs a systematic approach to investigation and prosecution of corruption cases.[30] Investigations commence with the assessment of complaints to determine their validity, followed by evidence collection through surveillance, interviews, financial analysis, and document reviews, all conducted with strict confidentiality. If sufficient evidence is gathered, suspects may be arrested and questioned. The ICAC collaborates closely with the Department of Justice, which evaluates the evidence to decide whether prosecution is warranted. Legal proceedings are then conducted in accordance with Hong Kong's criminal justice system.

In the period between 2000 and 2009, Quah saw the total number of corruption reports received by the ICAC decline from 4,390 in 2000 to 3,450 in 2009.[31] The private sector remained the sector most vulnerable to corruption in Hong Kong during that ten-year period, with the proportion of corruption reports accounting for around 60% of the total cases. Starting from 2011, the complaint figure instead of report figure has been presented by the ICAC to reflect more clearly the corruption situation, as a corruption report may contain multiple complaints in respect of different government departments/public bodies/industries. Therefore, the figures may not be comparable between decades (pre/post-2011). However, on the whole, the complaint figure has been on the decline since 2011 (see Figure 6.3). The number of total corruption complaints received in 2011 was 4,010, dropping to 2,001 in 2023. In 2023, among the 2,001 complaints received, government departments, public bodies, and the private sector respectively accounted for 23%, 6%, and 72% of the complaints.

As previously discussed, many attributed the success of Hong Kong in curbing corruption to the enforcement capacity of its regulator, ICAC. This can be measured by the

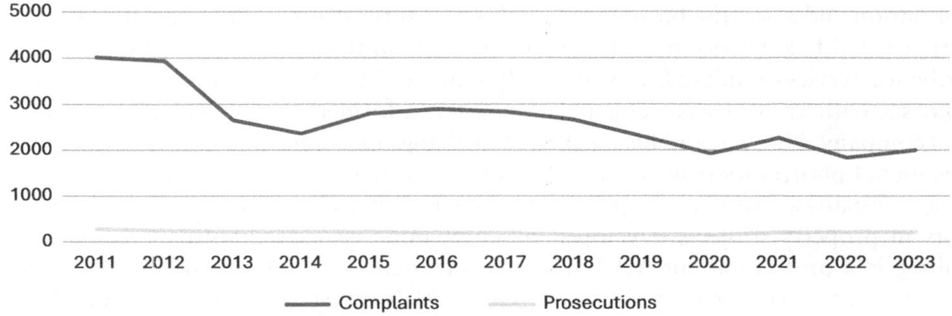

Figure 6.3 Corruption Complaints/Reports Received (Excluding Election Cases) and Prosecutions by the ICAC since 2011.

Table 6.1 Budget and Staffing of the ICAC in Selected Years

	2008	*2015*	*2022*
Budget (in millions)	USD 97.7	USD 126.01	USD 165.47
Personnel	1,263	1,351	1,400

Source: Quah (2021) and ICAC.

input and output into and from the regulator. In terms of input, it is important to see if the regulator is adequately staffed and resourced. Its budget and personnel in 2008, 2015, and 2022 are given in Table 6.1. By adjusting these figures with respect to the population of selected Asian countries, Quah reveals that Hong Kong had by far the highest per capita expenditures and staff-population ratios among Singapore, South Korea, Taiwan, the Philippines, Indonesia, and India in 2014.[32] There are also enforcement outputs. Since 1974 (until the end of 2021), in total 16,309 people have been prosecuted by the ICAC.[33] In the last decade, there were on an average around 200 people prosecuted and around 100 people convicted per year.[34] According to the POBO, the penalty for the offences can be up to a fine of HKD 1 million (roughly 99,800 GBP and 128,658 USD at the time of writing) and imprisonment for ten years.[35] Furthermore, a confiscation order of assets can be made.[36]

In recent years, some high-profile/value cases include the dummy insurance agents' scheme.[37] In this case, a group of individuals conspired to defraud two insurers of commissions totalling about HKD 52 million (roughly 5.1 million GBP and 6.7 million USD at the time of writing) by making false representations about the handling agents of 478 insurance policies. The mastermind, Lo Yin-wa, a former branch manager of FWD Life Insurance Company, recruited dummy agents who did not source any clients but were falsely represented as handling agents. This allowed them to claim commissions, incentives, bonuses, and allowances from the insurers. The ICAC's investigation uncovered the fraudulent scheme, leading to charges of conspiracy to defraud and money laundering against Lo and 12 other individuals.

Furthermore, there are cases involving civil servants. A former Hong Kong police officer, ex-sergeant Li Hung-fat, was convicted of accepting a HKD 500,000 bribe (roughly 50,000 GBP and 64,000 USD at the time of writing) to help a businessman with a debt collection issue involving a triad society.[38] Li abused his position to gather information and assist the businessman, who was at the centre of a financial dispute. The court rejected Li's defence that the money was a loan from his brother and ruled it was a bribe for services rendered. Li was finally sentenced to 18 months in prison. There are also cases with an overseas element. In one case, a former deputy general manager of a listed company, Ng Wai, and his mother, Han Shang-min, were charged with accepting an investment opportunity from an Australian businessman in exchange for showing favour in the company's overseas property investments.[39] Ng allegedly recommended investments in property projects developed by companies associated with the businessman, resulting in a profit of about AUD 2.9 million (roughly 1.4 million GBP and 1.8 million USD) from the investment opportunity. The ICAC's investigation revealed that Ng and his mother conspired to accept the advantage, leading to charges of conspiracy for an agent to accept an advantage.

With rising cross-border corruption activities, international cooperation has become essential in combating corruption. The basis of international liaison and mutual assistance is covered by the Mutual Legal Assistance in Criminal Matters Ordinance (Cap 525), the United Nations Convention against Corruption (UNCAC), and the United Nations Convention against Transnational Organised Crime. Under these regulatory instruments, ICAC officers can provide support for corruption-related investigations upon requests from overseas law enforcement and judicial authorities, or vice versa.[40] For example, in 2023, the ICAC managed eight such requests while receiving assistance for two of its own from foreign counterparts.[41]

The UNCAC plays a crucial role in fostering international cooperation to combat corruption. It provides a comprehensive legal framework to support mutual legal assistance,[42] extradition,[43] asset recovery,[44] and information sharing[45] among member states, facilitating collaboration in investigations,[46] prosecutions, and judicial proceedings.[47] UNCAC also emphasises cross-border preventive measures,[48] such as promoting transparency, integrity, and strong anti-corruption institutions, while also more generally encouraging the harmonisation of anti-corruption laws and policies to close legal loopholes.

International coordinated efforts to tackle corruption can also be enabled by the International Association of Anti-Corruption Authorities (IAACA). Since January 2022, the ICAC has held the presidency of the IAACA, spearheading global anti-corruption efforts and fostering international collaboration to advance the effective implementation of the UNCAC.[49] The IAACA performed this function by organising international or regional training activities, enabling anti-corruption agencies around the world and international organisations to exchange experiences on topics such as financial and forensic investigations, international anti-corruption cooperation, as well as anti-corruption education and youth engagement. Under the ICAC's leadership, IAACA's membership expanded from approximately 120 at the end of 2021 to nearly 170 by the end of 2023.[50] Its members encompass a wide range of specialised agencies worldwide, including those focused on law enforcement, corruption prevention, prosecution, auditing, and related fields. Today, IAACA stands as one of the largest international platforms for anti-corruption collaboration.

In the post-handover period, one notable focus has been the cooperation between mainland China and Hong Kong. The ICAC has maintained close connections with its counterparts in the mainland and Macao. In 2023, their chief Woo Ying-Ming paid official visits to the mainland to exchange views on the latest anti-corruption initiatives and developments with the National Commission of Supervision (NCS), the anti-corruption agency in China, and related central authorities and commissions of supervision of different provinces and cities.[51] Woo met the heads of the Guangdong Provincial Commission of Supervision, the Commission Against Corruption of Macao (CCAC), and the municipal commissions of supervision of those key cities in the Greater Bay Area of Guangdong. The NCS and CCAC committed to collaborating with the ICAC on various initiatives, such as organising joint practical workshops on law enforcement, developing a guide for doing business with integrity, and providing joint anti-corruption training programmes for enterprises in the region.

Heilbrunn differentiates among four types of anti-corruption commissions in the world.[52] First is the universal model with its investigative, preventative, and communicative functions. The universal model is typified by Hong Kong's ICAC. Second, the investigative model is characterised by a small and centralised investigative commission as operated in Singapore's Corrupt Practices Investigation Bureau. Both the universal and investigative models are organisationally accountable to the executive. Third, the parliamentary model includes commissions that report to parliamentary committees and are independent of the executive and judicial branches of state. The parliamentary model is epitomised by the New South Wales (Australia) Independent Commission Against Corruption. Finally, the multi-agency model includes a number of offices that are individually distinct, but together weave a web of agencies to fight corruption. The US has adopted this approach. Among the models, the universal model entails high costs that for many governments are simply prohibitive for the already limited budgets in certain countries. The ICAC is another piece of convincing evidence to showcase Hong Kong's strength and commitment to public enforcement so as to curb corruption.

5 The Worrying Signs?

Despite Hong Kong's achievements in curbing corruption as exemplified by various evidence above, Hong Kong's reputation has clearly been hampered by two top government officials involved in corruption scandals. The notable ones perhaps have been the conviction of former Chief Secretary of Hong Kong, Rafael Hui Si-Yan, and former Chief Executive, Donald Tsang Yam-Kuen. Hui was found guilty in 2014 of accepting HKD 8.5 million (roughly 848,000 GBP and 1 million USD at the time of writing) in bribes from executives of property developer Sun Hung Kai Properties. Hui was convicted on three counts of misconduct in public office, one count of conspiracy to commit misconduct in public office, and one count of conspiracy to offer an advantage to a public servant. He was sentenced to a seven-and-a-half-year jail term and a HKD 11.18 million fine – 1.1 million GBP and 1.4 million USD at the time of writing – (equivalent to the bribe he was found guilty of taking).[53] It is worth highlighting that out of these charges, misconduct in public office and conspiracy to commit misconduct in public office were brought under common law; and only conspiracy to offer advantages to a public servant was brought under Section 4(1)(a) of the POBO (as well as Section 159A of the Crimes Ordinance). Meanwhile, Tsang was found guilty of a charge of misconduct in public office over his failure to disclose the lease of a luxury flat in mainland China from the shareholder of a broadcast company whose licence applications he approved.[54] He was sentenced to 20 months' imprisonment (later reduced to 12 months). However, Tsang's conviction and sentence were subsequently overturned by the Court of Final Appeal (the highest court in Hong Kong).[55] Despite this, the confidence of the public in the integrity of government officials has clearly been dented (which might explain the result of the relevant public opinion poll discussed above).

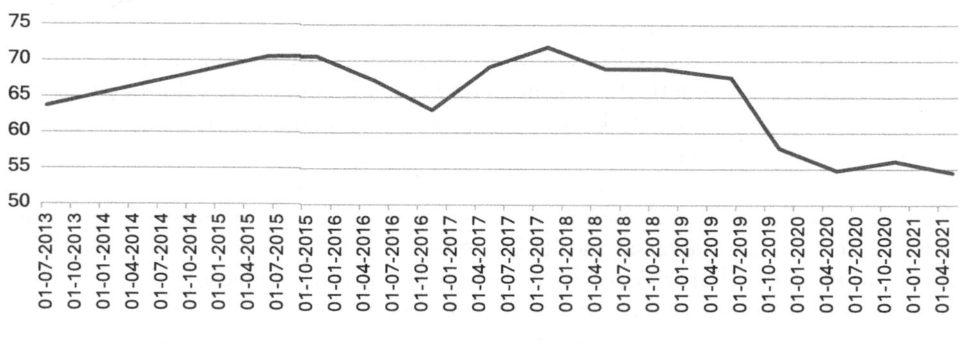

Figure 6.4 Performance of the ICAC in Local Public Opinion Poll throughout the Years.

Another public opinion poll also shows that public confidence in the work of the ICAC has been decreasing in recent years (see Figure 6.4).[56] According to empirical evidence, the ICAC is significantly more active in conducting investigations when it enjoys relatively high levels of public support than under low levels of public support.[57] It is worth noting that at roughly the same time as the episodes of Hui and Tsang, the once fearsome regulator was plagued by its own scandal.[58] An investigation commenced in 2013 when the ICAC received complaints against Timothy Tong, who was the former ICAC chief during 2012–2015. The accusations related to using public funds for entertainment activities, lavish overseas trips, as well as his acceptance and offering of gifts to mainland officials.

6 Conclusion

In 2013, a BBC reporter asked the following headline question in his article, 'Can Hong Kong stay corruption-free under China?'[59] On the one hand, as discussed above, the city-state has a very competent anti-corruption agency enforcing a set of functional anti-corruption laws (the POBO plus notably the common law offence of misconduct in public office). The ICAC is adequately resourced and has a large number of personnel to discharge its various functions. All these arguably have not changed after Hong Kong's reunification with China in 1997. On the other hand, if the CPI can be relied upon, there is still a clear gap between the (perceived) level of corruption in Hong Kong and mainland China. Since the interactions, both political and commercial, between Hong Kong and mainland China have been on the rise since 1997, it is almost inevitable that the former will be affected by the latter. As mentioned above, the cases of Tsang and Tong both had a 'mainland Chinese element' in them. Before making a serious accusation against China, one perhaps needs to understand the complex Chinese notion of *guanxi*.[60] Corruption is prohibited by law but cultivating/using *guanxi* is common in China. Unless a fine line can be drawn between the two, it is fair to expect that Hong Kong can only be more and more influenced by this Chinese culture in the process of the city-state's integration into its motherland, thereby further increasing the perceived level of corruption.

Notes

1 See, for example, OECD, 'Issues Paper on Corruption and Economic Growth' (2013). Available at: https://www.oecd.org/g20/topics/anti-corruption/issues-paper-on-corruption-and-economic-growth.htm.
2 Arvind Jain, 'Corruption: A Review' (2001) 15 *Journal of Economic Surveys* 71, 73.
3 Jain 92–93.
4 Andrei Shleifer and Robert Vishny, 'Corruption' (1993) 108 *Quarterly Journal of Economics* 599, 599.
5 Shleifer and Vishny 615–616.
6 Paolo Mauro, 'Corruption and Growth' (1995) 110 *Quarterly Journal of Economics* 681; Pranab Bardhan, 'Corruption and Development: A Review of Issues' (1997) 35 *Journal of Economic Literature* 1320.
7 Jain (n 2) 76–77.
8 See the Methodology Note of the Index.
9 In this local public opinion poll, the public perception on the degree of corruption is measured. The higher the score means the society is more 'corruption-free'.
10 Transparency International, 'Corruption Perception Index 2022' (2023). Available at https://www.transparency.org/en/cpi/2022.
11 Jon Quah, 'Controlling Corruption in City-states: A Comparative Study of Hong Kong and Singapore' (1994) 22 *Crime, Law and Social Change* 391.

12 Quah 408–409.
13 Abdul-Gafaru Abdulai, 'Political Will in Combating Corruption in Developing and Transition Economies' (2009) 16 *Journal of Financial Crime* 387, 388.
14 Abdulai 399.
15 Hong Kong Government, 'ICAC' (2022). Available at: https://www.gov.hk/en/about/abouthk/factsheets/docs/icac.pdf.
16 A detailed account of the case was given by the ICAC. Independent Commission Against Corruption, 'Landmark Cases' (2023). Available at: https://www.icac.org.hk/en/law/case/index.html.
17 Independent Commission Against Corruption.
18 Hong Kong Government (n 15).
19 The ICAC is empowered by Independent Commission against Corruption Ordinance (Cap 204) to investigate the offences of bribery involving civil servants, public bodies and private sector employees.
20 See Sections 10 & 10A–G, of the ICAC Ordinance.
21 Section 2 of the POBO.
22 Section 2 of the POBO. 'Entertainment' means the provision of food or drink, for consumption on the occasion when it is provided, and of any other entertainment provided at the same time, for example, singing and dancing. Although the acceptance of entertainment does not breach the POBO, individual departments will still stipulate the conditions for staff's acceptance of entertainment.
23 Section 9 of POBO stipulates that no agent (usually an employee) shall solicit or accept any advantage without the permission of his principal when conducting his principal's affairs or business; the offeror of the advantage is also guilty of an offence.
24 Wing-Chi Hui, 'Combating Corruption: The Hong Kong Experience' (2014) 6 *Tsinghua China Law Review* 239.
25 Michael Jackson, 'Anti-Corruption Law and Enforcement in Hong Kong Keeping It Clean' in Jiaxing Hu and Matthias Vanhullebusch (eds) *Finance, Rule of Law and Development in Asia: Perspectives from Singapore, Hong Kong and Mainland China* (Brill Academic Publishers, 2016) 485–490.
26 Jackson 491.
27 Jackson 493.
28 Ian Scott, 'The Hong Kong ICAC's Approach to Corruption Control' in Adam Graycar and Russell Smith (eds) *Handbook of Global Research and Practice in Corruption* (Edward Elgar, 2011) 412.
29 This approach was seen in *Shum Kwok Sher v HKSAR*; *Sin Kam Wah v HKSAR*, as well as a further 33 cases between 2003 and 2008. See Scott 412.
30 An enforcement flowchart can be found on the website of the ICAC. Independent Commission against Corruption, 'Investigation Procedures' (2024). Available at: https://www.icac.org.hk/en/rc/op/index.html.
31 Jon Quah, *Curbing Corruption in Asian Countries: An Impossible Dream?* (Emerald, 2011) 246.
32 Jon Quah, 'Best Practices for Combating Corruption: Learning from Singapore and Hong Kong' in Krishna Tummala (ed.) *Corruption in the Public Sector: An International Perspective* (Emerald, 2021) 16–17.
33 Data from the ICAC.
34 Data from the ICAC.
35 See Section 12 of POBO. This maximum penalty applies for the offence under Section 10.
36 Section 12AA of POBO.
37 Independent Commission Against Corruption, 'Mastermind and 12 Others Charged by ICAC in $52m Dummy Agents Commissions Fraud Plead Guilty in District Court' (2024). Available at: https://www.icac.org.hk/en/p/press/index_id_2010.html.
38 The Standard, 'Ex-sergeant Jailed 18 Months over HK$500,000 Bribe in "Private Investigation"' (2023). Available at: https://www.thestandard.com.hk/breaking-news/section/4/202176/Ex-sergeant-jailed-18-months-over-HK$500,000-bribe-in-%E2%80%98private-investigation%E2%80%99.
39 Independent Commission Against Corruption, 'Recent ICAC Cases' (2024). Available at: https://hkbedc.icac.hk/en/integrity_focus/recent_icac_cases/812.
40 See e.g. Mutual Legal Assistance in Criminal Matters Ordinance (Cap 525) para. 12.1.

41 Independent Commission Against Corruption, 'Annual Report 2023' (2024). Available at: https://www.icac.org.hk/icac/annual-report/2023/pdf/AR2023_Full.pdf.
42 UNCAC art. 46.
43 UNCAC art. 44.
44 UNCAC Chapter V.
45 UNCAC Chapter VI.
46 UNCAC art. 49.
47 UNCAC art. 47.
48 UNCAC Chapter II.
49 Independent Commission Against Corruption (n 41).
50 Independent Commission Against Corruption (n 41).
51 Independent Commission Against Corruption (n 41).
52 John Heilbrunn, 'Anti-corruption Commissions: Panacea or Real Medicine to Fight Corruption?' (2004) World Bank Institute Working Paper Series 37234. Available at: http://siteresources.worldbank.org/WBI/Resources/wbi37234Heilbrunn.pdf.
53 Herbert Smith Freehills, 'Property Tycoon and Former Chief Secretary Jailed in Hong Kong's Highest-Level Corruption Trial' (2014). Available at: https://hsfnotes.com/asiadisputes/2014/12/24/property-tycoon-and-former-chief-secretary-jailed-in-hong-kongs-highest-level-corruption-trial/.
54 BBC, 'Former Hong Kong Leader Donald Tsang Jailed again for Misconduct' (2018). Available at: https://www.bbc.co.uk/news/world-asia-china-44896124.
55 *HKSAR v Tsang Yam Kuen, Donald* [2019] HKCFA 24.
56 In this public opinion poll, the public were asked to rate their satisfaction with the Independent Commission against Corruption as a disciplinary force. 0 stands for very dissatisfied; 100 stands for very satisfied.
57 Jian Xu and Jing Xu, 'Differential Public Support and the Independence of Anti-Corruption Agencies' (2024) 16 *European Political Science Review* 72.
58 SCMP, 'Former Hong Kong Anti-corruption Commissioner Timothy Tong Hin-ming to Face No Further Criminal Probe' (27 January 2016). Available at: https://www.scmp.com/news/hong-kong/law-crime/article/1905876/former-hong-kong-anti-corruption-commissioner-timothy-tong.
59 BBC, 'Can Hong Kong Stay Corruption-Free under China?' (2013). Available at: https://www.bbc.co.uk/news/world-asia-china-23223457.
60 Flora Huang and Horace Yeung, *Institutions and Economic Growth in Asia* (Routledge, 2018) 63–64.

Bibliography

Abdulai, Abdul-Gafaru, 'Political Will in Combating Corruption in Developing and Transition Economies' (2009) 16 *Journal of Financial Crime* 387.

Bardhan, Pranab, 'Corruption and Development: A Review of Issues' (1997) 35 *Journal of Economic Literature* 1320.

BBC, 'Can Hong Kong Stay Corruption-Free under China? (2013). Available at: https://www.bbc.co.uk/news/world-asia-china-23223457.

BBC, 'Former Hong Kong Leader Donald Tsang Jailed Again for Misconduct' (2018). Available at: https://www.bbc.co.uk/news/world-asia-china-44896124.

Heilbrunn, John, 'Anti-corruption Commissions: Panacea or Real Medicine to Fight Corruption?' (2004) World Bank Institute Working Paper Series 37234. Available at: https://siteresources.worldbank.org/WBI/Resources/wbi37234Heilbrunn.pdf.

Herbert Smith Freehills, 'Property Tycoon and Former Chief Secretary Jailed in Hong Kong's Highest-Level Corruption Trial' (2014). Available at: https://hsfnotes.com/asiadisputes/2014/12/24/property-tycoon-and-former-chief-secretary-jailed-in-hong-kongs-highest-level-corruption-trial/.

Hong Kong Government, 'ICAC' (2022). Available at: https://www.gov.hk/en/about/abouthk/factsheets/docs/icac.pdf.

Huang, Flora and Yeung, Horace, *Institutions and Economic Growth in Asia* (Routledge, 2018).

Hui, Wing-Chi, 'Combating Corruption: The Hong Kong Experience' (2014) 6 *Tsinghua China Law Review* 239.

Independent Commission Against Corruption, 'Landmark Cases' (2023). Available at: https://www.icac.org.hk/en/law/case/index.html.
Independent Commission Against Corruption, 'Annual Report 2023' (2024). Available at: https://www.icac.org.hk/icac/annual-report/2023/pdf/AR2023_Full.pdf.
Independent Commission Against Corruption, 'Investigation Procedures' (2024). Available at: https://www.icac.org.hk/en/rc/op/index.html.
Independent Commission Against Corruption, 'Mastermind and 12 Others Charged by ICAC in $52m Dummy Agents Commissions Fraud Plead Guilty in District Court' (2024). Available at: https://www.icac.org.hk/en/p/press/index_id_2010.html.
Independent Commission Against Corruption, 'Recent ICAC Cases' (2024). Available at: https://hkbedc.icac.hk/en/integrity_focus/recent_icac_cases/812.
Jackson, Michael, 'Anti-Corruption Law and Enforcement in Hong Kong Keeping It Clean' in Jiaxing Hu and Matthias Vanhullebusch (eds) *Finance, Rule of Law and Development in Asia: Perspectives from Singapore, Hong Kong and Mainland China* (Brill Academic Publishers, 2016) 479–515.
Jain, Arvind, 'Corruption: A Review' (2001) 15 *Journal of Economic Surveys* 71.
Mauro, Paolo, 'Corruption and Growth' (1995) 110 *Quarterly Journal of Economics* 681.
OECD, 'Issues Paper on Corruption and Economic Growth' (2013). Available at: https://www.oecd.org/g20/topics/anti-corruption/issues-paper-on-corruption-and-economic-growth.htm.
Quah, Jon, 'Controlling Corruption in City-states: A Comparative Study of Hong Kong and Singapore' (1994) 22 *Crime, Law and Social Change* 391.
Quah, Jon, *Curbing Corruption in Asian Countries: An Impossible Dream?* (Emerald, 2011).
Quah, Jon, 'Best Practices for Combating Corruption: Learning from Singapore and Hong Kong' in Krishna Tummala (ed.) *Corruption in the Public Sector: An International Perspective* (Emerald, 2021) 7–22.
SCMP, 'Former Hong Kong Anti-corruption Commissioner Timothy Tong Hin-ming to Face No Futher Criminal Probe' (27 January 2016). Available at: https://www.scmp.com/news/hong-kong/law-crime/article/1905876/former-hong-kong-anti-corruption-commissioner-timothy-tong.
Scott, Ian, 'The Hong Kong ICAC's Approach to Corruption Control' in Adam Graycar and Russell Smith (eds) *Handbook of Global Research and Practice in Corruption* (Edward Elgar, 2011) 401–415.
Shleifer, Andrei and Vishny, Robert, 'Corruption' (1993) 108 *Quarterly Journal of Economics* 599.
The Standard, 'Ex-sergeant Jailed 18 Months over HK$500,000 Bribe in "Private Investigation"' (2023). Available at: https://www.thestandard.com.hk/breaking-news/section/4/202176/Ex-sergeant-jailed-18-months-over-HK$500,000-bribe-in-%E2%80%98private-investigation%E2%80%99.
Transparency International, 'Corruption Perception Index 2022' (2023). Available at: https://www.transparency.org/en/cpi/2022.
Xu, Jian and Xu, Jing, 'Differential Public Support and the Independence of Anti-corruption Agencies' (2024) 16 *European Political Science Review* 72.

7 Is It Possible to Fight Corruption in a Post-Communist Captured State? The Case of Bulgaria

Radosveta Vassileva

1 Introduction

Bulgaria provides an opportunity for a case study on the challenges of tackling corruption for several notable reasons. First, it is one of only two countries (along with Romania) which joined the EU *without* fulfilling the accession criteria on the rule of law.[1] That is why, Bulgaria and Romania were put under the Cooperation and Verification Mechanism (CVM) – a special mechanism under which the EU Commission assumed an obligation to help these countries catch up with other EU members in the areas of the rule of law and the fight against corruption.[2]

Moreover, Bulgaria has a plethora of seemingly well-armed bodies dedicated to anti-corruption efforts. Examples include the Prosecutor's Office (PO), the police,[3] the Anti-Corruption Commission, the State Agency for National Security (DANS),[4] the former Centre for the Prevention of Corruption and Organised Crime,[5] and the Judicial Inspectorate at the Supreme Judicial Council. Moreover, Bulgaria not only set up a National Council on Anti-Corruption Policies in 2015,[6] but also, on occasion, it has formed parliamentary committees on the prevention of corruption.

Despite the guidance from the EU Commission under the CVM and the abundance of various bodies focused on anti-corruption efforts, Bulgaria's fight against corruption seems doomed. The country is traditionally regarded as one of the most corrupt EU members by reputable rankings, such as *Transparency International*'s Corruption Perceptions Index (CPI).[7] A special Eurobarometer survey from 2022 shows that 88% of Bulgarians consider corruption to be 'widespread'.[8] Furthermore, the US government is paying close attention to the rampant corruption in Bulgaria – the Office of Foreign Assets Control of the US Department of the Treasury has sanctioned Bulgarian politicians, a former Minister of Finance, a former lead officer at DANS, as well as other influential public figures for corruption under the Global Magnitsky Human Rights Accountability Act.[9]

This chapter purports to critically evaluate Bulgaria's institutional anti-corruption framework to shed light on why the country has neither seen tangible results in the prevention, nor in the prosecution of corruption, and to consider what reforms are necessary. It argues that Bulgaria developed many of the above-mentioned anti-corruption bodies with a threefold purpose. First, it created the false impression that it had the political will to fight corruption, which was important vis-à-vis the CVM. Second, it diluted responsibility while ensuring these institutions remained captured. Most importantly, Bulgaria diverted attention from one of its long-standing rule of law challenges – the vertical, Soviet structure of its PO, which is politically dependent and which is seen by experts as a major source of corruption and blackmail because it shields those in power

DOI: 10.4324/9781003324843-10

from criminal liability and initiates bogus criminal proceedings against their opponents. Regrettably, by pretending to step up its anti-corruption framework, the governing majority ensured Bulgaria's captured state remained intact.

2 The Idiosyncrasies of the Post-communist Captured State

Before delving into Bulgaria's dubious anti-corruption efforts, some preliminary remarks seem necessary. Bulgaria is often described as a 'captured state'.[10] According to the *Transparency International*'s Glossary, 'state capture' occurs when '[p]owerful individuals, groups and organisations undemocratically [shape] a nation's policies, legal institutions and economies to illicitly enrich themselves with impunity'.[11]

Nevertheless, a related, more nuanced concept seems to denote better the nature of Bulgaria's widespread corruption – 'the post-communist mafia state'. In his influential book *Post-Communist Mafia State: The Case of Hungary*, Magyar explains the dynamics of the rule of law crisis in Hungary.[12] He defines the country as a 'post-communist mafia state', which is a 'subtype of autocratic regimes'.[13] While the term 'mafia state' defines 'the way in which the state functions', 'post-communist' refers to the 'circumstances of its formation'.[14] In Magyar's view, the fundamental feature of the mafia state is the specific way in which power is accumulated 'in the hands of the adopted political family by means of mafia culture elevated on the rank of central politics…'.[15] The mafia state engages in the 'hostile takeover of institutions' – that is why, 'the institutions of public authority cease to be the sites where real decisions are taken…'.[16]

Similarly to Hungary, Bulgaria was a communist state until 1989 – it was governed according to a one-party state model where all institutions acted as rubber stamps for the Bulgarian Communist Party. Below, for instance, we will see that the communist heritage of Bulgaria's PO in terms of structure, powers, and culture is one of the key obstacles hampering the prosecution of corruption. Moreover, parallels could be drawn between the regime built by Viktor Orbán in Hungary and the regime of Boyko Borissov in Bulgaria – these politicians rose to power in the same period and endeavoured to solidify autocratic regimes. Between 2009 and 2021, Borissov has led three governments in Bulgaria. At the time of writing of this chapter, Bulgaria is governed by a caretaker government presided over by a former President of Parliament from the GERB party, the party which Prime Minister Borissov heads.

GERB's zeal to capture state institutions and to remove checks and balances, ensuring the longevity of autocracy in Bulgaria, can be compared to the assault on the rule of law in Hungary by Orbán's Fidesz party. In this light, what metrics, such as the CPI or the Eurobarometer, cannot reflect is that, in Bulgaria, corruption is not merely a question of widespread perception – the country is permanently shaken by money laundering, bribery, and inexplicable wealth scandals, implicating ministers, members of parliament, the judiciary, the secret services, and even heads of anti-corruption bodies who are not held accountable.[17]

There are, however, several significant differences between the Hungarian and the Bulgarian rule of law crises. Unlike Bulgaria, Hungary was deemed to fulfil the accession criteria on the rule of law at the time of its EU accession in 2004. Besides, in contrast to Orbán, Borissov never engaged in overt confrontation with the EU. Unlike Fidesz's hostile takeover of institutions, GERB managed to capture institutions through more covert means – namely, by carrying out reforms in bad faith while claiming to comply with the CVM's recommendations.

3 On the Surface: The CVM and GERB's Political Will for Reforms

While a detailed overview of the CVM is beyond the scope of this chapter, it should be underlined that this was a mechanism anchored in dialogue between the EU Commission and Bulgaria. Its goal for Bulgaria was to help it achieve six benchmarks which were set at the time of accession – judicial independence, legal framework, continued judicial reform, and the fight against high-level corruption, general corruption, and organised crime.[18] This dialogue was evidenced by regular reports by the EU Commission, which discussed the progress made and which made concrete recommendations about future reforms.[19]

Since its accession to the EU and largely because of the CVM, Bulgaria has seen a range of reforms allegedly aimed at strengthening its anti-corruption efforts. The most notable, large-scale one was the adoption of the Law on Countering Corruption and Confiscating Illegally Acquired Assets (for brevity hereon Anti-Corruption Law) in 2018 whose main achievement was the establishment of a superstructure – the Anti-Corruption Commission which united some of the prior scattered anti-corruption bodies.[20] This is the main law governing the country's anti-corruption framework. It should be noted that this law was amended in 2023 to divide the commission into two bodies.[21] However, we focus on the 2018 reform because sufficient time has passed since its adoption to evaluate its impact and because the CVM was still underway at the time.

In a special report, endorsing the 2018 law, Bulgaria's Ministry of Justice argued that the main motivation for the reform was to 'better coordinate' the fight against corruption at the highest ranks of government and to comply with the EU Commission's recommendations in the January 2017 CVM report.[22] Thus, on the surface, Bulgaria demonstrated its political will and strong commitment to reforms. In the 2018 CVM report, the EU Commission even noted that Bulgaria '[had] made significant progress' in the high-level corruption benchmark because of the adoption of the 2018 law.[23]

4 A Closer Look: Deceptive Appearances

When one examines the substance of the 2018 reform consolidating the Anti-Corruption Commission, one quickly discerns an example of legislative manoeuvres aimed at imitating reforms, diluting responsibility, and ensuring institutions are susceptible to political influences.

4.1 Imitating Reforms and Diluting Responsibility

It is notable that in the 2022 report on Bulgaria by the Group of States against Corruption (GRECO), which was set up by the Council of Europe to monitor the compliance of its members with its anti-corruption standards, the evaluation team asserts that it is 'left with the impression that the separation of tasks between the [National Council on Anti-Corruption Policies] and the Anti-Corruption Commission was not clearly understood by interlocutors interviewed on-site, including representatives of the Anti-Corruption Commission'.[24] The former body was set up in 2015 and also purports to prevent corruption – the decree establishing it contains articles similar in spirit to some of the provisions of the Anti-Corruption Law, blurring their respective obligations.[25]

Regrettably, this is not the only example of a lack of coordination and dilution of responsibility. One of the consequences of the 2018 reform was incorporating a directorate previously part of DANS (Bulgaria's secret services), which was responsible for investigating corruption, in the Anti-Corruption Commission.[26] The 2018 Anti-Corruption Law amended the Law on DANS, removing its powers to investigate corruption.[27] However, shortly after the Anti-Corruption Law entered into force, DANS self-restored some of its powers to investigate via an ordinance.[28]

Another institution, which was merged with the Anti-Corruption Commission following the 2018 reform, is the Centre for the Prevention of Corruption and Organised Crime. This body under the auspices of the Bulgarian government was set up in 2010.[29] As visible from Articles 3(1) and Article 3(4) of a subsequent decree establishing its Rules of Conduct, this centre was tasked with developing 'complex solutions' to corruption issues by relying on a sophisticated cyber model known as BORCOR.[30] Nevertheless, from early on, the work of this Centre was marked by a lack of transparency.[31] Besides, after the merger with the Anti-Corruption Commission, independent media reported that the experts from this Centre had abandoned the cyber model and had been assigned the development of a programme promoting anti-corruption values at Bulgarian kindergartens and pre-schools.[32]

There is literature supporting the argument that initiatives focused on early childhood education may have a role to play in the fight against corruption in the long run.[33] Education is seen as a powerful tool promoting anti-corruption values in the United Nations Convention against Corruption, too.[34] However, to those knowing the Bulgarian context, this new assignment may be seen as a manoeuvre hiding the failure of the prior cyber initiative. Moreover, considering that no high-ranking public official has been held accountable for corruption to this day, there may be concerns that resources are invested in initiatives that do not threaten the establishment to minimise resources for activities that can combat corruption in the current government.

4.2 *Capture*

Even more problematically, anti-corruption reforms seem underpinned by the desire to capture institutions and subject them to the whims of the governing majority. When one examines how the lead officers of Bulgarian anti-corruption bodies are appointed, one sees that these appointments either depend on the governing majority in Parliament or on the executive. To this end, it should be noted that Bulgaria is a parliamentary republic in which the government itself is elected by the majority in parliament. In the case of a country whose politics has been dominated by the same political party for 16 years, such as Bulgaria, it is easy to understand why all these bodies are overshadowed by the same centre of power.

Pursuant to former Article (8)5 of the Anti-Corruption Law, the President of the Anti-Corruption Commission was elected by Parliament by a simple majority. Meanwhile, pursuant to former Article 8(6) of the same law, the Vice-President and the remaining three members of the Commission were elected by Parliament upon a proposal by the same President. This manner of appointment severely increased the risks of political involvement in the work of the Anti-Corruption Commission since not only were all members elected by the same governing majority, but also four of them were selected by one person (the Commission's head). One may reason by analogy to an Opinion by the Venice Commission, which commented on Bulgaria's Judicial Inspectorate (JI) at the Supreme Judicial Council, which is tasked with monitoring the ethical values of magistrates. As JI's members are elected by Parliament in a similar procedure, the Venice Commission has warned of '[increased] risk of political attachment'.[35]

Sadly, the 2023 reform of the Anti-Corruption Law may have exacerbated the problem of political attachment – pursuant to Article 8(3) of the current Anti-Corruption Law, members of the Anti-Corruption Commission are elected by two-thirds of the members of Parliament. This may imply that they will owe favours to more political groups – not just to the governing majority.

Beyond political attachment, biased appointment procedures may explain why candidates with dubious credentials and ethical values have been appointed in the past. For instance, the *ApartmentGate* scandal, which shook Bulgaria in 2019, implicated both the head and the vice-head of the Anti-Corruption Commission.[36] The *ApartmentGate* scandal involved the purchase of luxurious properties at below-the-market prices by the President of Parliament, the Minister of Interior, state officials, and heads of anti-corruption bodies.

Finally, other anti-corruption bodies, independent of the Anti-Corruption Commission, are also politically attached. For instance, the introduction to this chapter mentioned that the Bulgarian police is also vested with powers to counter corruption via its General Directorate Combating Organised Crime. However, it is subordinate to the Minister of Interior. Similarly, pursuant to Article 8(1) of the Law on DANS, the candidate for head of this service is proposed by the Council of Ministers. The National Council on Anti-Corruption Policies is also under the auspices of the government – its head and vice-head are sitting ministers.[37]

5 Soviet Gorilla-in-the-Room: Bulgaria's PO

Bulgaria's questionable reforms of anti-corruption bodies may also be seen as attempts to deviate attention away from one of its long-standing rule of law challenges – the structure, excessive powers, communist culture, and political dependencies of the PO. The specific features of this institution, which has not been reformed in depth since Bulgaria became a democratic state on paper in 1989, may shed light on why the country has not seen the prosecution of high-level corruption. Regrettably, the EU Commission did not properly insist on a comprehensive reform via the CVM, either.

5.1 No Checks and Balances

The PO has the complete monopoly over criminal investigations in Bulgaria.[38] However, it has a vertical, hierarchical structure in which all decisions – whether to start an investigation, whether to put an end to investigation, whether to press charges, etc. – depend on one person (the General Prosecutor).[39] While hierarchical structures of prosecution services are common in Europe, emerging international guidelines on prosecutorial independence and impartiality require 'an adequate system of checks and balances', which does not exist in Bulgaria.[40] Not only can the General Prosecutor impose his views and compromise the impartiality of lower-standing prosecutors, but also the prosecutorial decisions in this pre-trial (investigation) phase are not subjected to judicial oversight, which promotes arbitrary actions. The PO can turn a blind eye to crimes or press charges without proof to harass those who are inconvenient for the regime or those who are willing to expose the crimes of prosecutors.

The systemic problems of this institution preventing effective investigations, including the propensity to start bogus criminal proceedings or to shield those implicated in crimes from liability, have been captured by a series of judgements against Bulgaria by the European Court of Human Rights (ECtHR).[41] A cosmetic reform to the Code of Criminal Procedure and to the Law on the Judiciary in 2023 pretended to address some of these issues by creating a special mechanism for the investigation of a sitting General Prosecutor.[42] However, this seems to be one more example of a pseudo-reform designed to deceive that a change has taken place. Evidence to this end is provided by the very procedure of how a magistrate to investigate a General Prosecutor is selected – namely, they are chosen from a list of 22 pre-approved judges by the Supreme Court of Cassation, many of whom are implicated in controversies themselves.[43]

5.2 *Political Dependencies*

The model of Bulgaria's PO, which was inspired by the Soviet prosecutorial model, was introduced to Bulgaria in 1947.[44] In communist times, the PO was the voice of the totalitarian regime – thus, it was faithful to the Bulgarian Communist Party by design. After the end of communism, in 1991, Bulgaria set up a Supreme Judicial Council responsible for the election and promotion of all magistrates in the country. Following a cosmetic constitutional reform in 2023, this body was divided into two separate councils – a Supreme Judicial Council (SJC) and a Supreme Prosecutorial Council (SPC). However, in July 2024, Bulgaria's Constitutional Court declared these amendments anti-constitutional.[45]

Even if the 2023 constitutional amendments had remained in force, the newly set up councils would have been politically captured by virtue of the way members of such bodies were supposed to be elected.[46] The amendments did not seem to take into consideration earlier concerns about the SJC voiced by the Venice Commission.[47] Moreover, their compliance with international guidelines on prosecutorial independence and impartiality, which require that prosecution services be 'free from political interference', could be questioned.[48]

Overall, the politicisation of the SJC, including failed attempts to reform the institution, may shed light on why the General Prosecutor is traditionally faithful to the governing majority. Moreover, in case he deviates from the party line, he can easily be replaced.[49]

6 Conclusion and Recommendations

The case of Bulgaria illustrates the difficulties of preventing and prosecuting corruption in a post-communist captured state. Sadly, in such states, political elites are committed to the takeover of institutions vested with powers to combat corruption to ensure they can enrich themselves illicitly with impunity. Bulgaria's case also shows that a governing majority acting in bad faith may rely on deceptive manoeuvres to pretend compliance with anti-corruption recommendations by supranational institutions like the EU Commission. To this end, neither the overabundance of anti-corruption bodies nor the legislative hyperactivity allegedly aimed at strengthening the anti-corruption framework indicate that the country is genuinely committed to fighting corruption.

Bulgaria is in dire need of in-depth reforms which can be encouraged by the EU Commission, which is best placed to exert pressure on the local government thanks to different tools, such as soft law rule of law mechanisms,[50] or infringement procedures. However, Bulgaria's bitter CVM experience shows why the principle of mutual trust embedded in the EU Treaties should not be used as an excuse to take the promises of the local government at face value. This chapter suggests three priorities for reform that could be considered in more detail in future work:

1 Amending the relevant legislation to clearly differentiate between the obligations of the diverse anti-corruption bodies to put an end to the dilution of responsibility;
2 Amending the Anti-Corruption Law to ensure that members of the Anti-Corruption Commission are not just elected by Parliament. In this way, political capture will be made more difficult;[51] and
3 Reforming the SJC and restructuring the PO to ensure prosecutorial independence, coupled with introducing safeguards against prosecutorial arbitrariness in line with emerging international guidelines.[52] This will strengthen the effectiveness of investigations into high-level corruption and pave the way for its prosecution.

Notes

1 Bulgaria and Romania acceded the EU in 2007.
2 On the origin and development of the CVM, see Radosveta Vassileva, 'Threats to the Rule of Law: The Pitfalls of the Cooperation and Verification Mechanism' (2020) 3 EPL 741–768; The mechanism was terminated in 2023.
3 Under Article 39(2), point 9 of the Law on the Ministry of Interior, the General Directorate Combating Organised Crime can investigate corruption in the state administration.
4 Under Article 3(1) of Ordinance No. I-5 of 26 September 2018, DANS endeavours to examine complaints against the corruption of its employees.
5 In 2018, it became part of the Anti-Corruption Commission.
6 Council of Ministers' Decree No. 136 of 29 May 2015.
7 Since its accession to the EU, Bulgaria had been consistently ranked as the most corrupt EU member until 2020. It was surpassed by Hungary only in 2021. See Transparency International, 'CPI' (Official Website of Transparency International). https://www.transparency.org/en/cpi/2022, accessed 16 June 2023.
8 EU Commission, 'Special Eurobarometer 523' (Official Website of the EU Commission, 2022). https://europa.eu/eurobarometer/surveys/detail/2658, accessed 16 June 2023.
9 US Department of the Treasury, 'Treasury Sanctions Influential Bulgarian Individuals and Their Expansive Networks for Engaging in Corruption' (Official Website of the US Department of the Treasury, 2 June 2021). https://home.treasury.gov/news/press-releases/jy0208, accessed 16 June 2023; US Department of the Treasury, 'Treasury Sanctions Corrupt Elites across Bulgarian Political Spectrum' (Official Website of the US Department of the Treasury, 10 February 2023). https://home.treasury.gov/news/press-releases/jy1264, accessed 16 June 2023.
10 See Alexander Stoyanov et al., *State Capture: Assessment Diagnostics* (Centre for the Study of Democracy, 2019).
11 Transparency International, 'Glossary' (Official Website of Transparency International). https://www.transparency.org/en/glossary, accessed 19 June 2023.
12 Bálint Magyar, *Post-Communist Mafia State: The Case of Hungary* (CEU Press, 2016).
13 Magyar 73.
14 Magyar 2.
15 Magyar 3.
16 Magyar 16.
17 For instance, the *ApartmentGate* scandal involved the purchase of luxurious properties at below-the-market prices by the President of Parliament, the Minister of Interior, state officials, and heads of anti-corruption bodies, which raises suspicions of bribery and corruption. See Kerin Hope et al., 'Bulgaria's "Apartmentgate" Infuriates Struggling Citizens' (*FT*, 25 April 2019). https://www.ft.com/content/30083814-5ea0-11e9-a27a-fdd51850994c, accessed 23 June 2023.
18 See 2006/929/EC: Commission Decision of 13 December 2006 establishing a mechanism for cooperation and verification of progress in Bulgaria to address specific benchmarks in the areas

of judicial reform and the fight against corruption and organised crime (notified under document number C(2006) 6570).

19 Vassileva (n 2) 748–749.

20 Promulgated in State Gazette No. 7 of 19 January 2018.

21 Amendments promulgated in State Gazette No. 84 of 6 October 2023.

22 Ministry of Justice, *Draft Law on Countering Corruption and Confiscating Illegally Acquired Property: Comprehensive Preliminary Impact Assessment* (Ministry of Justice, 2017) 3.

23 EU Commission, Report from the Commission to the European Parliament and the Council on Progress in Bulgaria under the Cooperation and Verification Mechanism (COM(2018) 850 final).

24 GRECO, *Fifth Evaluation Report on Bulgaria* (GrecoEval5Rep(2022) 9) para 45.

25 Compare Article 3 of Council of Ministers' Decree No. 136 of 29 May 2015 to Article 30 of the former Anti-Corruption Law.

26 §5(6) of the final provisions.

27 §21 of the final provisions.

28 Article 3 of Ordinance No. I-5 of 26 September 2018 by DANS.

29 Council of Ministers' Decree 158 of 29 July 2010.

30 Council of Ministers' Decree 280 of 30 November 2010.

31 For a critical evaluation, see Antoaneta Tsoneva et al., *BORCOR between Myths and Corruption Realities* (Institute for Public Environment Development, 2012).

32 Ivan Petrov, 'Former BORCOR Continues to Waste Money' (*Sega*, 15 March 2019). https://www.segabg.com/category-bulgaria/bivshiyat-borkor-produlzhava-da-harchi-bezsmisleno-pari, accessed 5 June 2023.

33 Yayuk Rahayu, 'The Analysis of Anti-Corruption Education in Kindergarten DEK Padang' in *Proceedings of the International Conference of Early Childhood Education (ICECE 2019)* (Atlantis Press, 2019) 71–74.

34 Article 13, para 1(c).

35 Venice Commission, *Opinion No. 1098 / 2022 on the Draft Amendments to the Judicial System Act Concerning the Inspectorate to the Supreme Judicial Council* (Venice, 21–22 October 2022) para 21.

36 Hope et al. (n 17).

37 Article 4, Council of Ministers' Decree No. 136 of 29 May 2015.

38 Article 127 of Bulgaria's Constitution.

39 Venice Commission, *Opinion No. 515 / 2009 on the Draft Law Amending and Supplementing the Law on Judicial Power* (Venice, 13–14 March 2009) para 3.

40 Consultative Council of European Judges (CCJE) and Consultative Council of European Prosecutors (CCPE), *Challenges for Judicial Independence and Impartiality in the Member States of the Council of Europe* (SG/Inf(2016)3rev, 24 March 2016) para 118.

41 See *Kolevi v Bulgaria*, App No. 1108/02 (ECtHR, 5 November 2009) which concerns the framing of a prosecutor who tried to expose the crimes in office and corruption of the General Prosecutor; See *SZ v Bulgaria*, App No. 29263/12 (ECtHR, 3 March 2015), *Z v Bulgaria*, App No. 39257/17 (ECtHR, 28 May 2020), *X and Others v Bulgaria*, App No. 22457/16 (ECtHR, 2 February 2021) on investigations which were suspiciously compromised by the PO.

42 Amendments promulgated by State Gazette 48 of 2 June 2023.

43 Investigative journalists, members of the Organized Crime and Corruption Reporting Project, broke the news that the husband of the current magistrate selected to investigate complaints against the acting General Prosecutor is facing a criminal trial, which raises concerns about her own impartiality considering the General Prosecutor's influence in the justice system. See BIRD, 'The Ex-husband of "Ad Hoc" Prosecutor Taleva Is on Trial. Are There Dependencies?' (*BIRD*, 6 March 2024). https://bird.bg/ad-hoc-daniela-taleva/, accessed 21 March 2024.

44 Vassileva (n 2) 749–750.

45 Constitutional Court of Bulgaria, Decision 13 of 26 July 2024 on constitutional case 1/2024.

46 For instance, according to the short-lived amendments, six out of the ten members of the SPC were supposed to be elected by Parliament.

47 The Venice Commission has reported concerns that part of the country's legal profession considers that SJC's composition entails 'the risk of a SJC dominated by members elected by a political body, a factor likely to affect both the independence of the Council and that of the

judiciary in general', Venice Commission, *Opinion on the Draft to Amend and Supplement the Constitution (in the Field of the Judiciary) of the Republic of Bulgaria* (Venice, 23–24 October 2015) para 36.

48 CCJE and CCPE (n 40) para 35.

49 The dismissal of General Prosecutor Ivan Geshev in 2023 provides ample illustration. In 2022, under his leadership, the PO refused to press charges for money laundering against Borissov despite evidence gathered by the Ministry of Interior of a short-lived opposition government. See Milana Nikolova, 'Arrest, and Release, of Former Bulgarian PM Leaves Many Questions Unanswered' (*Emerging Europe*, 11 April 2022). https://emerging-europe.com/news/arrest-and-release-of-former-bulgarian-pm-leaves-many-questions-unanswered/, accessed 24 June 2023; However, when in 2023 Geshev threatened to press charges against Borissov on the same facts after a personal conflict between them erupted, the SJC was quick to dismiss him from office.

50 For instance, the Rule of Law Reports mechanism.

51 A source of inspiration could be Bulgaria's Constitutional Court where one-third of the judges are elected by Parliament, one-third of the judges are appointed by Bulgaria's President, and one-third are elected by the judiciary.

52 See CCJE and CCPE (n 40). See also CCPE, *Opinion No. 13(2018) on the Independence, Accountability and Ethics of Prosecutors* (Strasbourg, 23 November 2018).

Bibliography

BIRD, 'The Ex-husband of "Ad Hoc" Prosecutor Taleva Is on Trial. Are There Dependencies?' (*BIRD*, 6 March 2024), https://bird.bg/ad-hoc-daniela-taleva/, accessed 21 March 2024.

CCJE and CCPE, *Challenges for Judicial Independence and Impartiality in the Member States of the Council of Europe* (SG/Inf(2016)3rev, 24 March 2016).

CCPE, *Opinion No. 13(2018) on the Independence, Accountability and Ethics of Prosecutors* (Strasbourg, 23 November 2018).

EU Commission, Report from the Commission to the European Parliament and the Council on Progress in Bulgaria under the Cooperation and Verification Mechanism (COM(2018) 850 final).

EU Commission, 'Special Eurobarometer 523' (Official Website of the EU Commission, 2022), https://europa.eu/eurobarometer/surveys/detail/2658, accessed 16 June 2023.

GRECO, *Fifth Evaluation Report on Bulgaria* (GrecoEval5Rep(2022) 9).

Hope, K et al., 'Bulgaria's "Apartmentgate" Infuriates Struggling Citizens' (*FT*, 25 April 2019), https://www.ft.com/content/30083814-5ea0-11e9-a27a-fdd51850994c, accessed 23 June 2023.

Magyar, B, *Post-Communist Mafia State: The Case of Hungary* (CEU Press, 2016).

Ministry of Justice, *Draft Law on Countering Corruption and Confiscating Illegally Acquired Property: Comprehensive Preliminary Impact Assessment* (Ministry of Justice, 2017).

Nikolova, M, 'Arrest, and Release, of Former Bulgarian PM Leaves Many Questions Unanswered' (*Emerging Europe*, 11 April 2022), https://emerging-europe.com/news/arrest-and-release-of-former-bulgarian-pm-leaves-many-questions-unanswered/, accessed 24 June 2023.

Petrov, I, 'Former BORCOR Continues to Waste Money' (*Sega*, 15 March 2019), https://www.segabg.com/category-bulgaria/bivshiyat-borkor-produlzhava-da-harchi-bezsmisleno-pari, accessed 5 June 2023.

Rahayu, Y, 'The Analysis of Anti-Corruption Education in Kindergarten DEK Padang' in *Proceedings of the International Conference of Early Childhood Education (ICECE 2019)* (Atlantis Press, 2019).

Stoyanov, A et al., *State Capture: Assessment Diagnostics* (Centre for the Study of Democracy, 2019).

Transparency International, 'CPI' (Official Website of Transparency International), https://www.transparency.org/en/cpi/2022, accessed 16 June 2023.

Transparency International, 'Glossary' (Official Website of Transparency International), https://www.transparency.org/en/glossary, accessed 19 June 2023.

Tsoneva, A et al., *BORCOR between Myths and Corruption Realities* (Institute for Public Environment Development, 2012).

US Department of the Treasury, 'Treasury Sanctions Influential Bulgarian Individuals and Their Expansive Networks for Engaging in Corruption' (Official Website of the US Department of the Treasury, 2 June 2021), https://home.treasury.gov/news/press-releases/jy0208, accessed 16 June 2023.

US Department of the Treasury, 'Treasury Sanctions Corrupt Elites across Bulgarian Political Spectrum' (Official Website of the US Department of the Treasury, 10 February 2023), https://home.treasury.gov/news/press-releases/jy1264, accessed 16 June 2023.

Vassileva, R, 'Threats to the Rule of Law: The Pitfalls of the Cooperation and Verification Mechanism' (2020) 3 EPL 741–768.

Venice Commission, *Opinion No. 515 / 2009 on the Draft Law Amending and Supplementing the Law on Judicial Power* (Venice, 13–14 March 2009).

Venice Commission, *Opinion on the Draft to Amend and Supplement the Constitution (in the Field of the Judiciary) of the Republic of Bulgaria* (Venice, 23–24 October 2015).

Venice Commission, *Opinion No. 1098 / 2022 on the Draft Amendments to the Judicial System Act Concerning the Inspectorate to the Supreme Judicial Council* (Venice, 21–22 October 2022).

Part Three

Corporate Crimes

Challenges and Solutions

8 Civil False Claims Act

An Effective Anti-Corporate Fraud Remedy?

Penelope Giosa

1 Introduction

Corporate fraud is not a modern concept. Several massive corporate frauds took place in the past, damaging in this way not only the relevant investors but also entire economies. The South Sea Company bubble[1] in 1720, which deceived even Sir Isaac Newton, is an illustrative example, as well as the City of Glasgow Bank scandal[2] in 1878. Corporate fraud refers to any behaviour by which one person intends to gain a *dishonest* advantage over another, while a company is involved.[3] It is argued that all companies have a number of potential fraudsmen and thieves, therefore they should not be complacent or assume that they cannot be a victim of fraud.[4] This is particularly true if we bear in mind that business organisations on average lose 5% of their annual revenue to fraud, which is more than US $4.5 trillion lost to fraud globally each year.[5] Also, according to the PwC 2020 Global Economic Crime and Fraud Survey, nearly half of the participants in the survey had suffered at least one fraud and the average fraud incidents per company are six over the past 24 months.[6]

Detecting fraud is not easy, therefore several regulatory agencies in the US, such as the Department of Health and Human Services, rely to a great extent on the whistle-blowers' assistance in order to detect corporate fraud.[7] The role of whistle-blowers in enforcing corporate fraud is very important, as they are often a valuable source of information about the fraudulent activities of a company,[8] which is preferable to searching for new information through costly investigations.[9] In the United States, the False Claims Act (FCA), which is a civil statute, allows private citizens to file suit on behalf of the government against firms, which have allegedly defrauded the government. The US experience with the FCA is long and successful, considering that nearly 12,000 lawsuits were made between 2000 and 2018 and over $2.2 billion were recovered in the fiscal year 2022.[10] Hence, it is not without reason that the FCA is often called the most effective tool for combating fraud against the federal government.[11] Its critical role in combatting corporate fraud was also established after the Congress substantially amended the FCA, when it enacted the Fraud Enforcement and Recovery Act of 2009 (FERA), which was designed to "increase accountability for the corporate and mortgage frauds".[12] FERA expanded the FCA's scope of liability in the sense that now liability is imposed upon "any person who … knowingly makes, uses, or causes to be made or used, a false record or statement material to a false or fraudulent claim…".[13] This means that any entity doing business with a party that receives federal funding, even for actions that took place prior to FERA, can be liable under the FCA.[14] Hence, FCA in parallel with criminal proceedings are used to police the conduct of companies, which accept or use federal funds or have

DOI: 10.4324/9781003324843-12

payment obligations to the federal government of the United States.[15] However, as it will be explained below, the whistle-blowers who are employees involved in the daily business operation of the fraudulent organisation, may lose their job. Thus, the financial reward used by the authorities to encourage whistle-blowers' reporting does not always work. Also, qui tam suits are not available in all industries and the FCA pleading standard for whistle-blowers is rather strict.

In view of the above, this chapter evaluates the effectiveness of the FCA at addressing corporate fraud. Section 2 explains the current qui tam provisions, which regard whistle-blowing against corporate fraud. Section 3 reviews the history and theoretical underpinnings of the FCA in the United States of America and provides a review of how the current qui tam provisions eventually came into force. Focus is given to how the FERA has increased accountability for the corporate frauds. Section 4 examines the efficiency limitations of qui tam suits under the FCA when it comes to corporate fraud and explains why despite FERA's attempt to expand liability under the FCA, there are still hurdles for whistleblowing against corporate fraud. This chapter will then conclude with a brief discussion of the findings.

2 Whistleblowing – Qui Tam Suits under the False Claims Act

The remarkable accomplishment of the FCA, as described in the Introduction, would not have been without the assistance of the qui tam provisions, which have increased the resources of the federal government to address fraud that regards government contracts and programmes.[16] Citizen whistle-blowers have become the greatest source for uncovering complex frauds against the government, and their cases account for about 70% of all the money recovered under the FCA.[17] A qui tam lawsuit begins when the whistle-blower files a lawsuit on behalf of the government in a U.S. District Court.[18] Under the FCA, whistle-blowers are referred to as "relators", because technically the government is still the plaintiff, and they act in place of government enforcement agencies.

The cases are filed under seal and during the 60-day seal period, the government investigates the relator's allegations made in the complaint and written disclosure and may elect to do one of the following: (a) to intervene in the suit and take over responsibility for the litigation, (b) to decline intervention and allow the relators to pursue the claim on their own, (c) to dismiss the litigation, even if the relator objects or (d) to try to settle the case.[19] Regardless of the government's election, the case is unsealed and the litigation proceeds as any other federal case, as soon as the governments makes a decision. This means that once the government completes its investigation and the seal is removed, the complaint must be served on each defendant, who must file a reply and then formal discovery commences.[20] If the government declines intervention, this means that the relators can continue the litigation *without* the participation and financial support of the government.[21]

In any case, the relator is entitled to a share of the eventual recovery, which ranges between 15% and 30% of the recovery, plus the attorneys' fees and costs.[22] So, if the government intervenes, the relator receives between 15% and 25% of the recovery, whereas if the government does *not* intervene, the relator receives between 25% and 30% of the recovery. Also, there is a statute of limitations for filing a claim, according to which a claim must be filed within six years from the date of the violation of the FCA, or three years after the government knows about or should have known about the violation.[23] Also, it should be noted that 29 states have adopted FCAs similar to the federal law.[24]

3 False Claims Act: A Historical Review

The FCA, which is also called the "Lincoln Law", the "Informer's Act" or the "qui tam" statute, was effective in 1863 and has undergone significant revisions since its enactment, the most extensive of which occurred in 1943 and 1986.[25] The Congress enacted the FCA during the Civil War in order to stop dishonest suppliers to the Union military at a time when the government did not have many resources available to effectively investigate and prosecute fraud against the federal government.[26] *Qui tam* is short for the Latin phrase "qui tam pro domino rege quam pro se ipso in hac parte sequitur", meaning "who brings the action for the king as well as himself".[27] After the end of the Civil War, the use of the FCA declined in importance as robust enforcement mechanisms started applying and were effective enough to investigate and prosecute fraud without the assistance of whistle-blowers.[28] However, in the 1930s, when the military build-up of World War II began, the number of qui tam cases began to increase again.[29]

Yet not all these cases were legitimate and so the rising abuse of the FCA led to the first major amendment of the civil statute in 1943. One of the most important changes that took place in 1943 was the introduction of the "public disclosure bar". This means that the federal courts did not have jurisdiction over qui tam suits, which were based on existing indictments and not on new evidence or information provided by the party at issue.[30] The other major change was that the Department of Justice (DOJ) would have the right to intervene in any suit within 60 days of filing.[31] Depending on whether the government elected to intervene or not, the whistle-blower's share was determined accordingly. Hence, if the Attorney General (AG) decided to intervene, the whistle-blower's share was capped at 10% of the total recovery, whilst if the AG declined to intervene, the whistle-blower could recover at most 25% of the total recovery.[32] Within these ranges, the court could exercise its discretion to determine a fair and reasonable compensation.[33]

In 1986, Congress amended the FCA a second time to enhance the power of whistle-blowers and increase the financial incentives, as there was a dramatic increase in unreported fraud by government contractors, mainly in the area of defence procurement.[34] Hence, the FCA enabled a private individual having knowledge of past or present fraud against the federal government to bring a claim on the government's behalf and recover compensatory damages, civil penalties and triple damages. In this way, the recoverable damages increased from double to triple. The statutory penalties were also increased from $2,000 per false claim to a range from $5,000 to $10,000 per false claim and the whistle-blower's recovery was increased to a maximum of 25% – in cases where the government intervened, and 30% – in cases where the government elected *not* to intervene.[35] Additionally, whistle-blowers were able to recover their attorney fees and costs and they were allowed to bring a qui tam suit, even if the government was in possession of the information, as long as the whistle-blower was the original source of this information.[36] Another significant amendment that resolved the courts' disagreement about whether it was necessary for the government to prove specific intent to defraud or not was the requirement to prove that the defendant had (a) actual knowledge of the information's falsity, (b) deliberate ignorance of it or (c) reckless disregard of the information's truth.[37] Last but not least, a private right of action was given to anyone subject to discharge or discrimination in the terms and conditions of employment for participating or aiding in an FCA enforcement action.[38]

4 FERA and Its Impact on Corporate Fraud

In 2009, the Congress enacted the FERA, which was designed to "increase accountability for the corporate and mortgage frauds that ... contributed to the recent economic collapse".[39] The FERA contains the largest expansion of liability under the FCA in almost three decades.[40] This was achieved by removing two key provisions, which prevented FCA from operating as a "boundless" "all-purpose antifraud statute".[41]

The first provision removed was the requirement that the allegedly false claim should be presented to the government for payment. The amendment contemplates that liability may attach to claims that are submitted to a "contractor, grantee, or other recipient" of federal funds, even if the false claim was not submitted to the government itself.[42] As a result, the definition of the "claim" for payment was broadened to include claims for money or property expended on the government's behalf or used for a government purpose, regardless of whether the government had title to it, provided that the government gave the money or property or would reimburse a portion of it.[43] Hence, the FCA now makes it clear that liability attaches upon the submission of a false claim for money or property, "any part of which is provided by the Government without regard to whether the wrongdoer deals directly with the Federal Government; with an agent acting on the Government's behalf; or with a third party contractor, grantee, or other recipient" of federal funds.[44]

The second provision significantly lowered the threshold for finding an FCA violation by removing the intent requirement, according to which a subcontractor or a business had to act with the specific intent "to get" a false claim "paid or approved by the government".[45] The old provision imposed liability on any person "conspiring to defraud the Government by getting a false or fraudulent claim allowed or paid".[46] Also, under its former version, the FCA prohibited individuals from knowingly making, using, or causing to be made, a false or fraudulent claim.[47] Instead of the intent requirement, FERA contemplated that the false statement must now be "material" to government's payment decision, which means that the whistle-blower no longer needs to show that the government actually relied on a false record or statement, but only that the false claim made was capable of influencing the payment of the claim at issue.[48]

Thanks to these two amendments, a company can now be liable under the FCA, when someone in the company acts knowingly in causing a business or contractor to submit a false claim, even if the department of the company, which is responsible for processing and submitting the claim for payment is not aware of the corporate fraud.[49] What is more, a large number of companies are now subject to potential liability under the FCA; even companies which are not government contractors, but only subcontractors and vendors working with grantees or recipients of federal funds, can now be liable for corporate fraud under the FCA.

5 FERA and FCA: Panacea for Corporate Fraud?

The previous sections have demonstrated that the amendments to the FCA, along with the enactment of FERA in 2009 have effectively engaged private individuals in government litigation and improved whistle-blower incentives. Additionally, it is important to note that the US legislature has prohibited employers from including terms in employment contracts that prevent employees from reporting misconduct or wrongdoing to relevant authorities. An illustrative example is 5 U.S. Code § 2302 Prohibited Personnel

Practices and the Securities and Exchange Commission (SEC). SEC has fined companies for including such provisions discouraging organisations from including confidentiality clauses that deter whistleblowing. However, this section will highlight the efficiency limitations of qui tam suits under the FCA in addressing corporate fraud, despite efforts by US legislature to broaden liability under the FCA.

The first limitation is that qui tam suits are not available in all industries, but only in those, where the government is a significant buyer.[50] As explained, the False Claims Act (FCA) primarily applies to entities that conduct business with the federal government.[51] In instances where companies operate without federal government contracts or funding, whistleblowers lack the powerful financial incentives offered by the FCA to report regulatory violations against them.[52] This limitation is particularly evident when examining whistleblower activity across sectors. The healthcare industry, where the federal government is a predominant payer through programmes like Medicare and Medicaid, consistently sees a significantly higher proportion of fraud detection attributed to whistleblowers. Hence, in the healthcare sector, whistle-blowers account for 41% of fraud detection cases, while in other industries, where whistle-blowers cannot easily avail themselves of the rewards from qui tam lawsuits, they only account for 14%.[53]

Secondly, according to empirical research, it is company employees who are the most active whistle-blowers, while those with the strongest incentives to act, such as short sellers and equity holders, are less frequent in their actions.[54] Yet, the burden of whistleblowing is significant for company employees, who may face consequences such as "distancing and retaliation from fellow workers and friends, personal attacks on their character during a protracted dispute, and the need to change careers.[55] According to a new study, more than 80% of employees, who have witnessed or suspected financial crime, including corporate fraud, have chosen to stay silent and not blow the whistle, with nearly half of those respondents citing a fear of retaliation as a key reason.[56] Another older survey has also shown that in 82% of cases where the identity of the whistle-blower was revealed, the employee "was fired, quit under duress or had significantly altered responsibilities".[57] Therefore, while the qui tam provisions under the FCA use financial rewards to encourage whistle-blowers to report fraud, the financial benefits are not the primary concern for company employees who choose to blow the whistle.[58]

Of course, the monetary rewards serve as a financial insurance for employees in case of retaliation and qui tam provisions provide employment protection for fired employees. However, simply being fired for blowing the whistle does not automatically entitle them to that protection.[59] A claim of retaliation must involve: (1) a victim who is an "employee, contractor, or agent;" (2) who suffers, or is threatened with, some form of adverse employment action ("is discharged, demoted, suspended, threatened, harassed, or in any other manner discriminated against in the terms and conditions of employment"); (3) "because of;" (4) the conduct of the victim or an associate ("lawful acts done by employee, contractor, agent or associated others"); (5) relating to a protected activity ("lawful acts ... in furtherance of an action under this section [i.e., a qui tam action] or other efforts to stop one or more violations of this subchapter [i.e., the False Claims Act]").[60] This means that under the FCA, only employees who can prove a direct causal link between their whistleblowing activities and the retaliation they experienced are eligible for legal protection.[61] A significant point of contention among lower federal appellate courts is the precise interpretation of this 'because of' causation.[62] Some courts argue for a strict 'but-for' standard, requiring that the retaliation would not have occurred without the protected act. Others favour a more lenient "motivating factor" standard, where the protected act simply needs to have been one of the reasons for the retaliation, even if other factors were also present. This nuanced standard diminishes company employees' incentives to blow the whistle, as they know that even if they later file a claim of retaliation against their employers, it is not guaranteed that they will win.

Moreover, even anti-retaliation measures can be unrealistic incentives. Employers often use waivers or arbitration agreements, which, despite some recent limitations for specific claims (e.g., sexual harassment), still largely prevent employees from suing.[63] Furthermore, anti-retaliation cases often face an uphill battle. When successful, these cases typically offer compensatory damages, aiming to return the employee to the position prior to the retaliation, and may also include remedies like reinstatement and the recovery of legal fees and costs.[64] Another significant issue is the fragmented nature of US whistleblower laws. While robust protections exist for federal employees and numerous federal statutes cover private sector whistleblowers in various contexts, state-level protections for private employees still vary considerably.[65] This regulatory patchwork hinders corporate fraud reduction, despite the highly effective and financially rewarding qui tam provisions of the FCA.

Thirdly, the pleading standard for False Claims Act (FCA) whistleblowers remains stringent under Federal Rule of Civil Procedure 9(b), which requires that "in alleging fraud or mistake, a party must state with particularity the circumstances constituting fraud or mistake." This means relators must identify "dates, names of persons, names of products, statements made, documents used, and amounts at issue," often requiring "representative samples of the allegedly false claims with a high degree of detail."[66] (Wood) Meeting this standard is particularly challenging for non-employee whistleblowers, such as the general public, media, industrial and legal regulators, customers, suppliers, and competitors, as it necessitates access to internal company information.[67] Empirical evidence consistently shows that employees are significantly more likely to detect corporate fraud than auditors, highlighting the critical role of insider information.[68] Consequently, insider relators, particularly company employees, are better positioned to meet Rule 9(b)'s heightened pleading standard by "alleging particular details of a scheme to submit false claims paired with reliable indicia that lead to a strong inference that claims were actually submitted."[69] This leads to a persistent tension: while insiders possess the necessary information, they often face career disincentives despite the potential for substantial monetary rewards through *qui tam* payments. It is important to note, however, that the application of Rule 9(b) in FCA cases continues to be a point of divergence among US federal circuit courts, with some circuits adopting a more flexible approach requiring 'reliable indicia' rather than specific false claims, while others maintain a stricter interpretation.[70] The Supreme Court has repeatedly declined to resolve this circuit split, meaning the precise burden on relators still varies significantly depending on the jurisdiction.

6 Conclusion and Recommendations

This chapter explored to what extent the FCA in the US is an effective tool to address the corporate fraud. To this end, this chapter reviewed the history and theoretical underpinnings of the FCA and highlighted how the current qui tam claims work. Moreover, it has explained how the FERA has increased the accountability for corporate frauds.

As has been shown, since 2009, when the Congress enacted the FERA, the accountability for corporate fraud has dramatically increased. Firstly, this is because of the liability expansion, which can now attach to claims that are submitted to a "contractor, grantee, or other recipient" of federal funds, even if the false claim is not submitted to the government itself. Secondly, it is because the intent requirement was removed and as a result, even the department of a company, which is responsible for processing and submitting the fraudulent claim for payment, is now liable for corporate fraud, though it may be unaware of the relevant fraud.

However, despite the great progress that was made in the area of corporate fraud thanks to the FERA, there are still several challenges for those who want to step forward and blow the whistle about corporate fraud incidents. This chapter has identified that the limited scope of the FCA, which applies only to industries where the government is a significant buyer, such as the healthcare industry; this is a serious challenge for whistle-blowers in other industries, who cannot make use of the monetary rewards from qui tam lawsuits. The serious consequences that company employees, who are the most active whistle-blowers, usually face when they report corporate fraud, such as dismissal, distancing and retaliation from colleagues, is another challenge. In that case, it is questionable whether the monetary rewards offset the negative effects of whistleblowing on the whistle-blowers' career and life. To make matters worse, this chapter has shown that a claim for retaliation cannot easily succeed and vindicate the whistle-blowers' decision to reveal the truth. Also, since the negotiating power of employers is greater than the one of employees, it is easier for the former to include in the employment contracts employee waivers or arbitration agreements, which prevent employees from suing. But even when a claim for retaliation is possible, it can offer compensatory damages that will restore the employee back to the position prior to the retaliation. This means that the loss of future earnings suffered by the whistle-blower is not covered, even if the claim for retaliation succeeds. The variation in whistle-blower laws across the states of the US is another challenge that should be overcome, as well as the strict pleading standard from the FCA whistle-blowers, who must state with particularity the circumstances constituting corporate fraud.

Against this background, it is submitted that the amendments to the FCA, as well as the enaction of FERA in 2009 have promoted whistleblowing against corporate fraud, but still the balance between the monetary rewards from qui tam lawsuits and the fear of retaliation, which is predominant in case of corporate fraud, has not been meaningfully struck. Therefore, the legal system in the US should offer further protection to whistle blowers from retaliation, make it easier for retaliation claims to succeed and ensure that compensation for whistleblowers extends beyond mere actual financial losses to encompass loss of future earnings– such as through front pay for lost income and coverage for costs associated with a necessary change of occupation. Furthermore, compensation for other economic damages, like medical treatment expenses, and for intangible harm such as pain and suffering, would provide more comprehensive relief and significantly strengthen incentives for employees to report corporate fraud. Moreover, the companies should build a culture where their employees will feel comfortable to report even their suspicions of corporate fraud, by creating more secure and confidential internal reporting channels.

Notes

1 For further information, see Steven Toms, "Financial Scandals: A Historical Overview" (2019) 49(5) *Accounting and Business Research* 477–499.
2 Toms, pp. 477–499.
3 Michael J. Comer, *Corporate Fraud* (McGraw-Hill Book Company 1977), p. 380.
4 Comer p. 7.

5 Association of Certified Fraud Examiners, "Report to the Nations-2020 Global Study on Occupational Fraud and Abuse". Available at: https://acfepublic.s3-us-west-2.amazonaws.com/2020-Report-to-the-Nations.pdf.
6 PwC, "Fighting Fraud: A Never-Ending Battle 2020". Available at: https://www.global-screeningsolutions.com/industries/global-economic-crime-and-fraud-survey-2020-1.pdf; Larry Li and Adela McMurray, *Corporate Fraud Across the Globe,* (Palgrave Macmillan 2022), p. 23
7 Jonas Heese, Ranjani Krishnan and Hari Ramasubramanian, "The Department of Justice as a Gatekeeper in Whistleblower-Initiated Corporate Fraud Enforcement: Drivers and Consequences" (2021) 71 *Journal of Accounting and Economics* 1–24.
8 Heese et al.
9 Paolo Buccirossi et al., "Whistleblower Rewards, False Reports and Corporate Fraud" (2021) 51 *European Journal of Law and Economics* 411–431.
10 Department of Justice, "False Claims Act Settlements and Judgments Exceed $2 Billion in Fiscal Year 2022". Available at: www.justice.gov/opa/pr/false-claims-act-settlements-and-judgments-exceed-2-billion-fiscal-year-2022; Department of Justice, "Justice Department Recovers over $2.8 Billion from False Claims Act Cases in Fiscal Year 2018". Available at: www.justice.gov/opa/pr/justice-department-recovers-over-28-billion-false-claims-act-cases-fiscal-year-2018, accessed 8 September 2023.
11 Justin P. Tschcoepe, "A Fraud against One Is Apparently a Fraud against All: The Fraud Enforcement and Recovery Act's Unprecedented Expansion of Liability under the False Claims Act" (2010) 47(3) *Houston Law Review* 742. Andrew C. Call et al., "Whistleblowers and Outcomes of Financial Misrepresentation Enforcement Actions" (2018) 56(1) *Journal of Accounting Research* 123–171; Patrick Leahy Hearing on the "False Claims Act Corrections Act of 2007: Strengthening the Government's Most Effective Tool against Fraud for the 21st Century" (2008) in Ian M. Ortiz (ed), *Fighting Fraud with Qui Tam and the False Claims Act* (Nova Science Publishers 2010)
12 S. REP. No. 111-10, at 1 (2009).
13 FERA, Pub. L. No. 111-21, sec. 4(a)(1), 123 Stat. 1617, 1621 (2009) [codified as amended at 31 U.S.C.A. ß 3729(a)(1)(B) (West Supp. 2010)].
14 Cynthia Love, "The Fraud Enforcement and Recovery Act of 2009 and the Expansion of Liability under the False Claims Act" (2012) 2 *Utah Law Review*, 1130.
15 Craig Margolis and Christina Ferma, "The False Claims Act: Why Should a Civil Statute Matter to Criminal Lawyers?" (2017) 31(4) *Criminal Justice* 29.
16 Michael Hertz, "False Claims Act Hearing" in Ian M. Ortiz (ed), *Fighting Fraud with Qui Tam and the False Claims Act* (Nova Science Publishers 2010), p. 23.
17 Leahy (fn 11) p. 20.
18 Heese et al. (fn 7).
19 31 U.S.C. §3729 et seq; Rhoad and Fornataro (fn 41) p. 17.
20 Caitlin Hickey, "Incentivizing Whistleblowing in the United States" (2015) 27(4) *Neue Kriminalpolitik* 390.
21 31 U.S.C. §3729 et seq; Rhoad and Fornataro (fn 41) p. 17.
22 Robert Rhoad and Matthew Fornataro, "A Gathering Storm: The New False Claims Act Amendments and Their Impact on Healthcare Fraud Enforcement" (2009) 21(6) *Health Lawyer*, p. 17.
23 Hickey (fn 20).
24 Adriana S. Cordis and Elizabeth M. Lambert, "Whistleblower Laws and Corporate Fraud: Evidence from the United States" (2017) 41(4) *Accounting Forum* 293. These states are California, Colorado, Connecticut, Delaware, Florida, Georgia, Hawaii, Iowa, Illinois, Indiana, Louisiana, Massachusetts, Maryland, Michigan, Minnesota, Montana, North Carolina, New Hampshire, New Jersey, New Mexico, Nevada, New York, Oklahoma, Rhode Island, Tennessee, Texas, Virginia, Washington and Wisconsin.
25 Robin Page West, *Advising the Qui Tam Whistleblower - From Identifying a Case to Filing under the False Claims Act* (American Bar Association 2009), p. 1.
26 West p. 1.
27 West p. 1.
28 Tschcoepe (fn 11).
29 Tschcoepe (fn 11).
30 Love (fn 14) p. 1132.

31 James B. Helmer, Jr. and Robert Clark Neff, Jr., "War Stories: A History of the Qui Tam Provisions of the False Claims Act, The 1986 Amendments to the False Claims Act and Their Application in the United States ex rel. Gravitt v. General Electric Co. Litigation" (1991) 18 *Ohio Northern University Law Review* 39.
32 Joel M. Androphy, "History of the False Claims Act" in Joel M. Androphy (ed), *Federal False Claims Act and Qui Tam Litigation* (Law Journal Press 2023), pp. 2–74.
33 Androphy.
34 Androphy; Ann McRitchie, "Government Dismissal Authority of False Claims Act Qui Tam Claims: An Analysis of the Current Political and Judicial Debate" (2022) 51(4) *Public Contract Law Journal* 523.
35 Stephen A. Wood, "The False Claims Act: The Government's Main Weapon against Contractor Fraud" (2022) 51(4) *The Brief* 28.
36 Wood p. 29.
37 Wood p. 29; 31 U.S.C. §3729(b).
38 U.S.C. §3730(h).
39 Senate Report. No. 111-10, at 1 (2009). Available at: www.congress.gov/congressional-report/111th-congress/senate-report/10/1?q=%7B%22search%22%3A%5B%22S.+3170%22%5D%7D.
40 Tschcoepe (fn 11).
41 Allison Engine Co. v. United States ex rel. Sanders, 128 S. Ct. 2123, 2130 (2008); Robert Rhoad and Matthew Fornataro, "A Gathering Storm: The New False Claims Act Amendments and Their Impact on Healthcare Fraud Enforcement" (2009) 21(6) *Health Lawyer* 16.
42 Rhoad and Fornataro (fn 41) p. 16; Christopher A. Riley and Joann E. Johnston, "Fraud Enforcement and Recovery Act of 2009: Expanding Fraud and False Claims Act Liability and Increasing Enforcement in the Wake of the Economic Crisis" (2009) 28(7) *Banking and Financial Services Policy Report* 4; Tschcoepe (fn 11) p. 760.
43 Wood (fn 35) p. 3.
44 Senate Report No. 111-10, at 11 (2009). Available at: www.congress.gov/congressional-report/111th-congress/senate-report/10/1?q=%7B%22search%22%3A%5B%22S.+3170%22%5D%7D; FERA, Pub. L. No. 111-21, sec. 4(a)(1), 123 Stat. 1617, 1621 (2009).
45 Rhoad and Fornataro (fn 41), 16.
46 31 U.S.C. §3729(a)(3) (2006).
47 31 U.S.C. §3729(a)(2) (1988).
48 31 U.S.C. §3729(a)(1)(B) (1988) and §3729(b)(4).
49 Wood (fn 35) p. 4.
50 Alexander Dyck, Adair Morse and Luigi Zingales, "Who Blows the Whistle on Corporate Fraud?" (2010) 65(6) *The Journal of Finance* 2246.
51 David Kwok, "A Fair Competition Theory of the Civil False Claims Act" (2015) 94 *Nebraska Law Review* 397.
52 Kwok p. 397.
53 Dyck et al. (fn 50) p. 2215.
54 Dyck et al. (fn 50) p. 2214.
55 Dyck et al. (fn 50) p. 2245.
56 Medius, "Whistleblowing: 80% of Financial Professionals Stay Silent on Suspected Internal Fraud Fearing Retaliation". Available at: https://www.medius.com/whistleblowing/, accessed 17 August 2024.
57 Dyck et al. (fn 50) p. 2240.
58 Dyck et al. (fn 50); Li and McMurray (fn 6) p. 109.
59 Terrence M. O'Connor, *Federal Procurement Ethics: The Complete Legal Guide, Revised Edition* (Berrett-Koehler Publishers 2009), p. 159; 31 U.S. Code §3730(h).
60 31 U.S. Code §3730(h); Charles Doyle, "Qui Tam: An Abridged Look at the False Claims Act and Related Federal Statutes" (2018) Library of Congress public edition, Washington, DC: Congressional Research Service, p. 9.
61 Doyle p. 9.
62 Doyle p. 9.
63 Hickey (fn 20) pp. 388–398.
64 Hickey (fn 20) p. 392; Richard E. Moberly, "Unfulfilled Expectations: An Empirical Analysis of Why Sarbanes-Oxley Whistleblowers Rarely Win" (2007) 49(1) *William and Mary Law*

Review 65–155; Richard E. Moberly, "Sarbanes-Oxley's Whistleblower Provisions - Ten Years Later" (2012) 64(1) *South Carolina Law Review* 1–54.
65 Cordis and Lambert (fn 24) p. 291.
66 For further information about the categorisation of whistle-blowers into four groups based on the cost and level of difficulty in accessing the fraud information, please see Li and McMurray (fn 6) p. 246
67 Wood (fn 35) p. 33.
68 Dyck et al. (fn 50) p. 2226.
69 Michael Lockman, "In Defence of a Strict Pleading Standard for False Claims Act Whistleblowers" (2015) 82(3) *The University of Chicago Law Review* 1569; United States v Kanneganti, 565 F3d 180, 190 (5th Cir 2009).
70 Lockman (fn 69), 1577.

References

Androphy JM, "History of the False Claims Act" in Joel M. Androphy (ed) *Federal False Claims Act and Qui Tam Litigation* (Law Journal Press 2023), pp. 2–74.

Association of Certified Fraud Examiners, "Report to the Nations-2020 Global Study on Occupational Fraud and Abuse". Available at: https://acfepublic.s3-us-west-2.amazonaws.com/2020-Report-to-the-Nations.pdf.

Buccirossi P et al., "Whistleblower Rewards, False Reports and Corporate Fraud" (2021) 51 *European Journal of Law and Economics* 411–431.

Call AC et al., "Whistleblowers and Outcomes of Financial Misrepresentation Enforcement Actions" (2018) 56(1) *Journal of Accounting Research* 123–171.

Comer MJ, *Corporate Fraud* (McGraw-Hill Book Company 1977).

Cordis AS and Lambert EM, "Whistleblower Laws and Corporate Fraud: Evidence from the United States" (2017) 41(4) *Accounting Forum* 289–299.

Department of Justice, "Justice Department Recovers over $2.8 Billion from False Claims Act Cases in Fiscal Year 2018". Available at: www.justice.gov/opa/pr/justice-department-recovers-over-28-billion-false-claims-act-cases-fiscal-year-2018.

Department of Justice, "False Claims Act Settlements and Judgments Exceed $2 Billion in Fiscal Year 2022". Available at: www.justice.gov/opa/pr/false-claims-act-settlements-and-judgments-exceed-2-billion-fiscal-year-2022.

Doyle C, "Qui Tam: An Abridged Look at the False Claims Act and Related Federal Statutes" (2018) Library of Congress public edition, Washington, DC: Congressional Research Service.

Dyck A, Morse A and Zingales L, "Who Blows the Whistle on Corporate Fraud?" (2010) 65(6) *The Journal of Finance* 2213–2253.

Heese J, Krishnan R and Ramasubramanian H, "The Department of Justice as a Gatekeeper in Whistleblower-Initiated Corporate Fraud Enforcement: Drivers and Consequences" (2021) 71 *Journal of Accounting and Economics* 1–24.

Helmer JB and Neff RC, "War Stories: A History of the Qui Tam Provisions of the False Claims Act, The 1986 Amendments to the False Claims Act and Their Application in the United States ex rel. Gravitt v. General Electric Co. Litigation" (1991) 18 *Ohio Northern University Law Review* 35–75.

Hertz M, "False Claims Act Hearing" in Ian M. Ortiz (ed), *Fighting Fraud with Qui Tam and the False Claims Act* (Nova Science Publishers 2010).

Hickey C, "Incentivizing Whistleblowing in the United States" (2015) 27(4) Neue Kriminalpolitik 388.

Kwok D, "A Fair Competition Theory of the Civil False Claims Act" (2015) 94 *Nebraska Law Review* 355–400.

Leahy P, Hearing on the "False Claims Act Corrections Act of 2007: Strengthening the Government's Most Effective Tool against Fraud for the 21st Century" in Ian M. Ortiz (ed), *Fighting Fraud with Qui Tam and the False Claims Act* (Nova Science Publishers 2010).

Li L and McMurray A, *Corporate Fraud across the Globe* (Palgrave Macmillan 2022).

Lockman M, "In Defence of a Strict Pleading Standard for False Claims Act Whistleblowers" (2015) 82(3) *The University of Chicago Law Review* 1559–1607.

Love C, "The Fraud Enforcement and Recovery Act of 2009 and the Expansion of Liability under the False Claims Act" (2012) 2 *Utah Law Review* 1129–1154.

Margolis C and Ferma C, "The False Claims Act: Why Should a Civil Statute Matter to Criminal Lawyers?" (2017) 31(4) *Criminal Justice* 26–29.

McRitchie A, "Government Dismissal Authority of False Claims Act Qui Tam Claims: An Analysis of the Current Political and Judicial Debate" (2022) 51(4) *Public Contract Law Journal* 521–552.

Medius, "Whistleblowing: 80% of Financial Professionals Stay Silent on Suspected Internal Fraud Fearing Retaliation". Available at: https://www.medius.com/whistleblowing/.

Moberly RE, "Unfulfilled Expectations: An Empirical Analysis of Why Sarbanes-Oxley Whistleblowers Rarely Win" (2007) 49(1) *William and Mary Law Review* 65–155.

Moberly RE, "Sarbanes-Oxley's Whistleblower Provisions - Ten Years Later" (2012) 64(1) *South Carolina Law Review* 1–54.

O'Connor TM, *Federal Procurement Ethics: The Complete Legal Guide*, Revised Edition (Berrett-Koehler Publishers 2009).

Page West R, *Advising the Qui Tam Whistleblower- From Identifying a Case to Filing under the False Claims Act* (American Bar Association 2009).

PwC, "Fighting Fraud: A Never-Ending Battle 2020". Available at: https://www.global-screeningsolutions.com/industries/global-economic-crime-and-fraud-survey-2020-1.pdf.

Rhoad R and Fornataro M, "A Gathering Storm: The New False Claims Act Amendments and their Impact on Healthcare Fraud Enforcement" (2009) 21(6) *Health Lawyer* 14–22.

Riley CA and Johnston JE, "Fraud Enforcement and Recovery Act of 2009: Expanding Fraud and False Claims Act Liability and Increasing Enforcement in the Wake of the Economic Crisis" (2009) 28(7) *Banking and Financial Services Policy Report* 1–7.

Senate, "Report. No. 111-10" (2009). Available at: www.congress.gov/congressional-report/111th-congress/senate-report/10/1?q=%7B%22search%22%3A%5B%22S.+3170%22%5D%7D.

Toms S, "Financial scandals: A Historical Overview" (2019) 49(5) *Accounting and Business Research* 477–499.

Tschcoepe JP, "A Fraud against One Is Apparently a Fraud against All: The Fraud Enforcement and Recovery Act's Unprecedented Expansion of Liability under the False Claims Act" (2010) 47(3) *Houston Law Review* 741–778.

Wood SA, "The False Claims Act: The Government's Main Weapon against Contractor Fraud" (2022) 51(4) *The Brief*.

9 Unethical and Unlawful Behaviour by Global Banks

Implications for Human Rights

Stephen Schneider

1 Introduction

In recent years, increased attention has been paid to the human rights implications of services provided by multinational financial institutions (MFIs). This is largely the result of MFIs conducting business in countries with egregious human rights abuses. As Sullivan and Birtwell explain:[1]

> For the finance sector, the more difficult (and contentious) issue relates to situations where the provision of loans, insurance or other financial services exposes the financial institution to the human rights concerns of that business, sector or country. That is, even though they may not have particular control or influence over the activities of a client, financial institutions (because of their scale and profile) may find themselves linked with human rights violations perpetrated by that client.

This chapter explores ways that MFIs may contribute to human rights abuses by providing financial services within countries ruled by repressive regimes. It begins by briefly examining the extant literature and cases, distinguishing financial services provided to the private sector and those provided directly to governments implicated in human rights violations. It then analyses cases of MFIs guilty of a particularly blatant disregard for human rights: transgressing American trade sanctions against countries with repressive regimes.

2 Providing Financial Services to Correspondent Banks and Other Private Sector Businesses

In their report entitled *Human Rights Guidance Tool for the Financial Sector*, the United Nations Environment Programme (UNEP) provides some examples whereby financial services providers may be implicated in human rights violations by association:[2]

- the security personnel of a mining company reacts violently to on-site protests from local residents opposed to a mining development project which the bank is funding.
- general corporate funding is provided to a manufacturing company which has a reputation for compromising health and safety standards to maximize profits.
- project finance is provided for a new dam which will lead to the forced relocation of indigenous people.

DOI: 10.4324/9781003324843-13

According to Sullivan and Birtwell, 'project finance has been the source of some of the greatest controversies around the human rights performance of financial institutions.'[3]

> Large projects, in particular in developing countries, present challenges because of their scale, and the potential for impacts such as significant environmental damage, resettlement of project-affected populations, repression of opponents, militarisation of the project area, and increases in (violent) conflict. Attention has been focused on the financiers of such projects because of the perceived closeness of the relationship between the lending bank(s) and the specific project.

In short, notes the UNEP:[4]

> when providing funding or financial advice to a business client, a financial institution can be exposed to the human rights concerns which relate to that business and its sector. This is due to the provision of support being construed as an endorsement of the activities of the client, as well as facilitating the continuation and development of the business.

MFIs have been accused of indirectly abetting human rights violations through their dealings with correspondent banks or other private sector clients that are suspected of supporting terrorist groups and/or operate in countries where governments are accused of human rights abuses. HSBC provided U.S. correspondent accounts and other banking services to financial institutions in Saudi Arabia and Bangladesh, despite evidence they were processing transactions for al-Qaida and other terrorist groups.[5] HSBC personnel were aware of the allegations linking three banks to possible terrorist financing, but approved or maintained U.S. dollar accounts for them nevertheless.[6] Standard Chartered Bank (SCB) facilitated multiple transactions for the Dubai-based Al Zarooni Exchange, which the American government has barred due to evidence it was laundering money on behalf of terrorist organizations.[7]

3 Conducting Business with Governments Accused of Human Rights Abuses

MFIs may also be implicated in human rights violations when they conduct business directly with or otherwise support governments with poor human rights records. Kaleck and Saage-MaaB argue that financial services companies put themselves at particular risk when they do business with military regimes or dictatorships, which are typically the perpetrators of 'the most egregious human rights violations.'[8] The finance sector has been accused of

> facilitating the enrichment of corrupt and oppressive regimes through capital flight and money laundering, providing financial support for the trade in weapons, supporting extractive industries operating in conflict zones and financing projects that pose a threat to human rights in developing countries.[9]

Many corporations, including financial institutions, did business with the Nazi regime before and during the Second World War. This included Deutsche Bank, which helped finance the construction of the Auschwitz concentration camp, and the German insurance company Allianz, which insured buildings and other facilities in the death camp.[10] Stephens writes that 'most directly, financial corporations profited by retaining the assets of those killed by the Nazis.'[11]

> Banks and insurance companies pocketed the deposits of families who were exterminated or whose heirs were unaware of their relatives' accounts, as well as those who were unable to supply documentation to support their claims. In addition, banks profited from the mere fact that they were able to handle large accounts from Germany, investing the profits from assets stolen from Nazi victims as well as from goods produced by slave labour.

Kaleck and Miriam Saage-MaaB discuss how some banks were 'accused of variously aiding and abetting the Argentinean junta and the South African apartheid regime' through loans that helped 'encourage a policy of growing military expenditure.' They conclude these governments could 'not have supported their systemic human rights abuses and torture apparatus without the loans of (foreign) banks.'[12] In 2003, 32 banks and other corporations faced a civil suit in the U.S. courts, launched by South African citizens and civic organizations, for $400 billion in damages for their alleged role in supporting apartheid in South Africa.[13] Among the defendants were UBS and Barclays, two of the world's largest banks, which were accused of aiding the apartheid regime by providing financial support through the purchase of bonds and the provision of loans.[14] This civil suit was eventually dismissed by a U.S. district court judge, however. In her ruling, she wrote:[15]

> Supplying a violator of the law of nations with funds — even funds that could not have been obtained but for those loans — is not sufficiently connected to the primary violation to fulfill the requirement of aiding and abetting a violation of the law of nations.

Many MFIs have also furnished services to Saudi Arabia despite its numerous human rights abuses: gender-based discrimination, labour rights violations against migrant workers (including human trafficking), limiting freedom of expression and dissent, a highly unjust criminal justice system (through the use of the death penalty, lack of due process, and torture of prisoners), limits on religious freedoms, extra-judicial murder (in the case of Saudi dissident Jamal Khashoggi), and violations of international humanitarian law through its involvement in the conflict in Yemen.[16] HSBC helped the country issue its first international bonds in 2016.[17] In 2019, the bank arranged a $12 billion (USD) bond deal for Saudi Aramco, the kingdom's oil company, 'attracting $100 billion in orders and cooling talk of any investor boycott over human rights' according to the *Wall Street Journal*.[18] In 2022, a debut "green" bond from Saudi Arabia's Public Investment Fund attracted more than $22 billion (USD) in orders. Despite warnings about the environmental sustainability credentials of both the bond and the issuer, 28 banks helped to underwrite its issuance, led by BNP Paribas, J.P. Morgan, CitiGroup, Deutsche Bank, and Goldman Sachs.[19] By continuing to do business with the ruling monarchy and state-run oil and gas industry, these banks may be perceived as condoning human rights violations in this country.

4 Circumventing U.S. Government Trade Sanctions

MFIs have also exposed themselves to connivance in human rights abuses by evading American trade sanctions in pursuit of business in countries governed by repressive authoritarian governments, including those accused of supporting terrorism (Iran, Libya, Sudan, Myanmar, and North Korea). American and other Western banks not only repeatedly conducted financial transactions in countries subject to U.S. trade sanctions but purposely concealed the identity of these countries in their paperwork to circumvent American laws. In 2012, the U.S. Department of Justice sanctioned HSBC for circumventing trade sanctions by:[20]

> illegally conducting transactions on behalf of customers in Cuba, Iran, Libya, Sudan and Myanmar—all countries subject to sanctions enforced by the Office of Foreign Assets Control [OFAC] at the time of the transactions.

According to a 2012 report from the Senate Permanent Subcommittee on Investigations that was looking into a wide range of possible infractions committed by HSBC:[21]

> An outside auditor hired by the HSBC subsidiary in the U.S. [HBUS] has so far identified, from 2001 to 2007, more than 28,000 undisclosed OFAC sensitive transactions that were sent through HBUS involving $19.7 billion. Of those 28,000 transactions, nearly 25,000 involved Iran, while 3,000 involved other prohibited countries or persons.

Other prohibited countries for which HSBC illegally processed U.S. dollar transactions included Cuba, Sudan, Myanmar, and North Korea.[22]

HSBC staff and directors deliberately concealed the bank's ongoing business with clients in countries on the OFAC sanctions list. They removed potentially incriminating information from payment messages HSBC by omitting the names of sanctioned countries from American dollar payment messages sent to HBUS branches and other financial institutions in the US. A Department of Justice press release stated the bank went so far as to work "with at least one sanctioned entity to format payment messages, which prevented the bank's filters from blocking prohibited payments." In addition, HSBC branches outside the U.S. inserted cautionary notes in payment messages to HBUS that included: 'care sanctioned country,' 'do not mention our name in NY,' or 'do not mention Iran.'[23] Not only were HSBC branches in Europe and the Middle East intentionally circumventing U.S. laws, but management at the bank's global headquarters in London authorized these moves. The HSBC Group became aware of these illegal practices in 2000, and in 2003, the Director of Compliance wrote in a memo that these manoeuvres 'could provide the basis for an action against [HSBC] Group for breach of sanctions.'[24] However, as the Justice Department notes:[25]

> Notwithstanding instructions from the HSBC Group Compliance to terminate this practice, HSBC Group affiliates were permitted to engage in the practice for an additional three years through the granting of dispensations to HSBC Group policy.

Between 2005 and 2014, other MFIs headquartered in the U.K. or Europe were penalized for conducting business in countries on the OFAC sanctions list. These offenders included ABN Amro Holding,[26] Barclays,[27] Credit Suisse,[28] Deutsche Bank,[29] JPMorgan,[30] Standard Chartered,[31] Commerzbank,[32] Royal Bank of Scotland,[33] and BNP Paribus.[34] These MFIs purposely concealed or altered information to hide the identities of the sanctioned entities they were doing business with. The scope of the fines imposed by government authorities reflected the severity of the offences committed; as part of deferred prosecution agreements (DPA). Most of the MFIs accepted financial penalties totalling hundreds of millions of dollars. Under the terms of the DPA concluded with the U.S. Department of Justice in 2014, BNP Paribus, France's largest bank, agreed to pay a penalty of $8.9 billion USD for its role in transferring billions of dollars through the U.S. financial system on behalf of Sudanese, Iranian and Cuban entities subject to American sanctions.[35] In a press statement, the U.S. Department of Justice wrote: 'BNP ignored U.S. sanctions laws and concealed its tracks. And when contacted by law enforcement it chose not to fully cooperate.'[36] An assistant U.S. district attorney concluded that '[t]his conspiracy was known and condoned at the highest levels of BNP.'[37] In August 2012, the New York State Department of Financial Services determined that SCB had 'schemed with the Government of Iran' for almost a decade to 'hide from regulators roughly 60,000 secret transactions, involving at least $250 billion, and reaping SCB hundreds of millions of dollars in fees.' These actions:[38]

> left the U.S. financial system vulnerable to terrorists, weapons dealers, drug kingpins and corrupt regimes, and deprived law enforcement investigators of crucial information used to track all manner of criminal activity.

5 Discussion and Conclusion

Given the influence of multinational corporations is spreading over all aspects of commercial, financial, economic, and political life, increased attention has been paid to how they affect human rights. As Kinley and Joseph write, multinational corporations:[39]

> are very powerful entities in the current world order. Their impact on the well-being of communities and individuals, including in terms of human rights, is evident wherever they operate. While there is considerable scope for that impact to be positive, corporate activity is often perceived to have had, and has had, a detrimental impact on human rights protection.

The authors concede that 'the protection of human rights is not traditionally considered a responsibility of corporations.'[40] However, it has emerged as a significant issue within the context of corporate social responsibility.[41]

The United Nations Guiding Principles on Business and Human Rights (UNGP) is considered the global standard for controlling the risk of human rights violations directly or indirectly linked to private sector activity.[42] At the very least, under the UNGP companies are duty bound to conduct 'due diligence to identify, prevent, mitigate and account for how they address their impacts on human rights' as well as introduce 'processes to enable the remediation of any adverse human rights impacts they cause or to which they contribute.'[43] According to the UN Forum on Business and Human Rights:[44]

> corporate responsibility to respect human rights is a baseline expectation of all companies in all situations. Private sector banks and other financial institutions are expected to follow the UN Guiding Principles in the same way as any other company.

Juxtaposing the cases covered in this chapter against these standards exposes the failure of many MFIs to pass the most basic litmus test set by the UNGP. MFIs are complicit in human rights abuses indirectly when they conduct business with correspondent banks and other private sector entities in countries with atrocious human rights records or by providing financial services, through loans or by underwriting bond issuances, to repressive governments. The MFIs in question tolerated or ignored such violations, which is especially flagrant given their extensive risk assessment and due diligence resources. Some MFIs have even acted as if they are above the law. Circumventing U.S. trade sanctions, which are in place expressly to pressure authoritarian governments to become more respectful of democratic processes and human rights, undermines the very purpose of the sanctions, which in turn helps perpetuate these oppressive regimes. The fact that some banks also conspired to hide their transgressions exposes an appalling lack of social conscience, ethical business practices, and lawfulness.

Due to the immense power of MFIs, their investing and financing decisions can potentially have significant implications for either fuelling (or at least condoning) human rights abuses or, alternatively, helping to dissuade repressive regimes from engaging in such abuses. The evidence suggests that MFIs are more apt to be included in the former category; there is scant evidence that they have used their leverage to pressure client states that are fully integrated in the global finance system (i.e., Saudi Arabia), to reform and be more respectful of human rights.

Sullivan and Birtwell caution that 'in relation to customers, there are clearly practical limitations to how a financial institution can influence how the customer acts' concerning human rights abuses or other transgression.[45] Yet, as the world has become increasingly financialized banking and finance now drives and dominates the world's economy. As Dowell-Jones argues, because of the 'colossal scale of today's financial markets and financial institutions' it is easy to see why 'they are so relevant to human rights.'[46]

Some argue that UN guiding principles are insufficient precautions due to their voluntary nature. Notwithstanding the dismal of the civil suit launched against MFIs accused of supporting apartheid in South Africa, Zerk contends that, while global financial service providers and other multinational corporations may not be the 'front-line' abusers of human rights in authoritarian countries, 'they should nevertheless be held legally responsible on the basis that they assisted or facilitated the abuse in some material way.'[47]

Notes

1 Rory Sullivan & Philippa Birtwell, 'Human Rights', *CEO Briefing*, United Nations Environment Programme FI Human Rights Stream (June 2018) 4.
2 United Nations Environment Programme Finance Initiative, 'Human Rights Guidance Tool for the Financial Sector' (UNEP Finance Initiative, December 2014). Available at: http://www.unepfi.org, accessed 29 November 2024.
3 Sullivan & Birtwell (n 1) 4.
4 United Nations Environment Programme Finance Initiative (n 2).
5 United States Department of Justice, 'HSBC Holdings PLC. and HSBC Bank USA N.A. Admit to Anti-Money Laundering and Sanctions Violations, Forfeit $1.256 Billion in Deferred Prosecution Agreement' (United States Department of Justice Office of Public Affairs, 11 December 2012). Available at: https://www.justice.gov/news/press-releases, accessed 29 November 2024.
6 United States Senate, Permanent Subcommittee on Investigations, *U.S. Vulnerabilities to Money Laundering, Drugs, and Terrorist Financing: HSBC Case History*, Hearing before the Permanent Subcommittee on Investigations of the Committee on Homeland Security and Governmental Affairs (S. Hrg. 112-597, 12 July 2012) 239.
7 Richard Holmes and others, 'Standard Chartered's Iran Problems Didn't Go Away', *Buzzfeed News* (New York, 20 September 2021). Available at: https://www.buzzfeednews.com/article/richholmes/standard-chartered-bank-money-iran-fbi, accessed 27 September 2024.
8 Wolfgang Kaleck & Miriam Saage-MaaB, 'Corporate Accountability for Human Rights Violations Amounting to International Crimes: The Status Quo and its Challenges' (2010) 8 *Journal of International Criminal Justice* 699, 703.

9 Sullivan & Birtwell (n 1) 2.
10 Beth Stephens, 'The Amorality of Profit: Transnational Corporations and Human Rights' (2002) 20 *Berkeley Journal of International Law* 45, 50.
11 Stephens (n 10) 49–50.
12 Kaleck & Saage-MaaB (n 8) 706.
13 F&C Asset Management plc & KPMG LLP UK, *Banking on Human Rights: Confronting Human Rights in the Financial Sector* (F&C Asset Management plc; KPMG LLP UK, 2004) 6.
14 Erin Daly, '$400B Apartheid Case against UBS, Barclays Trimmed' (*Law360.com*, 8 April 2009). Available at: http://www.law360.com, accessed 21 March 2023.
15 In re South African Apartheid Litigation, 617 F. Supp. 2d 228 (S.D.N.Y. 2009).
16 Amnesty International, *Report 2022/23: The State of the World's Human Rights* (Amnesty International, 2023); Human Rights Watch, 'Saudi Arabia' (*Human Rights Watch*, n.d.). Available at: https://www.hrw.org/middle-east/n-africa/saudi-arabia, accessed 15 May 2023; United States Department of State, *2020 Country Reports on Human Rights Practices: Saudi Arabia* (United States Department of State, 2020).
17 Rory Jones & Margot Patrick, 'HSBC Carves Special Role as Banker to Saudis', *Wall Street Journal* (New York, 13 June 2019). Available at: https://www.wsj.com/articles/hsbc-carves-special-role-as-banker-to-the-saudis-11560425106, accessed 22 July 2022.
18 Jones & Patrick (n 17).
19 Dominic Webb, 'Investors Pile into Saudi PIF Greed Bonds Despite ESG Concerns', *Responsible Investor* (London, 6 October 2022). Available at: https://www.responsible-investor.com/investors-pile-into-saudi-pif-green-bond-despite-esg-concerns/, accessed 5 May 2023.
20 United States Department of Justice (n 5).
21 United States Senate, Permanent Subcommittee on Investigations (n 6) 6.
22 United States Senate, Permanent Subcommittee on Investigations (n 6) 6.
23 United States Department of Justice (n 5).
24 United States Department of Justice (n 5).
25 United States Department of Justice (n 5).
26 Glenn Simpson, 'ABN Amro to Pay $80 Million Fine Over Iran, Libya', *Wall Street Journal* (New York, 20 December 2005). Available at: https://www.wsj.com/articles, accessed 12 August 2023.
27 United States Department of Justice, 'Barclays Bank PLC Agrees to Forfeit $298 Million in Connection with Violations of the International Emergency Economic Powers Act and the Trading with the Enemy Act' (United States Department of Justice, Office of Public Affairs, 18 August 2010). Available at: https://www.justice.gov/news/press-releases, accessed 21 March 2023.
28 United States Department of Justice, 'Credit Suisse Agrees to Forfeit $536 Million in Connection with Violations of the International Emergency Economic Powers Act and New York State Law' (United States Department of Justice, Office of Public Affairs, 16 December 2009). Available at: https://www.justice.gov/news/press-releases, accessed 13 March 2023; Aaron Lucchetti & Jay Solomon, 'Credit Suisse to Pay U.S. $536 Million in Iran Probe', *Wall Street Journal* (New York, 17 December 2009). Available at: https://www.wsj.com/articles, accessed 21 May 2023; Claudio Gatti & John Eligon, 'Iranian Dealings Lead to a Fine for Credit Suisse", *New York Times* (New York, 15 December 2009). Available at: nytimes.com, accessed 23 April 2023.
29 Liz Moyer, 'Deutsche Bank to Pay 258-Million and Fire 6 in Settlement', *New York Times* (New York, 4 November 2015). Available at: nytimes.com, accessed 21 April 2023.
30 United States Department of the Treasury and Comptroller of the Currency, Consent Order AA-EC-13-04 in the Matter of JPMorgan Chase Bank, N.A. Columbus, OH; JPMorgan Bank and Trust Company, N.A., San Francisco, CA; Chase Bank USA, N.A., Newark, DE (United States Department of the Treasury and Comptroller of the Currency, 1 April 2013).
31 New York State Department of Financial Services, In the Matter of Standard Chartered Bank, New York Branch, New York, New York, Order Pursuant to Banking law § 39 (August 2012).
32 Leslie Caldwell, 'Assistant Attorney General Caldwell Remarks at the ACAMS Anti-Money Laundering & Financial Crime Conference' (United States Department of Justice Office of Public Affairs, 16 March 2015). Available at: https://www.justice.gov/news/press-releases, accessed 27 February 2023.
33 Matthew Goldstein, 'R.B.S. to Pay $100 Million to Settle Inquiries into Violations of Sanctions', *New York Times* (New York, 13 December 2013). Available at: nytimes.com, accessed 23 April 2023.

34 United States Department of Justice, 'BNP Paribas Agrees to Plead Guilty and to Pay $8.9 Billion for Illegally Processing Financial Transactions for Countries Subject to U.S. Economic Sanctions' (United States Department of Justice Office of Public Affairs, 30 June 2014). Available at: https://www.justice.gov/news/press-releases, accessed 21 March 2023.
35 United States Department of Justice, United States Attorney, Southern District of New York, Criminal Division, Plea Agreement Re: United States v. BNP Paribas S.A. (New York, 27 June 2024).
36 United States Department of Justice (n. 35).
37 Heidi Moore & Jill Treanor, 'BNP Paribas Pleads Guilty to Criminal Charges in Sanctions Case', *The Guardian* (London, 30 June 2014). Available at: https://www.theguardian.com, accessed 15 July 2014.
38 New York State Department of Financial Services (n 31).
39 David Kinley & Sarah Joseph, 'Multinational Corporations and Human Rights: Questions about Their Relationship' (2002) 27 *Alternative Law Journal* 7.
40 Kinley & Joseph (n 39) 7.
41 Kinley & Joseph (n 39) 7.
42 United Nations, 'U.N. Guiding Principles on Business and Human Rights' (United Nations Business and Human Rights Resource Centre, 30 November 2024). Available at: https://www.business-humanrights.org/en/big-issues/governing-business-human-rights/un-guiding-principles/, accessed 19 November 2024.
43 United Nations, *U.N. Guiding Principles on Business and Human Rights. Implementing the United Nations 'Protect, Respect and Remedy' Framework* (United Nations, Human Rights, Office of the High Commissioner, 2011) 16.
44 United Nations Forum on Business and Human Rights, Halifax Initiative, *Financing Human Rights Abuse: The Role of Public and Private Financial Institutions* (United Nations, 2012) 3.
45 Sullivan & Birtwell (n 1) 4.
46 Mary Dowell-Jones, 'Financial Institutions and Human Rights' (2013) 13(3) *Human Rights Law Review* 423.
47 Jennifer Zerk, *Corporate Liability for Gross Human Rights Abuses. Towards a Fairer and More Effective System of Domestic Law Remedies* (Report Prepared for The Office of the UN High Commissioner for Human Rights, 2014), 24.

Bibliography

Amnesty International, Report 2022/23*: The State of the World's Human Rights* (Amnesty International, 2023).

Caldwell L, 'Assistant Attorney General Caldwell Remarks at the ACAMS Anti-Money Laundering & Financial Crime Conference' (United States Department of Justice Office of Public Affairs, 16 March 2015). Available at: https://www.justice.gov/news/press-releases, accessed 27 February 2023.

Daly, E '$400B Apartheid Case against UBS, Barclays Trimmed' (*Law360.com*, 8 April 2009). Available at: https://www.law360.com, accessed 21 March 2023.

Dowell-Jones, M 'Financial Institutions and Human Rights' (2013) 13(3) *Human Rights Law Review* 423.

F&C Asset Management plc & KPMG LLP UK, *Banking on Human Rights: Confronting Human Rights in the Financial Sector* (F&C Asset Management plc; KPMG LLP UK, 2004).

Gatti C and J Eligon, 'Iranian Dealings Lead to a Fine for Credit Suisse", *New York Times* (New York, 15 December 2009). Available at: nytimes.com, accessed 23 April 2023.

Goldstein M, 'R.B.S. to Pay $100 Million to Settle Inquiries into Violations of Sanctions', *New York Times* (New York, 13 December 2013). Available at: nytimes.com, accessed 23 April 2023.

Holmes R and others, 'Standard Chartered's Iran Problems Didn't Go Away', *Buzzfeed News* (New York, 20 September 2021). Available at: https://www.buzzfeednews.com/article/richholmes/standard-chartered-bank-money-iran-fbi, accessed 27 September 2024.

Human Rights Watch, 'Saudi Arabia' (*Human Rights Watch*, n.d.). Available at: https://www.hrw.org/middle-east/n-africa/saudi-arabia, accessed 15 May 2023.

Jones R and M Patrick, 'HSBC Carves Special Role as Banker to Saudis', *Wall Street Journal* (New York, 13 June 2019). Available at: https://www.wsj.com/articles/hsbc-carves-special-role-as-banker-to-the-saudis-11560425106, accessed 22 July 2022.

Kaleck, W and M Saage-MaaB, 'Corporate Accountability for Human Rights Violations Amounting to International Crimes: The Status Quo and Its Challenges' (2010) 8 *Journal of International Criminal Justice* 699.

Kinley, D and S Joseph, 'Multinational Corporations and Human Rights: Questions about Their Relationship' (2002) 27 *Alternative Law Journal* 7.

Lucchetti, A and J Solomon, 'Credit Suisse to Pay U.S. $536 Million in Iran Probe', *Wall Street Journal* (New York, 17 December 2009). Available at: https://www.wsj.com/articles, accessed 21 May 2023.

Moore, H and J Treanor, 'BNP Paribas Pleads Guilty to Criminal Charges in Sanctions Case' *The Guardian* (London, 30 June 2014). Available at: https://www.theguardian.com, accessed 15 July 2014.

Moyer, L, 'Deutsche Bank to Pay 258-Million and Fire 6 in Settlement', *New York Times* (New York, 4 November 2015). Available at: nytimes.com, accessed 21 April 2023.

Simpson, G, 'ABN Amro to Pay $80 Million Fine over Iran, Libya', *Wall Street Journal* (New York, 20 December 2005). Available at: https://www.wsj.com/articles, accessed 12 August 2023.

Stephens, B, 'The Amorality of Profit: Transnational Corporations and Human Rights' (2002) 20 *Berkeley Journal of International Law* 45.

Sullivan, R and P Birtwell, 'Human Rights', *CEO Briefing*, United Nations Environment Programme FI Human Rights Stream (June 2018).

United Nations, *U.N. Guiding Principles on Business and Human Rights* (United Nations Business and Human Rights Resource Centre, 30 November 2024). Available at: https://www.business-humanrights.org/en/big-issues/governing-business-human-rights/un-guiding-principles/, accessed 19 November 2024.

United Nations, *U.N. Guiding Principles on Business and Human Rights. Implementing the United Nations 'Protect, Respect and Remedy' Framework* (United Nations, Human Rights, Office of the High Commissioner, 2011).

United Nations Environment Programme Finance Initiative, 'Human Rights Guidance Tool for the Financial Sector' (UNEP Finance Initiative, December 2014). Available at: https://www.unepfi.org, accessed 29 November 2024.

United Nations Forum on Business and Human Rights, Halifax Initiative, *Financing Human Rights Abuse: The Role of Public and Private Financial Institutions* (United Nations, 2012).

United States Department of Justice, 'Barclays Bank PLC Agrees to Forfeit $298 Million in Connection with Violations of the International Emergency Economic Powers Act and the Trading with the Enemy Act' (United States Department of Justice, Office of Public Affairs, 18 August 2010). Available at: https://www.justice.gov/news/press-releases, accessed 21 March 2023.

United States Department of Justice, 'BNP Paribas Agrees to Plead Guilty and to Pay $8.9 Billion for Illegally Processing Financial Transactions for Countries Subject to U.S. Economic Sanctions' (United States Department of Justice Office of Public Affairs, 30 June 2014). Available at: https://www.justice.gov/news/press-releases, accessed 21 March 2023.

United States Department of Justice, 'Credit Suisse Agrees to Forfeit $536 Million in Connection with Violations of the International Emergency Economic Powers Act and New York State Law' (United States Department of Justice Office of Public Affairs, 16 December 2009). Available at: https://www.justice.gov/news/press-releases, accessed 13 March 2023.

United States Department of Justice, 'HSBC Holdings PLC. and HSBC Bank USA N.A. Admit to Anti-Money Laundering and Sanctions Violations, Forfeit $1.256 Billion in Deferred Prosecution Agreement' (United States Department of Justice Office of Public Affairs, 11 December 2012). Available at: https://www.justice.gov/news/press-releases, accessed 29 November 2024.

United States Department of State, *2020 Country Reports on Human Rights Practices: Saudi Arabia* (United States Department of State, 2020).

United States Senate, Permanent Subcommittee on Investigations, *U.S. Vulnerabilities to Money Laundering, Drugs, and Terrorist Financing: HSBC Case History*, Hearing before the Permanent

Subcommittee on Investigations of the Committee on Homeland Security and Governmental Affairs (S. Hrg. 112-597, 12 July 2012).
Webb D, 'Investors Pile into Saudi PIF Greed Bonds Despite ESG Concerns', *Responsible Investor* (London, 6 October 2022). Available at: https://www.responsible-investor.com/investors-pile-into-saudi-pif-green-bond-despite-esg-concerns/, accessed 5 May 2023.
Zerk, J, *Corporate Liability for Gross Human Rights Abuses. Towards a Fairer and More Effective System of Domestic Law Remedies* (Report Prepared for the Office of the UN High Commissioner for Human Rights, 2014).

Cases

In re South African Apartheid Litigation, 617 F. Supp. 2d 228 (S.D.N.Y. 2009).
New York State Department of Financial Services, In the Matter of Standard Chartered Bank, New York Branch, New York, New York, Order Pursuant to Banking Law § 39 (August 2012).
United States Department of the Treasury and Comptroller of the Currency, Consent Order AA-EC-13-04 in the Matter of JPMorgan Chase Bank, N.A. Columbus, OH; JPMorgan Bank and Trust Company, N.A., San Francisco, CA; Chase Bank USA, N.A., Newark, DE (1 April 2013).
United States Department of Justice, United States Attorney, Southern District of New York, Criminal Division, Plea Agreement Re: United States v. BNP Paribas S.A. (New York, 27 June 2024).

10 A Critique of Corporate Criminal Liability in the US

How Fraud Swallows Everything: Policing What Corporations *Say* Instead of What They *Do*

J.S. Nelson

1 Introduction

This chapter argues that the disabling of substantive criminal regulation in the United States (US) has led to an irresponsible system in which companies are left to unsuccessfully police themselves, and it leaves regulators monitoring primarily what corporations say instead of what they do. Furthermore, the US overly relies on whistleblowers and the media to reveal corporate misconduct.

Focusing prosecutions on what companies say creates additional incentives for lying and volatile results that more substantive and solidly consistent regulation based on companies' underlying actions would not. The emerging US political approach of flooding the market with subsidies without many controls, as the country did with pandemic spending and green technology, also contributes to large amounts of fraud, and worsens the situation.

Based on this flawed foundation, patterns of US criminal fraud prosecutions will accelerate especially in areas where technological developments move fast, there is money in investing, and companies can most easily obfuscate facts in the pursuit of profits. Although there are good arguments that the United States does not have a credible system of white-collar criminal enforcement,[1] what enforcement the country has tends to be built around what entities *say* instead of what they *do*.

The practical issue is that the US tends not to pass new statutes that contain substantive regulation of business behaviour—for example, outlawing the actual use of production techniques that damage the environment. That approach would require both a consensus on banning a practice, which industry and labour may fight, and the hiring of additional personnel who would have to enforce the law by more directly inspecting companies. Instead, what the US tends to do, as with the 2022 Inflation Reduction Act,[2] is either use "carrots" to change the relative price of practices by flooding the market with subsidies—or it insists that companies disclose their practices on an issue, with the assumption that the market will discipline companies and punish them through damage to their reputations.[3]

But flooding the market with subsidies without many controls, as the US did with pandemic spending and "green" technology, leads to large amounts of fraud. As one author has described, because pandemic 'dollars came with few strings and minimal oversight,' the result was 'one of the largest frauds in American history, with billions of dollars stolen by thousands of people.'[4] In addition, the consensus of empirical work on market disclosures to enforce ethical behaviour shows that they do not work to protect others from corporate misbehaviour.[5]

DOI: 10.4324/9781003324843-14

This chapter argues that the disabling of substantive criminal regulation in the US has led to an irresponsible system in which companies are left to unsuccessfully police themselves. Prosecuting criminal fraud based on what companies say creates additional incentives for lying and volatile results that more substantive and solidly consistent regulation based on companies' underlying actions would not. We will see a growth in US criminal fraud prosecutions in areas where technological developments move fast, there is money in investing, and companies can most easily obfuscate facts in the pursuit of profits.

2 The Fragile Nature of US Fraud Prosecutions Based on What Companies Say

Unfortunately, for both performative purposes and short-term profit, US businesses have an incentive to lie to regulators rather than to comply under the US system.[6] It is often cheaper to tell the government and other oversight organizations that companies have made changes rather than for them to make such changes. A classic example is the 2015–2017 Volkswagen emissions cheating scandal. Even when the company was held liable for lying about its compliance with emissions standards, it never developed so-called "clean diesel" technology, and it escaped liability for the estimated 12,000 additional deaths that its violation of diesel emissions standards may have caused each year.[7]

Businesses recognize that there has been a hollowing out of US regulatory resources since at least the 1990s that effectively permits companies to regulate themselves.[8] US regulators largely police compliance by disciplining companies that do not do what they say that they do. That approach polices what such entities *say*, rather than spending resources for the government to find out what they do.

The US also overly relies on whistleblowers and the media to reveal corporate misconduct. Data show that local media across the US are disappearing, with thousands of local media companies being bought up.[9] Often, among the first services not to be funded after acquisition of a local media company is investigative reporting, which is vital to holding entities accountable for their actions in a community.

Meanwhile, the US Securities and Exchange Commission (SEC) and other agencies encourage whistleblowing by employees and parties with knowledge of misconduct. Whistleblowers' careers, however, are often destroyed—a particularly dangerous outcome when they may be among the most ethical people in the company or industry.[10] Whistleblowers face financial hardships with little reasonable possibility of winning an award in a timely way, or at all.[11]

The terror of whistleblowing also prompts companies to treat employees as potential enemies and poisons relationships in the workplace. For example, in 2021, after whistleblower Frances Haugen disclosed tens of thousands of documents showing that Facebook knew that its products caused harm and that the company had misrepresented itself to the public, one of the first things that Facebook (now Meta) did was to cut off other employees' access to similar information inside the company.[12] In 2022, Meta disbanded the unit entirely.[13]

Although imposing corporate criminal fraud liability for what businesses say they will do should theoretically make US companies less willing to advertise risky propositions, there is so much money to be made in the market for these investments that companies often make the statements anyway. This author has written separately on the scale and nature of corporate misconduct in, for example, "greenwashing" promises for environmental compliance and in returns for cryptocurrencies.[14]

Prosecuting these cases after the fact is built on the same flaws, and it provides little remedy. US corporate prosecutions have become 'unbound,' as Professor Baer notes, in that prosecutors faced with corporate misrepresentations and little substantive law, try to use what law exists to go after misstatements and other poor behaviour.[15] Professor Coffee, Jr. is also correct that US prosecutors have similarly distorted the boundaries of tort and criminal law to prosecute behaviour as criminal that may previously have been civilly fraudulent.[16] And Professors Diamantis and Thomas are correct when they say that the mess of this system means that the US does not have a principled corporate criminal law.[17]

Although criminal penalties continue to increase, shifting US criminal law to rely on statements is weakening the coherent impact of the law. The traditionally stronger substantive prohibitions of criminal law have become obfuscated by smokescreens of disclosure and ad-hoc application.

Disclosure in civil law is the abdication of values by the state and the delegation of those values to the marketplace. Disclosure used to be one of the features that distinguished civil regimes from criminal ones. As Professor Davis writes in the context of debates around the passage of the Foreign Corrupt Practices Act, civil '[d]isclosure regimes deter by enabling embarrassment, by triggering naming and shaming. They work by exposing wrongdoers to condemnation by customers, suppliers, peers, and the public at large.'[18] Importantly, what delegation to disclosure in enforcement means is no 'explicit denunciation by the state' of what companies are substantively doing.[19]

Academics criticize the collapse of distinctions in the law for criminalizing what would otherwise have been civil actions.[20] But this is a weakening and destabilization of the criminal law, even with its larger penalties—not a sign of its strength. In continuing to emphasize the disclosure approach of civil law, criminal law is increasingly diminished in its substantive prohibitions.[21] Especially as it relates to new areas of investment, criminal law is being limited in its reach to cover what used to be primarily civil. This is a sad reverse implication of Professor Coffee's observation regarding 'the disappearance of any clearly definable line between civil and criminal law.'[22]

3 Why US Fraud Prosecutions Continue to Cover New Territory

As many other parts of US white-collar law fail to retain their bite, fraud—based largely on statements—remains a malleable concept and an easier basis for prosecutions than many other grounds.[23] As Professor Buell describes, '[i]f malfeasance in the business world has a single concept at its core, it is fraud.'[24] Fraud, he concludes after a survey of its origins and applications, 'is deception, with the getting of something from another as the object of the deception.'[25] In the 'intentional and wrongful deception worked upon the fraud victim—either a lie or the concealment of important information that the seller was obligated to disclose'—the lie or omission is key.[26]

The US Department of Justice's (DOJ) own journal provides a nice summary of the dilemmas the government faces when prosecuting white-collar cases. It is not an accident that its general discussion of white-collar crime continually refers to standards and strategy for fraud—in some places, four times within a few sentences.[27]

Professor Podgor's research on criminal fraud reveals how imprecise the charge is. '[F]raud is not a crime with prescribed elements,' but instead a '"concept" at the core of a variety of criminal statutes.'[28] Application of fraud charges has been growing as 'generic statutes such as mail fraud and conspiracy to defraud [are] being applied to an ever-increasing spectrum of fraudulent conduct.'[29]

There are distinctions to be made between prosecution of the corporation versus individuals within the corporation. As Professor Buell notes, it 'is the nature of the corporation ... to divide and diminish responsibility.'[30] That division and diminishment of responsibility includes not only the protection of investors behind limited liability for loss of their assets in the corporation, but also the division and diminishment of responsibility for misconduct by agents of the corporation acting on the corporation's behalf.[31] Abuse of the corporate form has evolved for large-scale entities.[32] Rather than a single person hiding abuse through his control of the entire corporate form, the corporation hides its abuse by delegating to its agents' pieces of abusive behaviour.[33]

In regard to the corporation itself, Professor Arlen thus notes that:[34]

> a rule of 'pure strict vicarious criminal liability' best approximates the existing law governing corporate criminal liability, especially for those crimes which are of particular concern, such as securities fraud, government procurement fraud, and antitrust violations.

4 The Standards for US Criminal Fraud Charges

Turning to how these cases are charged, the essential difference between US federal civil and criminal law is not necessarily the acts to be proven, but the degree of motivation ('intent') necessary for the acts.

Federal-securities fraud provides a good example of how thin this distinction is between civil and criminal charges. Although securities are regulated through a series of federal statutes, securities fraud is primarily regulated through the Securities Act of 1933 ('1933 Act') and the Securities Exchange Act of 1934 ('1934 Act').[35]

The definition of fraud is broad for both civil and criminal federal cases. For example, pattern criminal jury instructions define "fraud," "fraudulent," or "defrauding" as 'to trick, deceive, injure, or damage in some way.'[36] A statement or representation is "fraud" when 'the person making it knew the statement to be untrue or knew the representations to be false at the time that the statement or representation was made.'[37]

For certain types of civil federal-securities fraud,[38] the moving party must merely prove scienter. Scienter for fraud, according to the US Supreme Court, is 'a mental state embracing an intent to deceive, manipulate or defraud.'[39] In many circuits, this scienter may be satisfied by severe recklessness or extreme departures from ordinary care.[40] In other civil fraud cases, scienter need not even be proven.[41]

Criminal fraud *mens rea* (required state of mind) is not significantly elevated over the civil standard of scienter. To commit a criminal violation of the 1933 Act, the defendant must have acted 'willfully.'[42] The 1934 Act proscribes penalties for behaviour that is performed 'willfully and knowingly.'[43] Federal courts, in their jury instructions for violations of both the 1933 and 1934 Acts, have interpreted these requirements to mean that the 'person making the statement or making the representation' must have been 'acting with the intent to trick, deceive, injure, or damage or is making the statement or representation with reckless indifference to its truth, accuracy, or falsity.'[44]

As in some civil cases, some criminal federal-securities-fraud courts permit recklessness to satisfy intent.[45] The Seventh Circuit has found criminal intent satisfied by circumstantial evidence of a defendant's knowledge of the scheme when taking over a company.[46]

Additionally, in federal-securities-fraud cases, a defendant need not be successful in defrauding his or her victims for conviction. If the defendant acted with fraudulent intent beyond a reasonable doubt, 'it is unimportant whether the defendant was successful and accomplished the plan or was unsuccessful and did not accomplish it.'[47] Under the US Supreme Court's "fraud on the market" theory, the government also need not prove direct reliance on a defendant's statement for fraud to have occurred if the fraud could have affected a security's market price.[48] It is, however, a complete defence to criminal fraud for the defendant to have: '[a]n honest belief or "good faith" belief ... that the statements or representations made were true' at the time that they were made.[49]

When criminal intent is not as hard a thing to prove, such as with fraud, the remaining difference between civil and criminal cases is in the level of proof required, from civil "preponderance of the evidence" to criminal "beyond a reasonable doubt."[50] Factual cases often easily satisfy the criminal standard of proof because many corporate fraud prosecutions rely, for example, on extensive written documentation.

Ultimately then, the practical issue determining whether the US government pursues a civil or criminal prosecution tends to be how strongly the government feels that it should signal its condemnation of the behaviour and what remedies it seeks.[51] The US Supreme Court has explicitly approved of the government's ability to choose whether it wants to pursue a civil or criminal case based on the same underlying course of conduct.[52]

Finally, there are a growing number of cases being brought by federal prosecutors under 18 U.S.C. §1348, which is modelled on the bank fraud statute[53] but penalizes securities and commodities fraud.[54] The importance of Section 1348 being modelled on the bank fraud statute, and not on mail, wire, or traditional federal-securities fraud, is that appellate courts are holding that it reaches securities and commodities schemes in which there is no evidence of direct misrepresentations or material omissions with a duty to disclose.[55] This quality provides prosecutors even more flexibility to charge fraud criminally in economic crimes involving investors.

5 Political and Economic Pressures around Criminal Fraud

By 2018, US government prosecutions against white-collar crimes had fallen to their lowest level in 20 years.[56] During the first year of the first Trump administration, DOJ's fines against corporations fell off 90%.[57] In addition, Professor Garrett notes that[58]:

> most of the cases with large penalties in the first twenty months of the Trump Administration were legacy cases that had been initiated and investigated under the Obama Administration.

What should make us think that federal government prosecutions of white-collar crime should pick up, especially in the area of fraud as a low-hanging fruit?

First, there is an increasing realization that asking corporations to police themselves is not working particularly well. According to Professor Soltes in 2019, if we measure the pervasiveness of illegal conduct from the likelihood that a large, publicly traded firm 'would be criminally sanctioned by the DOJ or face a civil enforcement action for accounting matters by the SEC,' those numbers would be '0.5 per cent and 1.1 per cent, in a given year.'[59] The likelihood that such a firm is civilly sued for alleged misconduct is under 5% per year.[60]

Meanwhile, benchmarking data from the internal reports of large firms indicate that they have around 124 substantive reports of legally actionable misconduct per year, or, on average, once every three days.[61] Using all available public data sources, merely one-out-of-nearly-13 (12.8) incidents are being reported, or 92% of incidents are not being reported. In 2018, using another data set of 608 firms, Professors Healy and Serafeim record that only 17% of firms (104 in 608) reported internal violations to regulators at all.[62]

Similarly, although it is difficult to collect accurate statistics on precisely how much white-collar crime occur each year, people and businesses are far more likely to be victims of white-collar crime than of either traditional property crime or violent crime. In a 2018 publication, 35% of businesses, and 25% of households, reported that they have been victims of white-collar crime.[63] Victimization rates for property crime and violent crime, by contrast, are 8% and a little over 1% (respectively).[64] Accordingly, nearly four-and-a-half times as many businesses have been victims of white-collar crime as of general property crime, and nearly 25 times as many households have been the victims of white-collar crime as of violent crime.

Second, damages from fraud seem to be growing. Fraud may be among the fastest-growing forms of white-collar crime. According to a 2020 report from accounting firm PwC, in a survey of more than 5,000 respondents across 99 territories, nearly half had suffered losses from fraud over the past 24 months, with an average of six times per company.[65] US healthcare fraud alone is estimated to cost between 3% and 10% of health care expenditures, which could total more than $300 billion a year.[66]

Third, there is new, tough talk on white-collar crime from the US DOJ, and the lowest-hanging fruit may be prosecutions for fraud. In 2021, Deputy Attorney General Lisa Monaco explained in her keynote policy address to the American Bar Association that the Biden administration is 'going to find ways to surge resources to the department's prosecutors' combatting white-collar crime.[67] Her specific example was a dedication of resources to combat criminal fraud with 'a new squad of FBI agents… embedded in the Department's Criminal Fraud Section.'[68] She also noted that, as part of the Biden administration's new aggressiveness toward white-collar crime, 'our prosecutors [are] preparing for more trials right now than at any time in the last decade.'[69]

Finally, pursuing misrepresentations about investments comports with the advice that federal prosecutors give each other about what makes the best white-collar cases. As the DOJ's internal journal advises, in thinking about pursuing cases that "will stick" "Look for the Big Lie."'[70] In white-collar cases, '[t]he common tactic [is to] create a dust storm of confusion, blame underlings, express a lack of business acumen and sophistication, and the like.'[71] Meanwhile, a federal prosecutor's 'most effective response stays true to that simple theme: there was a big lie, and this defendant cannot explain it, hide from it, or ultimately, defend it.' The prosecutor should be able to prove that the defendant 'wrote it, said it, posted it, or all three.' In legal terms, '[i]t was false, it was material, and it formed the backbone of his scheme. Everything else is just white noise.'

6 Conclusion

As losses mount under the US system based on what companies say, instead of what they do, fast-moving areas are especially attractive targets and "big lies" for prosecutors to pursue. Given the flawed foundation of the US system, we should expect more volatility to come.

Notes

1 *See generally*, *e.g*., Diamantis, M. and Thomas, W.R., 'But We Haven't Got Corporate Criminal Law!' (2022) 47(4) *J. Corp. L.* 991–1008; Hasnas, J., 'The Forlorn Hope: A Final Attempt to Storm the Fortress of Corporate Criminal Liability' (2021)47(4) *J. Corp. L.* 1009–1028.
2 *See* The Inflation Reduction Act of 2022 (IRA), Public Law No. 117–169.
3 *See*, *e.g*., Macey, J.R., 'Efficient Capital Markets, Corporate Disclosure, and Enron' (2004) 89 *Cornell L. Rev.* 394, 395.
4 Fahrenthold, D.A., 'Prosecutors Struggle to Catch Up to a Tidal Wave of Pandemic Fraud', *N.Y. Times* (16 August 2022).
5 It is an important, though separate, discussion that the market does not discipline companies as we imagine that it should. (*See*, *e.g*., Nelson, J.S., 'Disclosure-Driven Crime' (2019) 52 *U.C. Davis L. Rev.* 1489, 1523–24.)
6 Coffee, J.C. Jr, 'Crime and the Corporation: Making the Punishment Fit the Corporation' (2022) 47(4) *J. Corp. L.* 963. See also Coffee, J.C. Jr, 'Crime and the Corporation: Making the Punishment Fit the Corporation' (SSRN 7 September 2021), 1.
7 Nelson, J.S., 'Disclosure-Driven Crime' (2019) 52 *U.C. Davis L. Rev.* 1489, 1495; Knapton, S., 'Volkswagen Scandal: Nearly 12,000 Deaths Could be Avoided If Industry Met Emissions Targets', *Telegraph* (22 September 2015).
8 As a former managing director of Goldman Sachs, Robert Mass, related a conversation at the time with a regulator, he noted 'this looks to me like you're taking an obligation that was traditionally the government's obligation and basically saying you now have to do it.' And she replied, 'Absolutely. We've written the rules precisely to put it on you' ('Arguments for Various Models', *ComplianceNet Conference*, Online, 29 June 2021, 23:19).
9 Abernathy, P.M., *News Deserts and Ghost Newspapers: Will Local News Survive?* (University of Northern Carolina 2020).
10 *See* Eisenstadt, L.F. and Pacella, J.M., 'Whistleblowers Need Not Apply' (2018) 55 *Am. Bus. L.J.* 665, 668–69.
11 *See*, *e.g*., Baer, M.H., 'Reconceptualizing the Whistleblower's Dilemma' (2017) 50 *U.C. Davis L. Rev.* 2215, 2217.
12 Seetharaman, D., 'Facebook Limits Employee Access to Some Internal Discussion Groups', *Wall Street Journal* (14 October 2021).
13 Horwitz, J., 'Facebook Parent Meta Platforms Cuts Responsible Innovation Team', *Wall Street Journal* (8 September 2022).
14 *See* Nelson, J.S., 'Corporate Criminal ESG' (2024) 109 *Iowa L. Rev.* 1429; Nelson, JS, 'Cryptocommunity Currencies' (2020) 105 *Cornell L. Rev.* 909.
15 Baer, M., 'Corporate Criminal Law Unbounded' in R.F. Wright, K.L. Levine and R.M. Gold (eds) *The Oxford Handbook of Prosecutors and Prosecution* (OUP 2021), 476.
16 Coffee, Jr., 2021: 194.
17 Diamantis & Thomas, 2022: 3.
18 Davis, K.E., 'Why Does the United States Regulate Foreign Bribery: Moralism, Self-interest, or Altruism?' (2012) 67 *N.Y.U. Ann. Surv. Am. L.* 497, 500.
19 Davis, 2012: 500.
20 *See*, *e.g*., Gold, R.M., 'Volunteer Prosecutors' (2022) 59 *Am. Crim. L. Rev.* 1483, 1516; Haugh, T., 'Overcriminalization's New Harm Paradigm' (2015) 68 *Vand. L. Rev.* 1191, 1196; Larkin, Jr, P.J., 'Public Choice Theory and Overcriminalization' (2013) 36 *Harv. J.L. & Pub. Pol'y* 715, 720; Stuntz, W.J., 'The Pathological Politics of Criminal Law' (2001) 100 *Mich. L. Rev.* 505, 509.
21 *Cf*., Stuntz, 2001: 509.
22 Coffee, Jr, 1991: 193.
23 *See generally* Baer, M.H., 'Forecasting the How and Why of Corporate Crime's Demise' (2022) 47 *J. Corp. L.* 887.
24 Buell, S.W., *Capital Offenses: Business Crime and Punishment in America's Corporate Age* (W.W. Norton & Company 2016), 32.
25 Buell, 2016: 44.
26 Buell, 2016: 60.
27 Kirsch II, T.L. and Hollar, D.E., 'Prosecution of Individuals in Corporate Criminal Investigations' (2018) 66 *DOJ J. of Fed. L. and Prac.* (Special Edition on Corporate Crime) 3, 7–8.
28 Podgor, E.S., 'Criminal Fraud' (1999) 48 *Am. U. L. Rev.* 729, 730.

29 Podgor, 1999: 730–31.
30 Buell, 2016: 24.
31 Nelson, J.S., 'Paper Dragon Thieves' (2017) 105 *Geo. L. J.* 871, 892–93, 898–99; *accord* Henning, PJ, 'Why It Is Getting Harder to Prosecute Executives for Corporate Misconduct' (2017) 41 *Vt. L. Rev.* 503.
32 Nelson, 2017: 884, 901–08 [providing examples], 909–21[describing resulting problems with application of conspiracy law].
33 Nelson, 2017: 884, 901–02.
34 Arlen, J., 'The Potentially Perverse Effects of Corporate Criminal Liability' (1994) 23 *J. Legal Studies* 833, 840.
35 Securities Act of 1933, 2022, 15 U.S.C. §§77a-bbbb ("1933 Act"); Securities Exchange Act of 1934, 2022, 15 U.S.C. §§78a-qq ("1934 Act"). *See also generally* Drummonds, K., Havas, R., Maul, J., Porter, D. and Trunley, B., 'Securities Fraud' (2016) 53 *Am. Crim. L. Rev.*, 1733, 1734–35.
36 Securities fraud, 2022: §62:15.
37 Securities fraud, 2022: §62:15.
38 These cases would be, for example, under §10(b), Rule 10b-5, and §17(a)(1). (*See generally* Civil, 2021: §12:22.)
39 *Aaron*, 1980: 686 n.5.
40 *See, e.g., Nathenson*, 2001: 407.
41 These cases would be under §§17(a)(2) & (3). (*See generally* Civil, 2021.)
42 1933 Act: 15 U.S.C. §77x; Scienter, 2022: §7:48.10.
43 1934 Act: 15 U.S.C. §78ff(a). There is also a "no-knowledge" standard in the 1934 Act, which is an additional discussion beyond the scope of this chapter. (*See* 1934 Act: 15 U.S.C. §78ff(a); *see also generally* Standards, 2022: §7:3.)
44 Securities Fraud: Instructions Common to the Securities Act of 1933 and the Securities Exchange Act of 1934, 2022, 2B Fed. Jury Prac. & Instr. (O'Malley, et al.) §62:15 (6th ed., Aug.)
45 *See, e.g.*, Boyer (United States v. Boyer), 1982, 694 F.2d 58 (3d Cir.), 59.
46 *See* Wilson (United States v. Wilson), 2018, 879 F.3d 795 (7th Cir.), 804–05.
47 Securities Fraud, 2022: §62:15.
48 *See* Basic Inc. v. Levinson, 1988, 485 U.S. 224, 241–50.
49 Securities Fraud, 2022: §62:15.
50 *See generally* Policy background; Burdens of proof, 2021, 21B Fed. Prac. & Proc. Evid. (Wright & Miller) §5122 (2d ed., April Update).
51 Greenberg, B. and Torres, S., 'Parallel Proceedings in Health Care Fraud' (2018) 66 *DOJ J. of Fed. L. and Prac.* (Special Edition on Corporate Crime) 15, 16.
52 *See, e.g.*, Kordel (United States v. Kordel), 1970, 397 U.S. 1, 11. There may still be a double jeopardy issue in the government's pursing the same behaviour twice, but that is not the same as the government's freedom to choose how it will pursue behaviour that could be either civil or criminal.
53 *See* 18 U.S.C. §1344 (2021).
54 *See, e.g.*, Moser, S. and Weitz, J., '18 U.S.C. §1348—A Workhorse Statute for Prosecutors' (2018) 66 *DOJ J. of Fed. L. and Prac.* (Special Edition on Corporate Crime) 111, 111–12.
55 *See* Moser & Weitz, 2018: 113–19.
56 White-collar prosecutions, 2018.
57 Lartey, J., 'Corporate Penalties Dropped as Much as 94% under Trump, Study Says', *Guardian* (25 July 2018).
58 Garrett, B.L., 'Declining Corporate Prosecutions' (2020) 57 *Am. Crim. L. Rev.* 109, 115.
59 Soltes, E., 'The Frequency of Corporate Misconduct: Public Enforcement versus Private Reality' (2019) 26 *J. Fin. Crime* 923, 924.
60 Soltes, 2019: 924.
61 Soltes, 2019: 924.
62 See also Healy, P. and Serafeim, G., 'Agency Costs and Enforcement of Management Controls: Analyzing Punishments for Perpetrators of Economic Crimes' (20 March 2018), AAA 2017 Management Accounting Section (MAS) Meeting. Available at SSRN: https://papers.ssrn.com/sol3/papers.cfm?abstract_id=2801622 (accessed 27 March 2025), 6. See also Healy, P. and Serafeim, G., 'Who Pays for White-Collar Crime?' (2016) *Harv. Bus. Sch. Working Paper*.
63 *See* Cliff, G. and Wall-Parker, A., 'Statistical Analysis of White-collar Crime', *Oxford Research Encyclopaedia of Criminology* (OUP 2018), 7.

64 *See* Cliff et al., 2018: 7.
65 PricewaterhouseCoopers, *2020 Fighting Fraud: A Never-Ending Battle, PwC's Global Economic Crime and Fraud Survey* (PWC 2020), 3.
66 NHCAA, 'The Challenge of Health Care Fraud' (NHCAA, 2022). Available at https://www.nhcaa.org/tools-insights/about-health-care-fraud/the-challenge-of-health-care-fraud/ (accessed 27 March 2025).
67 Monaco, L.O., Keynote Address at ABA's 36th National Institute on White Collar Crime (28 October 2021). Available at https://www.justice.gov/archives/opa/speech/deputy-attorney-general-lisa-o-monaco-gives-keynote-address-abas-36th-national-institute (accessed 27 March 2025).
68 Monaco, 2021.
69 Monaco, 2021. Gurman, S., 'Deputy Attorney General Lisa Monaco Underscores DOJ's Tougher Line on Corporate Crime', *Wall Street Journal* (7 December 2021).
70 Zusman, K.A., 'Making It Stick: Protecting Your White Collar Convictions on Appeal' (2018) 66 *DOJ J. of Fed. L. and Prac.* (Special Edition on Corporate Crime) 65 [capitalization in original].
71 Zusman, 2018: 65 [capitalization in original].

Bibliography

Case Law (US)

Aaron v. Sec. and Exch. Comm'n, 1980, 446 U.S. 680.
Basic Inc. v. Levinson, 1988, 485 U.S. 224.
Boyer (United States v. Boyer), 1982, 694 F.2d 58 (3d Cir.).
Kordel (United States v. Kordel), 1970, 397 U.S. 1.
Nathenson v. Zonagen Inc., 2001, 267 F.3d 400 (5th Cir.).
Wilson (United States v. Wilson), 2018, 879 F.3d 795 (7th Cir.).

Statute (US)

Bank Fraud, 2021, 18 U.S.C. §1344.
The Inflation Reduction Act of 2022 (IRA), Public Law No. 117–169.
Securities Act of 1933, 2022, 15 U.S.C. §§77a-bbbb.
Securities Exchange Act of 1934, 2022, 15 U.S.C. §§78a-qq.

Articles, Books and Articles

Abernathy, P.M., *News Deserts and Ghost Newspapers: Will Local News Survive?* (University of Northern Carolina 2020).
'Arguments for Various Models', Panelists: Cynthia Williams, Jonathan Lipson, Robert Bird, Robert Mass, and Laurie Smiley, Chair: JS Nelson *(ComplianceNet Conference*, Online, 29 June 2021). Available at: https://www.compliancenet.org/2021 (accessed 25 March 2025).
Arlen, J., 'The Potentially Perverse Effects of Corporate Criminal Liability' (1994) 23 *J. Legal Studies* 833.
Baer, M.H., 'Reconceptualizing the Whistleblower's Dilemma' (2017) 50 *U.C. Davis L. Rev.* 2215.
Baer, M., 'Corporate Criminal Law Unbounded' in R.F. Wright, K.L. Levine and R.M. Gold (eds) *The Oxford Handbook of Prosecutors and Prosecution* (OUP 2021) 475–496.
Baer, M.H., 'Forecasting the How and Why of Corporate Crime's Demise' (2022) 47 *J. Corp. L.* 887.
Bromberg, A.R., Lowenfels, L.D. and Sullivan, M.J., Bromberg & Lowenfels on Securities Fraud §7:48.10 (2nd edn, Clark Boardman Callaghan 2022).
Buell, S.W., *Capital Offenses: Business Crime and Punishment in America's Corporate Age* (W.W. Norton & Company 2016).
Civil Injunctive Proceedings—Elements of a Cause of Action—Scienter, 2 *White Collar Crime* §12:22 (3rd edn, December 2021).

Cliff, G. and Wall-Parker, A., 'Statistical Analysis of White-collar Crime', *Oxford Research Encyclopaedia of Criminology* (OUP 2018).

Coffee Jr, J.C., 'Does Unlawful Mean Criminal: Reflections on the Disappearing Tort/Crime Distinction in American Law' (1991) 71 *B.U. L. Rev.* 193.

Coffee Jr, J.C., 'Crime and the Corporation: Making the Punishment Fit the Corporation' (SSRN 7 September 2021). Available at SSRN: https://ssrn.com/abstract=3914961 or https://doi.org/10.2139/ssrn.3914961 (accessed 27 March 2025).

Coffee Jr, J.C., 'Crime and the Corporation: Making the Punishment Fit the Corporation' (2022) 47(4) *J. Corp. L.* 963.

Davis, K.E., 'Why Does the United States Regulate Foreign Bribery: Moralism, Self-interest, or Altruism? (2012) 67 *N.Y.U. Ann. Surv. Am. L.* 497.

Diamantis, M. and Thomas, W.R., 'But We Haven't Got Corporate Criminal Law!' (2022) 47 *J. Corp. L.* 991.

Drummonds, K., Havas, R., Maul, J., Porter, D. and Trunley, B., 'Securities Fraud' (2016) 53 *Am. Crim. L. Rev.* 1733.

Eisenstadt, L.F. and Pacella, J.M., 'Whistleblowers Need Not Apply' (2018) 55 *Am. Bus. L.J.* 665.

Fahrenthold, D.A., 'Prosecutors Struggle to Catch Up to a Tidal Wave of Pandemic Fraud', *N.Y. Times* (16 August 2022).

Garrett, B.L., 'Declining Corporate Prosecutions' (2020) 57 *Am. Crim. L. Rev.* 109.

Gold, R.M., 'Volunteer Prosecutors' (2022) 59 *Am. Crim. L. Rev.* 1483.

Greenberg, B. and Torres, S., 'Parallel Proceedings in Health Care Fraud' (2018) 66 *DOJ J. of Fed. L. and Prac.* (Special Edition on Corporate Crime) 15.

Gurman, S., 'Deputy Attorney General Lisa Monaco Underscores DOJ's Tougher Line on Corporate Crime', *Wall Street Journal* (7 December 2021).

Hasnas, J., 'The Forlorn Hope: A Final Attempt to Storm the Fortress of Corporate Criminal Liability' (2021) 47(4) *J. Corp. L.* 1009–1028.

Haugh, T., 'Overcriminalization's New Harm Paradigm' (2015) 68 *Vand. L. Rev.* 1191.

Healy, P. and Serafeim, G., 'Who Pays for White-Collar Crime?' (2016) *Harv. Bus. Sch. Working Paper*.

Healy, P. and Serafeim, G., 'Agency Costs and Enforcement of Management Controls: Analyzing Punishments for Perpetrators of Economic Crimes' (20 March 2018), AAA 2017 Management Accounting Section (MAS) Meeting. Available at SSRN: https://papers.ssrn.com/sol3/papers.cfm?abstract_id=2801622 (accessed 27 March 2025).

Henning, P.J., 'Why It Is Getting Harder to Prosecute Executives for Corporate Misconduct' (2017) 41 *Vt. L. Rev.* 503.

Horwitz, J., 'Facebook Parent Meta Platforms Cuts Responsible Innovation Team', *Wall Street Journal* (8 September 2022).

Kirsch II, T.L. and Hollar, D.E., 'Prosecution of Individuals in Corporate Criminal Investigations' (2018) 66 *DOJ J. of Fed. L. and Prac.* (Special Edition on Corporate Crime) 3.

Knapton, S., 'Volkswagen Scandal: Nearly 12,000 Deaths Could Be Avoided If Industry Met Emissions Targets', *Telegraph* (London, 22 September 2015).

Larkin, Jr, P.J., 'Public Choice Theory and Overcriminalization' (2013) 36 *Harv. J.L. & Pub. Pol'y* 715.

Lartey, J., 'Corporate Penalties Dropped as Much as 94% under Trump, Study Says', *Guardian* (25 July 2018).

Macey, J.R., 'Efficient Capital Markets, Corporate Disclosure, and Enron' (2004) 89 *Cornell L. Rev.* 394.

Monaco, L.O., Keynote Address at ABA's 36th National Institute on White Collar Crime (28 October 2021). Available at https://www.justice.gov/archives/opa/speech/deputy-attorney-general-lisa-o-monaco-gives-keynote-address-abas-36th-national-institute (accessed 27 March 2025).

Moser, S. and Weitz, J., '18 U.S.C. §1348—A Workhorse Statute for Prosecutors' (2018) 66 *DOJ J. of Fed. L. and Prac.* (Special Edition on Corporate Crime) 111.

Nelson, J.S., 'Paper Dragon Thieves' (2017) 105 *Geo. L. J.* 871.

Nelson, J.S., 'Disclosure-Driven Crime' (2019) 52 *U.C. Davis L. Rev.* 1489.

Nelson, J.S., 'Cryptocommunity Currencies' (2020) 105 *Cornell L. Rev.* 909.
Nelson, J.S., 'Corporate Criminal ESG' (2024) 109 *Iowa L. Rev.* 1429.
NHCAA, 'The Challenge of Health Care Fraud' (NHCAA 2022). Available at https://www.nhcaa.org/tools-insights/about-health-care-fraud/the-challenge-of-health-care-fraud/ (accessed 27 March 2025).
Podgor, E.S., 'Criminal Fraud' (1999) 48 *Am. U. L. Rev.* 729.
Policy Background; Burdens of Proof, 2021, 21B Fed. Prac. & Proc. Evid. (Wright & Miller) §5122 (2nd edn, April Update).
PricewaterhouseCoopers, 2020 *Fighting Fraud: A Never-Ending Battle, PwC's Global Economic Crime and Fraud Survey* (PWC 2020).
Securities Fraud: Instructions Common to the Securities Act of 1933 and the Securities Exchange Act of 1934, 2022, 2B Fed. Jury Prac. & Instr. (O'Malley, et al.) §62:15 (6th edn, August).
Seetharaman, D., 'Facebook Limits Employee Access to Some Internal Discussion Groups', *Wall Street Journal* (14 October 2021).
Soltes, E., 'The Frequency of Corporate Misconduct: Public Enforcement Versus Private Reality' (2019) 26 *J. Fin. Crime* 923.
Standards of Culpability; Willfully and Knowingly, 2022, 21 Sec. Crimes §7:3 (December).
Stuntz, W.J., 'The Pathological Politics of Criminal Law' (2001) 100 *Mich. L. Rev.* 505.
TRAC, 'White Collar prosecutions Fall to Lowest in 20 Years' (TRAC Reports 24 May 2018). Available at https://tracreports.org/tracreports/crim/514/ (accessed 27 March 2025).
Zusman, K.A., 'Making It Stick: Protecting Your White Collar Convictions on Appeal' (2018) 66 *DOJ J. of Fed. L. and Prac.* (Special Edition on Corporate Crime) 65.

11 Corporate Criminal Liability

Shifting the Burden of Cost to the Private Sector

Georgia Bufton

1 Introduction

Tackling fraud has become a key priority for the Government.[1] Previous attempts to tackle the threat presented by fraud have been described as disjointed and lacking in an overarching strategy to prevent, investigate and prosecute these crimes.[2] This chapter examines the limitations of common law principles underpinning corporate accountability, with particular emphasis on the identification doctrine. It critiques how this traditional framework fails to address the evolving, decentralized nature of contemporary corporate governance. In response, this chapter explores the "failure to prevent" (FTP) model, which has gained traction in regulating corporate criminal behaviour. This approach shifts the focus from individual culpability to a broader understanding of corporate responsibility. By analysing the development and application of FTP offences, key comparisons between legislative frameworks for bribery and fraud are highlighted thus illustrating how these offences are expanding corporate criminal liability whilst promoting a more comprehensive approach to corporate governance and accountability.

2 Legislative Context

Spurred on by the Russian invasion of Ukraine in 2022, a significant amount of legislation has been passed in the UK over a short period; namely the Economic Crime (Transparency and Enforcement) Act 2022[3] (ECTEA) and the Economic Crime and Corporate Transparency Act (ECCTA) 2023.[4] The ECTEA was to address the remaining holes in the first *ECA*.[5] Noteworthy, the ECCA[6] struggled around debates between the proposed introduction of an FTP[7] offence; it was later cut down only to cover the government's current definition of large organizations.

In the UK, there are currently two main "FTP" offences: failure to prevent bribery under the BA and failure to prevent the facilitation of tax evasion under the CFA. A new FTP fraud offence will come into effect on 1 September 2025. These offences are an uneasy compromise in the UK that 'aims to address the well-known deficiencies of the common law's approach to corporate criminal liability'.[8] The courts have taken a significantly narrow interpretation of whose behaviour within an organization can attract corporate liability; some significant prosecutions have fallen apart on this point.[9]

To address these issues, in November 2020, the Law Commission[10] was asked by the Government to review the law on corporate criminal liability and specifically whether an FTP economic corporate crime offence should be introduced. The Law Commission decided[11] that there was no argument for a general FTP economic crime offence, as FTP offences as well as a regulatory regime already existed under the Money Laundering

DOI: 10.4324/9781003324843-15

Regulations 2007.[12] The Law Commission suggested that there was scope for an FTP fraud offence and the Fraud Strategy clearly indicated that the Government were committed to exploring this. Therefore, the ECCTA included an amendment around the FTP fraud offence. It is now hoped that that this offence will partly address these issues in UK law, whilst instilling fraud prevention and promoting cultural change. This Act forms part of a trilogy of new legislation supporting the two Economic Crime Plans.[13] The ECCTA forms part of a complex landscape and aims to fill in the existing gap between fraud and FTP. Arguably, the ECCTA (notably Schedules 12 and 13) has helped describe the landscape in this ever-evolving area.

3 The Identification Doctrine

The attribution of corporate criminal liability is a significant challenge for prosecutors. According to the directing mind and will test,[14] a corporate could only be held criminally liable if the commission of an offence could be attributed to a natural person that represents its 'directing mind and will' at the time the offence was committed.[15] This represents a limited number of individuals, making it challenging to meet, especially for large corporations with intricate and decentralized management structures. The Serious Fraud Office (SFO) has long criticized the test as archaic and inadequate.[16]

As succinctly summarized by the Law Commission, 'the governing principle is that those who control or manage the affairs of a company are regarded as embodying the company itself'.[17] As seen in the case of *Tesco v Nattrass*[18] and *Meridian v Securities Commission*,[19] the courts have grappled with this doctrine, as it permits criminal liability to be imposed on a company for an offence that requires the requisite state of mind to commit the offence.[20]

4 Limitations

Due to its narrow scope of application, the identification doctrine typically covers those in senior management positions who are considered the 'directing mind and will' of the company thus making it extremely difficult to hold corporates accountable in cases where low-level employees commit misconduct.[21] Furthermore, the difficulty in establishing guilt is challenging which often leads to acquittals or failure in prosecuting; especially those with complex structures in place.[22] It can be argued that the identification doctrine encourages poor corporate structures as some companies may deliberately structure their operations in a way which will insulate senior management from direct involvement in criminal activities.[23]

4.1 Introduction of a 'Senior Manager' Test

The ECCTA has expanded the identification doctrine so that a corporation could be guilty of a certain criminal offence if the offence is committed by a 'senior manager' acting within the actual or apparent scope of their authority.[24] This significantly expands the group of individuals through which liability can be attributed to a company, thus making it easier for prosecutors to successfully pursue corporate wrongdoing.

Under ECCTA, a 'senior manager' is defined as an individual who plays a significant role[25] in the:

- Making of decisions about how the whole or a substantial part of the activities of the body, corporate or partnership are to be managed or organized, or
- Actual managing or organizing of the whole or a substantial part of those activities.[26]

The ECCTA describes 'significant role' under its revised identification doctrine; it attributes responsibility and liability to individuals in positions of influence within a company, ensuring greater accountability in corporate governance.[27] The term refers to individuals who play significant roles either in decision-making or operational management. This definition aligns with that used under the Corporate Manslaughter and Corporate Homicide Act 2007 (CMCHA).[28] While the Act provides statutory guidance, case law has yet to fully test the practical implications of what constitutes a 'significant role'. The definition of 'senior management' is derived from the CMCHA. The Explanatory Notes to the CMCHA indicate that this definition encompasses individuals within the direct chain of management, as well as those in strategic or regulatory compliance roles.[29]

The introduction of a senior manager test represents a significant shift from the existing framework; this will be the equivalent of removing a very large and painful thorn from the side of the Serious Fraud Office, that have markedly struggled to prosecute corporations as a result of the current – and extremely limited – directing mind and will definition. Moreover, this change could significantly expand the range of employees whose criminal actions may be imputed to the corporation in question. The CMCHA provides a solid model for the senior management definition within the ECCTA. The CMCHA explicitly considers the role of senior management in health and safety failures.[30] This focus on accountability at the very top of the chain can be directly relevant to economic crimes, where senior management's decisions and oversight significantly impact corporate conduct.[31]

With the spotlight currently placed on fraud – which makes up over 40% of crime within the UK,[32] the UK Government has 'committed in the Economic Crime Plan 2 and the Fraud Strategy to introduce reform to the identification principle for all criminal offences in due course';[33] the Criminal Justice Bill 2023[34] seeks to do this in Clause 14.[35] It is mandatory that organizations are aware of the heightened risk brought about by the extension of corporate criminal liability in this area.

4.2 *Prosecutions Are Central to the Long-Term Impact*

One of the key intentions of the new FTP fraud offence under the ECCTA is to drive a change in corporate culture, whilst encouraging companies to prevent fraud from happening in the first instance. Giving evidence to the UK Parliamentary Justice Committee in May 2024, the SFO Director Nick Ephgrave was clear: 'I want [the SFO] to be the first organization to take a prosecution forward based on the duty to prevent fraud…that would be a wonderful thing to do'.[36]

While prosecutions are central to the long-term impact of the ECCTA, previous usage of the existing FTP offences show little success regarding the number of prosecutions, since only a small number of prosecutions have been brought under FTP bribery, and none have been brought under the FTP facilitation of tax evasion.

The primary advantage of the introduction of FTP fraud will be deterrence, rather than a substantial increase in the number of prosecutions. Lord Garnier stated that the unimpressive figures of prosecutions for FTP offences are insignificant; he believes that the intention behind this suite of reforms is to 'create an atmosphere where people mitigate in advance the dangers of those criminal offences being committed'.[37]

The use of Deferred Prosecution Agreements (DPAs) will likely continue as it is considered a 'generally desirable outcome for a corporate and wider society'; it also 'compensates for the paucity of corporate convictions'.[38] DPAs were introduced under the provisions of Schedule 17 of the Crime and Courts Act 2013,[39] and allow for a prosecution to be suspended for a defined period provided the organization meets certain specified conditions. Such terms and conditions can be broad, involving fines and remedial actions. Questions have been raised regarding whether DPAs are regarded as a 'soft option for corporates to absolve themselves of responsibility and to avoid the risk of potential prosecution'.[40] Alternatively, DPA's have been described as striking a balance 'between the need to communicate the severity of a corporate defendant's conduct and the need to avoid unintended consequences of a criminal conviction'.[41]

The reform of the identification doctrine on a statutory footing for economic crimes aims to simplify the process for authorities to hold corporates accountable for primary fraud and bribery offences. Although the term 'senior manager' has now been defined, it will still be subject to judicial interpretation; in relation to which, the courts may still lean towards a narrow interpretation as demonstrated in *Serious Fraud Office v Barclays PLC*.[42] What remains to be seen, and what will be closely followed, is the long-term impact of this offence. If there is no threat of prosecution, then the offence itself ceases to become a credible deterrent. The Government's Impact Assessment of the new FTP fraud offence concluded, that, although the changes to the identification principle are anticipated to lead to an increase in corporate prosecutions, the rise in the number of additional cases is expected to be minimal.[43]

4.3 *Failure to Prevent Fraud – Increasing the Scope of Corporate Criminal Liability*

The ECCTA 'introduces a new offence, at s.199, whereby an organization can be convicted of failure to prevent fraud if an associate or employee commits a specified fraud offence'.[44] By way of background, it is 'modelled on the existing corporate failure-to-prevent offences, comprising bribery and tax evasion, which are, in contrast, of general application'.[45] A fraud offence is confined to a list of offences set out in Schedule 13.[46] The number of listed offences is small and includes tax evasion, false accounting, false statements by company directors, fraudulent trading and fraud contrary to section 1 of the Fraud Act.[47] An interesting omission to this list is money laundering offences within the Proceeds of Crime Act[48] and conspiracy to defraud.[49]

The new FTP offence applies to large organizations;[50] for the purposes of the ECCTA, a 'large organization' is defined as one that meets two out of the three following criteria, during the financial year of the entity concerned that preceded the year of the fraud offence:

a turnover of more than £36 million;
b balance sheet total of more than £18 million; and
c more than 250 employees.[51]

There is a defence available to the FTP fraud offence which requires the body to prove that at the time of the offence it had in place 'such prevention procedures as it was reasonable in all the circumstances to expect the body to have in place' or that 'it was not reasonable in all the circumstances to expect the body to have any prevention procedures in place'.[52] In contrast to the adequate procedures defence under the BA,[53] the requirements governing the FTP fraud defence appear less constricted. Employees, agents, subsidiaries and any other person performing services for or on behalf of the organization are all included under the umbrella of associated persons.[54] Noteworthy

> in all scenarios, the associated person must commit the relevant fraud offence with the intention, whether direct or indirect, of benefitting the relevant body or any person to whom, or to whose subsidiary, the associated person provides services on behalf of the relevant body.[55]

4.4 *Definition of a 'Relevant Body'*

In contrast to the senior manager test, the FTP fraud offence applies to 'relevant bodies' which are described by section 199(1),[56] as a body, corporate or partnership, wherever incorporated or formed. Certainly, this is a broad definition – broader than that used in section 75 of the BA. Under section 75 of the BA, the relevant body refers to the type of entity that can be held liable for bribery offences; it clarifies that a 'relevant body' includes both commercial and non-commercial organizations that may be charged under the provisions of the BA. There is no requirement for the body to be incorporated within the UK or to conduct any business or part of a business within the UK. By contrast, Lord Garnier's proposal[57] defines the relevant body similarly to the definition that is contained in the BA, as a body with a UK Nexus. A UK Nexus refers to the connections or link between the activities of a corporation and the UK; the concept of this is important for determining jurisdiction and ensuring that companies are held accountable for their actions within the framework of UK law.

Certain offences termed 'fraud offences' are covered within Schedule 13 of the Act.[58] An organization will be liable where a specific fraud is:

a Committed by an 'associate;'
b For the benefit of the organization or any person to whom services are provided on behalf of the organization; and
c The organization did not have reasonable fraud prevention procedures in place (unless it was not reasonable to expect them to have such procedures).

The definition of an 'associate' is significantly wider than that of an associated person; it includes presumptions surrounding which categories of individuals will be considered associates.[59] For FTP offences, any employee, agent or subsidiary of the relevant body will be considered an associate. Additionally, a person may be deemed an associate if they perform services for, on behalf of, the relevant body which will be determined based on all relevant circumstances.

5 Conclusion

The governance landscape has changed. There appears to be considerably more political will to do more in this arena; this will be seen in court-related proceedings in due course.

Taken together, the FTP fraud offence and changes to the identification doctrine give prosecutors the ability to bring corporate charges for the behaviour of more individuals within an organization. The most significant changes that the ECCTA introduced are the FTP fraud offence and the replacement of the common law's directing mind and will test for corporate criminal liability with a new statutory senior manager test.

Drawing these points together, the key takeaway for corporates is that the ECCTA makes it apparent that those with significant strategic and operational responsibilities would most likely fall within the scope of what a senior manager is. Whilst one could argue that as the CEO and CFO of a company will undertake roles holding significant strategic and operational responsibilities, that does not necessarily mean that they should automatically be considered a senior manager. Naturally, in all cases, this would require a specific analysis of the actual roles and responsibilities that an individual has and their specific involvement within the transaction or deal in question.

Clearly, the purpose of the ECCTA is to make corporate structures and control less opaque, to oblige corporate bodies and partnerships to do much more in the prevention of financial crime being committed on their behalf, in their names or using their structures and to make these individuals ultimately more accountable when they fail to do so.

Notes

1 Fraud Reform Program Accounting Officer Assessment. (22 March 2021). Available at: Fraud Reform Programme Accounting Officer Assessment - GOV.UK.
2 House of Commons Justice Committee, Fraud and the Justice System. Fourth Report of Session 2019–2020.
3 Economic Crime (Transparency and Enforcement) Act 2022.
4 Economic Crime and Corporate Transparency Act 2023.
5 Economic Crime and Corporate Transparency Act 2023.
6 Economic Crime and Corporate Transparency Act 2023.
7 Economic Crime and Corporate Transparency Act 2023.
8 Cronin 2024.
9 Serious Fraud Office v Rolls-Royce PLC and another [2017] Lloyd's Rep FC 249.
10 The Law Commission is a statutory, independent body and its role is to review and recommend reforms to the law in England and Wales.
11 Law Commission, 'Corporate Criminal Liability: An Options Paper' (10 June 2022). Available at: https://corporatejusticecoalition.org/wp-content/uploads/2022/07/Corporate-Criminal-Liability-Options-Paper_LC.pdf (accessed 27 March 2025).
12 The Money Laundering Regulations 2007 (SI 2007/2157).
13 Policy Paper, 'Economic Crime Plan, 2019 to 2022, 12th July 2019, HM Treasury and Home Office'. Available at: https://assets.publishing.service.gov.uk/media/5d2701f4e5274a5864497e3a/2019-22_Economic_Crime_Plan.pdf (accessed 27 March 2025); 'Economic Crime Plan, 2023–2026, 30th March 2023, HM Treasury and Home Office'. Available at: https://assets.publishing.service.gov.uk/media/642561b02fa8480013ec0f97/6.8300_HO_Economic_Crime_Plan_2_v6_Web.pdf (Accessed 27 March 2025).
14 Tesco Supermarkets Ltd v Nattrass [1971] UKHL 1, [1972] AC 153; Lim, E, 'A Critique of Corporate Attribution: "Directing Mind and Will" and Corporate Objectives' (2011) SSRN. Available at SSRN: https://ssrn.com/abstract=2368181 (accessed 27 March 2025).
15 Tesco Supermarkets Ltd v Nattrass [1971] UKHL 1, [1972] AC 153; Lim 2011.
16 Serious Fraud Office, 'Control Liability—Is It a Good Idea and Does It Work in Practice?' (6 September 2016).
17 Law Commission, *Legislating the Criminal Code: Involuntary Manslaughter* (Law Com No. 237, 1996) para 6, 27.
18 Tesco Supermarkets Ltd v Nattrass [1971] UKHL 1, [1972] AC 153.
19 Meridian v Securities Commission [1995] 2 AC 500.
20 Intent, recklessness or dishonesty dependent on the offence in question; Serious Fraud Office v Barclays Plc [2018] EWCH 3055 (QB).
21 Gobert, J, 'Corporate Criminality: Four Models of Fault' (1994) 14 *Legal Studies* 393.
22 Wells, C, *Corporations and Criminal Responsibility* (OUP 2001).
23 Radhi, R, Abbas, A, *How Can Restorative Justice and the Unified Theory of Punishment Help Us Make Sense of Corporate Crime and Punishment?* Doctoral Thesis, Durham University, 2019.
24 Economic Crime and Corporate Transparency Act 2023, s 196(1).

25 Economic Crime and Corporate Transparency Act 2023, s 6.
26 Economic Crime and Corporate Transparency Act 2023 HL Bill 156. Available at: https://bills.parliament.uk/publications/51963/documents/3729 (accessed 27 March 2025).
27 The term refers to individuals who play significant roles either in: decision making about how the whole or a substantial part of the corporation's activities are managed or organized or operational management of the whole or a substantial part of those activities.
28 Corporate Manslaughter and Corporate Homicide Act 2007.
29 Explanatory Notes to the Corporate Manslaughter and Corporate Homicide Act 2007. Available at: https://www.legislation.gov.uk/ukpga/2007/19/section1/notes?view=plain (accessed 27 March 2025).
30 The following provisions ensure that liability under Corporate Manslaughter Corporate Homicide Act considers the actions or inactions of senior management: Section 1(3) Definition of Senior Management. Section 1(1) Offence of Corporate Manslaughter. Section 1(4)(c) Management and Organization of Activities.
31 Roper, V, 'The Corporate Manslaughter and Corporate Homicide Act 2007—A 10-Year Review' (2018) 82(1) *The Journal of Criminal Law* 48–75.
32 UK Government, *Fraud Strategy: Stopping Scams and Protecting the Public.* Available at: https://www.gov.uk/government/publications/fraud-strategy/fraud-strategy-stopping-scams-and-protecting-the-public (accessed 27 March 2025).
33 Criminal Justice Bill 2023. Available at: https://bills.parliament.uk/bills/3511 (accessed 27 March 2025).
34 Criminal Justice Bill [HL] 2023–2024.
35 Clause 14 of the Criminal Justice Bill 2023 expands the 'Identification Doctrine' (which relates to the criminal liability of senior managers of bodies corporate and partnerships) to all offences (expanding the reforms made by the Economic Crime and Corporate Transparency Act to apply to all crimes, not just economic crimes); Criminal Justice Bill 2023: ECHR Memorandum November 2023 (updated 14 May 2024). Available at: https://www.gov.uk/government/publications/criminal-justice-bill-overarching-documents/criminal-justice-bill-echr-memorandum-november-2023-accessible-version (accessed 27 March 2025).
36 House of Commons Justice Committee Oral Evidence: Work of the Serious Fraud Office, HC 743. Available at: https://committees.parliament.uk/oralevidence/14850/pdf/ (accessed 27 March 2025).
37 Simmons and Simmons Podcast Series: Forthcoming Changes to Corporate Criminal Law, https://www.simmons-simmons.com/en/publications/clnedzjm4005iu6x4bacn4ryg/podcast-series-forthcoming-changes-to-corporate-criminal-law.
38 WilmerHale, 'Bribery Act 2010: Ten Years On' (21 May 2021). Available at: https://www.wilmerhale.com/en/insights/blogs/wilmerhale-w-i-r-e-uk/20210521-bribery-act-2010-ten-years-on (accessed 27 March 2025).
39 Crime and Courts Act 2013, Schedule 17.
40 White & Case, 'Deferred Prosecution Agreements 5 Years On – The Americanization of UK Corporate Crime Enforcement' (10 May 2019). Available at: https://www.whitecase.com/insight-alert/deferred-prosecution-agreements-5-years-americanisation-uk-corporate-crime (accessed 27 March 2025).
41 Bourton, S, Hall, D, Johnson, D, Ryder, N, 'Corporate Criminal Liability and the Identification Doctrine – A Critical Reflection'. Available at: https://uwe-repository.worktribe.com/preview/10607029/Corporate%20criminal%20liability%20and%20the%20identification%20doctrine%20-%20A%20critical%20reflection.pdf (accessed 27 March 2025).
42 Serious Fraud Office v Barclays PLC [2018] EWHC 3055 (QB).
43 Home Office, The Impact Assessment on the Reform to the Identification Doctrine (2023) (IA No.: HO IA 0463). Available at: https://assets.publishing.service.gov.uk/media/648c20455f7bb7000c7fabca/5_IDD_Impact_Assessment.pdf (accessed 27 March 2025).
44 Cronin 2024.
45 Cronin 2024.
46 A 'listed offence' Economic Crime and Corporate Transparency Act 2023 Chapter 56. Available at: https://www.legislation.gov.uk/ukpga/2023/56 (accessed 25 March 2025).
47 Fraud Act 2006, s 1.
48 Proceeds of Crime Act 2002.
49 Proceeds of Crime Act 2002, s327(2).

50 Economic Crime and Corporate Transparency Act, s201.
51 Economic Crime and Corporate Transparency Act 2023, s199.
52 Economic Crime and Corporate Transparency Act 2023, s199(4).
53 Bribery Act 2010, s7(2).
54 The Economic Crime and Corporate Transparency Act broadly includes employees, agents, subsidiaries, and any other person performing services for or on behalf of an organization. Any individual or entity performing services for the organisation can fall under this umbrella. It is the organisations responsibility to implement preventative measures across all tiers of its operation.
55 Herbert Smith Freehills, 'Economic Crime and Corporate Transparency Act 2023: Who Is an Associated Person for the Failure to Prevent Fraud Offence?' (Herbert Smith Freehills, 22 March 2024). Available at: https://www.herbertsmithfreehills.com/notes/fsrandcorpcrime/2024-03/economic-crime-and-corporate-transparency-act-2023-who-is-an-associated-person-for-the-failure-to-prevent-fraud-offence (accessed 27 March 2025).
56 Economic Crime and Corporate Transparency Act 2023, s199(1).
57 Economic Crime and Corporate Transparency Bill Volume 831: 27 June 2023.
58 Economic Crime and Corporate Transparency Act 2023, Sch 13 – Offences of fraudulent trading, participating in fraudulent business carried on by a sold trader, offences of fraud, obtaining services dishonestly, false accounting, the making of sale statements by company directors, cheating the public revenue, aiding and abetting, counselling or procuring any such offence.
59 Economic Crime and Corporate Transparency Act 2023, s199(7)–(9).

Bibliography

Articles and Books

Gobert, J, 'Corporate Criminality: Four Models of Fault' (1994) 14 *Legal Studies* 393.
Lim, E, 'A Critique of Corporate Attribution: "Directing Mind and Will" and Corporate Objectives' (2011) SSRN. Available at SSRN: https://ssrn.com/abstract=2368181 (accessed 27 March 2025).
Roper, V, 'The Corporate Manslaughter and Corporate Homicide Act 2007—A 10-Year Review' (2018) 82 *The Journal of Criminal Law* 48.
Wells, C, *Corporations and Criminal Responsibility* (OUP 2001).

Legislation and Bills

Bribery Act 2010.
Corporate Manslaughter and Corporate Homicide Act 2007.
Criminal Finances Act 2017.
Criminal Justice Bill 2023.
Criminal Justice Bill 2023: ECHR Memorandum November 2023.
Economic Crime and Corporate Transparency Act 2023.
Economic Crime (Transparency and Enforcement) Act 2022.
Fraud Act 2004.
The Money Laundering Regulations 2007 (SI 2007/2157).

Case Law

Hewlett-Packard Co v Autonomy Corp Ltd (2018).
Meridian v Securities Commission [1995] 2 AC 500.
Serious Fraud Office v Barclays PLC [2018] EWHC 3055 (QB).
Tesco Supermarkets Ltd v Nattrass [1971] UKHL 1, [1972] AC 153.
United States v Ebbers, 458 F.3d 110 (2d Cir. 2006).
United States v Skilling, 561 US 358 (2010).

Reports and Policy Papers

HM Treasury and Home Office, *Economic Crime Plan 2019 to 2022* (12 July 2019).

HM Treasury and Home Office, *Economic Crime Plan 2023-2026* (30 March 2023).

Home Office, The Impact Assessment on the Reform to the Identification Doctrine (2023) (IA No: HO IA 0463).

House of Commons Justice Committee, *Fraud and the Justice System* (HC 12, Fourth Report of Session 2022–2023).

House of Commons Justice Committee, *Oral Evidence: Work of the Serious Fraud Office* (HC 743).

Law Commission, *Legislating the Criminal Code: Involuntary Manslaughter* (Law Com No. 237, 1996) para 6, 27.

Law Commission, *Corporate Criminal Liability: An Options Paper* (10 June 2022). Available at: https://corporatejusticecoalition.org/wp-content/uploads/2022/07/Corporate-Criminal-Liability-Options-Paper_LC.pdf (accessed 27 March 2025).

Serious Fraud Office, 'Control Liability—Is It a Good Idea and Does It Work in Practice?' (6 September 2016).

Online Sources

Herbert Smith Freehills, 'Economic Crime and Corporate Transparency Act 2023: Who Is an Associated Person for the Failure to Prevent Fraud Offence?' (Herbert Smith Freehills, 22 March 2024). Available at: https://www.herbertsmithfreehills.com/notes/fsrandcorpcrime/2024-03/economic-crime-and-corporate-transparency-act-2023-who-is-an-associated-person-for-the-failure-to-prevent-fraud-offence (accessed 27 March 2025).

White & Case, 'Deferred Prosecution Agreements 5 Years On – The Americanization of UK Corporate Crime Enforcement' (White & Case, 10 May 2019). Available at: https://www.whitecase.com/insight-alert/deferred-prosecution-agreements-5-years-americanisation-uk-corporate-crime (accessed 13 December 2024).

WilmerHale, 'Bribery Act 2010: Ten Years On' (21 May 2021). Available at: https://www.wilmerhale.com/en/insights/blogs/wilmerhale-w-i-r-e-uk/20210521-bribery-act-2010-ten-years-on (accessed 13 December 2024).

UK Government, *Fraud Strategy: Stopping Scams and Protecting the Public*. Available at: https://www.gov.uk/government/publications/fraud-strategy/fraud-strategy-stopping-scams-and-protecting-the-public (accessed 27 March 2025).

Discussion Papers and Commentaries

Bourton, S, and others, 'Corporate Criminal Liability and the Identification Doctrine – A Critical Reflection'.

Cronin, A, 'Fixing Fraud: Flaws in the Economic Crime and Corporate Transparency Act and the Current Enforcement Approach' (November 2024) Institute of Economic Affairs Discussion Paper No. 129.

Roper, V, 'Economic Crime and Corporate Transparency Bill Volume 831: 27 June 2023'.

Doctoral Thesis

Radhi, R, Abdulmohsen, A, *How Can Restorative Justice and the Unified Theory of Punishment Help Us Make Sense of Corporate Crime and Punishment?* (Durham University 2019).

12 Are Traditional Laws Fit for Purpose? A Critique of International Law Governing the Criminal Liability of Digital Providers for Cyber-Sex-Trafficking

Michala Meiselles

1 Introduction

Digital platforms offer an interface. Beyond their role as commercial showcases, these platforms offer a locus where persons can engage with one another, replacing many traditional public places for discussion, debate, and trade. Populated by a broad array of providers, the digital ecosystem is home to a host of actors who exist, operate, transact, and interact. A vibrant marketplace lacking physical borders, the digital ecosystem is a space where universal laws are scarce, and those rules that exist are patchy.

Illegal content displayed on digital platforms is a critical issue for lawmakers and policymakers at the national and international levels, as is the legality of transactions and/or the subject matter of these transactions.[1] Cyber-sex-trafficking (CST) is one such concern. While the term 'sex trafficking' is not specifically defined by the Palermo Protocol,[2] it is generally taken to mean the act of trafficking for the purpose of sexual exploitation.[3] A devastating problem, CST is exacerbated by several factors. First, by a lack of agreement on the meaning and scope of this phenomenon. Secondly, by the absence of consensus about the best way to tackle the role and responsibilities of digital providers, and the lack of international regulation governing the liability of such providers, coupled with the patchwork nature of domestic laws governing this liability. Finally, by the versatility of digital media and the ability of criminals to leverage this versatility.[4] As Clough aptly puts it, cybercrime evolves as technology develops and the ways in which we use technology change.[5]

This chapter asks whether it is time to revisit the international legal framework we currently use, so we can address the role and responsibilities of digital providers for CST. To answer this question, this chapter explores the ways in which traffickers exploit the digital ecosystem, before critically assessing the current international legal framework. It concludes by drawing out the key challenges that lawmakers and policymakers face in their fight against CST.

This chapter aims to contribute to the ongoing debate by enhancing our understanding of the ways in which digital providers can be involved in CST, adding to the discourse over the role of the digital ecosystem in the commission of crimes against the person and the responsibilities of digital providers for user-to-user content (U2U). At the time of writing, this discourse is invaluable to two major international projects: in the European Union (EU) – Directive 2024/1712 (Anti-Trafficking Directive) – and internationally – United Nations Convention against Cybercrime (Cybercrime Convention).[6]

Since this chapter focusses on U2U transactions involving the promotion of commercial sexual services provided by trafficked victims, this chapter looks at a transaction

DOI: 10.4324/9781003324843-16

where one user aims to sell such services to others with the aid of a digital provider. Three key actors are typically involved in such digital transactions: seller, buyer, and digital provider. This chapter uses three terms: digital ecosystem, digital providers, and digital technologies. 'Digital ecosystem' refers to the Internet, social media *and* other digital media – current and future. 'Digital providers' describes the parties providing services in the digital ecosystem and 'digital technologies' refers to 'technologies in the form of social media platforms and applications, websites, communication apps, or other applications designed for the transfer of money, pictures, or text between individuals.'[7]

2 How Traffickers Exploit the Digital Ecosystem

Sex traffickers started integrating the Internet into their business operations several decades ago. In the early days of the Internet, traffickers used stand-alone sites.[8] Nowadays, they exploit digital media and tap into the potential offered by classified ad sites, to recruit victims, and to offer and/or sell services including sexual services.[9] By leveraging these different media, traffickers have increased the scope and reach of their criminal enterprises.[10]

Traffickers have integrated digital technologies[11] into their business model[12] exploiting these technologies during the recruitment, transportation, exploitation, and laundering phases of the trafficking process.[13]

First, during the recruitment phase, traffickers use digital technologies to *source*, *lure* and *coerce* victims. Often taking advantage of personal information that is publicly available and using the anonymity offered by online spaces to reach out to specific victims or groups of victims.[14] Frequently victims are lured in by online advertisements that look to recruit individuals to work in a variety of legitimate jobs.[15] Occasionally, traffickers approach victims directly.[16] During this process, digital technologies are used in a variety of ways: to approach and befriend the victim, to carry out interviews, to cultivate a relationship of trust and reduce inhibitions on behaviour, to alienate the victim from their support system and foster feelings of powerlessness, to facilitate blackmail, to normalize sexual acts, and to decrease the ability of the victim to identify the abusive nature of certain activities and incidents.[17]

Secondly, during the transportation phase, traffickers exploit digital technologies to *arrange* travel, visas, work permits, and accommodation, and to *communicate* and *transact* with stakeholders linked to their operations including government personnel (for visas and work permits), transporters (airlines, travel agents, and so forth), and parties linked to the housing of victims.[18]

Thirdly, during the exploitation stage, digital technologies provide sex traffickers with the ability to *promote* services provided by their victims to users.[19] Traffickers exploit the digital ecosystem to access a larger audience with a minimum amount of effort, using it to reach more obscure target audiences.[20] Online soliciting offers a sex buyer-friendly environment enabling 'virtual cruising' in which users make a choice from the comfort of their own environment (home, offices, hotel, and so on) relying on the discretion, relative secrecy, and general effortlessness offered by the Internet.[21]

Fourthly, by combining digital technologies with smartphone apps, traffickers can streamline their operations, connecting with victims and customers rapidly, and facilitating inter alia the receipt of payments from users and the movement of funds.[22] Fifthly, digital technologies have transformed exploitation, as webcams and livestreams have given rise to new forms of exploitation, reducing the need for victim transportation.[23]

Finally, these digital technologies allow traffickers to 'operate in multiple locations simultaneously while physically exploiting the victims in just one location' by streaming images of sex acts in real time or not through a computer with a webcam to other computers.[24]

3 Current International Legal Framework

Having reviewed how sex traffickers exploit the digital ecosystem to advance their operations, the following segment looks at the current International legal framework governing sex trafficking.[25]

The rules governing online content fall in the first instance to States and international organizations – such as the EU and the UN – with States acting individually or collectively through treaties to introduce rules governing online content and prohibitions around online behaviour.[26] Non-state actors also play a role in shaping the rules governing online behaviour, with platforms and applications defining community standards which act as 'boundary markers' to distinguish acceptable from harmful, dangerous, or illicit conduct.[27]

3.1 Palermo Protocol[28]

The Palermo Protocol is the core treaty governing human trafficking. Adopted by Resolution AIRES/55/25 of 15 November 2000 at the 55th General Assembly Session, this Protocol entered into force on 25 December 2003, providing the first internationally recognized definition of 'trafficking in persons.' With 117 signatories and 180 parties, the Palermo Protocol has effectively reached 'almost universal ratification'; resulting in over 90% of the Member States of the United Nations adopting into their domestic laws, an offence *criminalizing trafficking* alongside the definition of 'trafficking in persons' contained in Article 3 of the Palermo Protocol.[29]

According to the Palermo Protocol 'trafficking in persons' depends on the existence of three conditions.[30] First, the commission of a *specific material act*. In this case, the specific material act is that of 'recruitment, transportation, transfer, harbouring or receipt of persons.'[31] Secondly, these acts must involve the *suppression of consent*. In other words, the act must be perpetrated using certain means intended to suppress the consent of the adult victim, including 'the threat or use of force or other forms of coercion, of abduction, of fraud, of deception, of the abuse of power or of a position of vulnerability.'[32] Alternatively, such consent may be obtained by means of 'the giving or receiving of payments or benefits to achieve the consent of a person having control over another person, for the purpose of exploitation.'[33] This requirement applies when the trafficked victims are adults but does *not* apply when trafficked victims are children. Thirdly, these acts must be committed for a *specific purpose* namely the exploitation of the victims. The Palermo Protocol provides a non-exhaustive list of examples of exploitation including 'exploitation of the prostitution of others or other forms of sexual exploitation, forced labour or services, slavery or practices similar to slavery, servitude or the removal of organs.'[34]

The first category of exploitation – prostitution of others and other forms of sexual exploitation – is addressed in the Modern Slavery Act 2015 (in England and Wales);[35] in 22 U.S.C. §7102(12)[36] and 18 U.S.C §1591 (in the US);[37] and Article 225–6 of the French *Code Pénal* (in France).[38]

3.2 Anti-Trafficking Directive

Introduced in June 2024, Directive 2024/1712 updates the 2011 Directive.[39] It provides Member States with two years for transposition.[40] Aimed at ensuring Member States and the EU are better equipped to fight against new forms of exploitation, this multifaceted project provides law enforcement and judicial bodies with stronger tools to investigate and prosecute human trafficking and exploitation, while setting out to tackle the increased use of information and communication technologies in these criminal ventures.[41]

3.3 *Cybercrime Convention*

The culmination of years of work by UN's Member States with input from civil society, the academic community, and the private sector, the Draft Cybercrime Convention was agreed upon by the committee established by the General Assembly of the UN in August 2024, and the Convention itself was adopted in December 2024.[42] This Convention addresses the exploitation of information and communications technology systems for criminal offences including human trafficking. The most contemporary international legal framework on cybercrime, this multifaceted instrument calls on State Parties to criminalize certain cyberactivities including online child sexual abuse and exploitation.[43]

4 Critical Analysis of the Current International Legal Framework

This chapter asks whether it is time to revisit the international legal framework we currently use, so we can address the role and responsibilities of digital providers for CST. To answer this question, the following segment critically analyses the current legal framework governing CST, to identify the key challenges that lawmakers and policymakers face.

Since the introduction of the Palermo Protocol, the world has changed. Back when this Protocol was adopted, Internet usage was limited, and social media had yet to emerge. Whereas nowadays, social media and the Internet have assumed a pivotal role in our daily lives and are widely used by the bulk of the world's population. Now, mobile devices allow users to surf the Internet and access social media anytime and anyplace, with digital applications providing easy access to a plethora of social media.[44] Notwithstanding the concern of the international community and nations about the role and responsibilities of digital providers for CST, no uniform rules have emerged so far. This situation is the result of several key factors.[45]

4.1 *Challenges of Domestic Law*

By design, domestic law is traditionally confined to crimes committed within the boundaries of the jurisdiction itself. These jurisdictional constraints mean that, in practice, most nations will only prosecute crimes committed within their borders, though some jurisdictions also use extra-territorial jurisdictional rules to prosecute specific offences committed outside the affected jurisdiction.[46] In the UK, for example, pursuant to the Sexual Offences Act 2003, British citizens can be prosecuted for sexual offences committed against children outside the UK.[47] The same is true for female genital mutilation.[48]

A related challenge is the general lack of domestic law aimed at tackling the role and responsibilities of digital providers for human trafficking and CST activities on their platforms. While most jurisdictions have adopted the Palermo Protocol, criminalizing the activities of human traffickers, few have developed rules to address the liability of digital providers for their involvement in such operations.[49] This is the consequence of various causes. First, national laws do not necessarily consider the online nature and impact of such activities, especially when these transcend geographic and political borders. Secondly, lawmakers and policymakers are confronted with a problem that is of overwhelming dimensions; beyond the fact that the technology is dynamic and its evolution rapid, its impact is far-reaching, the number of users and victims is vast, and they are scattered across the globe.

4.2 *Speed of Change and the Absence of a Global Infrastructure*

A further challenge facing domestic, and by extension international, lawmakers and policymakers is the rapid evolution of digital media. Presented with an everchanging landscape, policymakers, and lawmakers are generally unable to legislate at a pace that matches up to the level of development. As we have seen criminals are adept at exploiting new technologies. Capitalizing on the versatility of these media, the speed of technological innovation, and the absence of a global infrastructure governing supervisory, investigation, and enforcement. Here INTERPOL plays an important role – supporting national law enforcement agencies – but its powers are limited.[50]

4.3 *Lack of Consensus*

In the context of CST, traffickers exploiting digital media are aided by several factors. First, the lack of consensus and the absence of international regulation governing the responsibility of digital providers for content generally, and user content specifically. Secondly, the patchwork nature of national laws in this context.

A general lack of consensus exists within and across States about what exactly amounts to CST, the scope of this offence, and who qualifies as a culprit. In this context, it has been a struggle to develop and agree on an effective framework addressing the role and responsibilities of digital providers, resulting in a lack of agreement – national and international – about: whether digital providers are liable for user content;[51] if they are liable, what form such liability should take[52]; and if digital providers are found criminally liable, whether there is a need for "knowledge"; which model of corporate criminal liability should be used; and what types of punishment should be imposed.[53]

This lack of agreement about the best way to tackle the liability of digital providers, results in legal uncertainties which are harmful to users and businesses,[54] and regulatory arbitrage, which occurs when actors structure their operations in a way that takes advantage of regulatory differences to reduce regulatory costs or evade liability.[55] The differences resulting from this lack of consensus arguably allow entities operating digital platforms (including websites and social media) with advertisements promoting and/or facilitating sex trafficking, to engage in forum shopping, by permitting them to pick jurisdictions where they can relocate their operations and platforms to mitigate regulatory costs and/or to avoid regulation, detection, prosecution, and enforcement entirely. This relocation has amplified the 'already-existing challenges law enforcement face' when gathering tips and evidence to investigate and prosecute those controlling or using online platforms.[56] Such investigations and prosecutions may be further exacerbated by the fact that those controlling online platforms use complex and opaque payment systems, mixing traditional and alternative payment methods – including virtual currencies, store-brand gift cards, and pre-paid debit products – alongside evasive techniques to facilitate illicit transactions – such as the use of third parties.[57]

Another challenge faced by law enforcement is the increased use of social media platforms which: use different levels of encryption of messages shared by users; allow 'user pseudo-anonymity' through the creation and use of false identities; and permit automatic content deletion which erases the message shortly after it has been viewed by the recipient.[58]

5 Conclusion

The digital ecosystem is a vibrant marketplace, which is largely free from regulation. It is not currently governed by a universal legal framework and is not subject to a global system of enforcement, so no overarching authority exists with the power to monitor, police, and protect individuals against harms in this sphere. Effectively leaving criminals and sex traffickers in a position to exploit this digital ecosystem in their operations by enabling them to use digital media to source, target, prey upon, and exploit victims; to promote services to users – with services provided digitally or in person; to receive user payments in exchange for these services; to transfer funds in and across jurisdictions; and to raise funding for their operations.

Most jurisdictions have adopted the Palermo Protocol criminalizing the activities of human traffickers. Even so, this chapter shows that there still exists a divergence in the jurisdictional approaches to the general treatment of digital providers associated with the commission of this crime and specifically to the criminalization of digital platforms advertising and/or promoting the services of adults and children for sexual exploitation. This state of affairs is largely rooted in a general disagreement about the extension of criminal liability and the fear of *guilt by association*; in this context, questions crop-up about where criminal liability begins and ends, and how remotely or closely a person has to be connected to the underlying offence to be responsible.[59] In the words of Baker:[60]

> Just how much has an individual to do in order to be included in the net of those who are regarded as accountable … just what and how much must she or he know, believe or suspect for it to be just to regard her or him as blameworthy? And what if she … has a change of mind? Should it be possible to withdraw from the involvement in the criminal enterprise, thereby avoiding liability for it, especially once an offence has been embarked upon; and, if so, why?

Notes

1 Protocol to Prevent, Suppress and Punish Trafficking in Persons, especially Women and Children, supplementing the United Nations Convention against Transnational Organized Crime (Palermo Protocol). See slso Jonathan Clough, 'Cybercrime' (2011) 37 *Commw L Bull* 671; Adam M. Bossler and Tamar Berenblum, 'Introduction: New Directions in Cybercrime Research' (2019) 42(5) *J Crim Justice* 495.

2 Article 3a of the Palermo Protocol defines 'trafficking in persons' and refers to various forms of exploitation including 'exploitation of the prostitution of others or other forms of sexual exploitation.'

3 Sex trafficking according to Goldman refers to 'paid sexual activity by minors or someone compelled or forced to engage in such activity' (Goldman 2018: FN15).

4 Bossler and Berenblum 2019: 495. C.f. Clough 2011: 672, and Avinash Krishna Goswami and Ritu Gautam, 'India's Cybercrime, Cybersecurity and Cyber Regulation' in Pradeep Kulshrestha, Anita Singh and Ritu Gautam (eds), *Cyber Crime, Regulation and Security: Contemporary Issues and Challenges* (The Law Brigade Publisher 2022), 48.

5 Clough 2011: 672.

6 Directive 2024/1712 of the European Parliament and of the Council of 13 June 2024 amending Directive 2011/36/EU on preventing and combating trafficking in human beings and protecting

its victims OJ L, 2024/1712, 24.6.2024 (Anti-Trafficking Directive 2024). The United Nations Convention against Cybercrime (Cybercrime Convention) is available at: https://www.unodc.org/unodc/en/cybercrime/convention/home.html (accessed 23 June 2025).

7 UNODC, 'Global Report on Trafficking in Persons' (2020), 119.

8 Emily Morgan, 'On FOSTA and the Failures of Punitive Speech Restrictions' (2020) 115 *Nw U L Rev* 503; Caitlyn Burnitis, 'Facing the Future with FOSTA: Examining the Allow States and Victims to Fight Online Sex Trafficking Act of 2017' (2020) 10 *U Miami Race & Soc Just L Rev* 139; Naoise Webster, 'Analysis of FOSTA's Constitutionality: How the Supreme Court Should Approach This Issue' (2020) 7 *NE L Rev* 15.

9 UNODC, 'Global Report on Trafficking in Persons' (2024), 97. See also UNODC, 'Global Report on Trafficking in Persons' (2020), 119, 121; Europol, 'Situation Report Trafficking in Human Beings in the EU' (2016) Document No. 765175: 12, 23.

10 Europol, 'Intelligence Notification: Trafficking in Human Beings and the Internet' (2014) Intelligence Notification 15/2014, 1. Offenders use these media in multiple ways, which Yar classifies by reference to their distinctive features, as person-centred and content-centred offences (Yar 2018: 7). Person-centred offences cover behaviours in which the offender targets a person, or persons, or groups who are then subjected to a range of harms (Yar 2018: 7). Content-centred offences cover online distribution of content which is legally prohibited or over which the party sharing the content has no rights or ownership (Yar 2018: 7).

11 The term 'digital technologies' is used in this chapter. A synonym for the term 'digital technologies' is the term 'Internet technologies' used by the UNODC which is a generic term describing 'technologies in the form of social media platforms and applications, websites, communication apps, or other applications designed for the transfer of money, pictures, or text between individuals' (UNODC, 'Global Report on Trafficking in Persons' (2020), 119).

12 Sigrid Raets and Jelle Janssens, 'The Economics of Human Trafficking in a Digitalised Age' in Ognian Shentov, Tanas Rusev and Georgios A. Antonopoulos (eds) *Financing of Organised Crime: Human Trafficking in Focus* (Centre for the Study of Democracy 2018), 86–87.

13 Alexis A. Aronowitz, *Human Trafficking, Human Misery: The Global Trade in Human Beings* (Praeger Publishers 2009), 9–10.

14 UNODC, 'Global Report on Trafficking in Persons' (2020), 119, 121. See also Europol, 'Situation Report Trafficking in Human Beings in the EU' (2016) Document No. 765175: 12; Aronowitz 2009: 130.

15 Europol, 'Intelligence Notification: Trafficking in Human Beings and the Internet' (2014) Intelligence Notification 15/2014, 2. See also Europol, 'Situation Report Trafficking in Human Beings in the EU' (2016) Document No. 765175, 12.

16 Jennifer Middleton, 'From the Street Corner to the Digital World: How the Digital Age Impacts Sex Trafficking Detection and Data Collection' in John Winterdyk and Jackie Jones (eds), *The Palgrave International Handbook of Human Trafficking* (Palgrave Macmillan 2020), 470–471.

17 Catherine Hamilton-Giachritsis, Elly Hanson, Helen Whittle and Anthony Beech, 'Everyone Deserves to be Happy and Safe. A Mixed Methods Study Exploring How Online and Offline Child Sexual Abuse Impact Young People and How Professionals Respond to It' (NSPCC 2017), 6. See also Middleton 2020: 471.

18 Europol, 'Intelligence Notification: Trafficking in Human Beings and the Internet' (2014) Intelligence Notification 15/2014, 2. See also Europol, 'Situation Report Trafficking in Human Beings in the EU' (2016) Document No. 765175, 12; Raets et al. 2018: 88; Aronowitz 2009: 55–56, 130–132.

19 UNODC, 'Global Report on Trafficking in Persons' (2020), 120–121. See also Hamilton-Giachritisis et al. 2017: 12; Yar 2018: 7; Europol, 'Intelligence Notification: Trafficking in Human Beings and the Internet' (2014) Intelligence Notification 15/2014, 2; Raets et al. 2018: 89–90; Aronowitz 2009: 55–56, 130–132.

20 Raets et al. 2018: 89–90.

21 Raets et al. 2018: 89–90. See also Middleton 2020: 472.

22 UNODC, 'Global Report on Trafficking in Persons' (2024), 96. See also UNODC, 'Global Report on Trafficking in Persons' (2020), 122–123; Hamilton-Giachritisis et al. 2017: 12 and Catherine Hamilton-Giachritiis, Elly Hanson, Helen Whittle, Filipa Alves-Costa, Andrea Pintos, Theo Metcalf and Anthony Beech, 'Technology Assisted Child Sexual Abuse: Professionals' Perceptions of Risk and Impact on Children and Young People' (2021) *Child Abuse Neglect*, 2, 5–7.

23 UNODC, 'Global Report on Trafficking in Persons' (2020), 119, 122.
24 European Parliamentary Research Service, 'Understanding EU Action against Human Trafficking' (2023), 8.
25 FOSTA (Allow States and Victims to Fight Online Sex Trafficking Act) Long title: A bill to amend the Communications Act of 1934 to clarify that section 230 of such Act does not prohibit the enforcement against providers and users of interactive computer services of Federal and State criminal and civil law relating to sexual exploitation of children or sex trafficking, and for other purposes. For a detailed review of FOSTA, its features and critique, see Lannier, S., Meiselles, M. Challenging the criminal liability of online services providers for sex trafficking – A comparison of the American and French approaches. (2025) 83 *Crime Law Soc Change* 38.
26 Yar 2018: 10.
27 Yar 2018: 11. See Giancarlo Frosio, 'Mapping Online Intermediary Liability' in Giancarlo Frosio (ed), *Oxford Handbook of Online Intermediary Liability* (Oxford Academic 2020), 3.
28 Protocol to Prevent, Suppress and Punish Trafficking in Persons, especially Women and Children, supplementing the United Nations Convention against Transnational Organized Crime (otherwise widely known as the Palermo Protocol). Certified copy available at https://treaties.un.org/doc/Treaties/2000/11/20001115%2011-38%20AM/Ch_XVIII_12_ap.pdf (accessed 12 March 2025). Status information available at https://treaties.un.org/pages/ViewDetails.aspx?src=TREATY&mtdsg_no=XVIII-12-a&chapter=18&clang=_en (accessed 12 March 2025).
29 UNODC, 'Global Report on Trafficking in Persons' (2020), 23.
30 Article 3(a), 2000 Protocol.
31 Article 3(a), 2000 Protocol.
32 Article 3(a), 2000 Protocol.
33 Article 3(a), 2000 Protocol.
34 Article 3(a), 2000 Protocol.
35 Scotland and Northern Ireland are only governed by parts of this Act. Sexual exploitation is defined in Modern Slavery Act section 3(3) which reads 'For the purposes of §2 a person is exploited only if one or more of the following subsections apply in relation to the person … (3) Something is done to or in respect of that person – (a) which involves the commission of an offence under (i) §1(1)(a) of the Protection of Children Act 1978 (indecent photographs of children), or (ii) Part 1 of the Sexual Offences Act 2003 (sexual offences), as it has effect in England and Wales, or (b) which would involve the commission of such an offence if it were done in England and Wales.'
36 22 U.S.C. §7102(12) is available at https://www.law.cornell.edu/uscode/text/22/7102 (accessed 12 March 2025). This Section defines 'severe forms of trafficking in persons' – in §§11 – as meaning sex trafficking, which is then defined in §§12 as 'the recruitment, harboring, transportation, provision, obtaining, patronizing, or soliciting of a person for the purpose of a commercial sex act.'
37 18 U.S.C §1591 is available at https://www.law.cornell.edu/uscode/text/18/1591 (accessed 12 March 2025). This Section addresses sex trafficking of children or by force, fraud or coercion.
38 This addresses the act of *proxénétisme* or pimping in English. Available at https://www.legifrance.gouv.fr/codes/article_lc/LEGIARTI000006417855 (accessed 12 March 2025). For a review of this aspect of French law, see Lannier, S., Meiselles, M. Challenging the criminal liability of online services providers for sex trafficking – A comparison of the American and French approaches. (2025) 83 *Crime Law Soc Change* 38.
39 Directive 2011/36/EU of the European Parliament and of the Council of 5 April 2011 on preventing and combating trafficking in human beings and protecting its victims and replacing Council Framework Decision 2002/629/JHA.
40 Pursuant to Article 2, Directive 2024/1712, Member States must introduce new legislation or update existing legislation so that it aligns with this Directive no later than 15 July 2026.
41 Commission press release 'Commission Welcomes Breakthrough Political Agreement on Stronger Rules to Fight Trafficking in Human Beings' (dated 23 January 2024). Available at https://ec.europa.eu/commission/presscorner/detail/ov/ip_24_343 (accessed 23 July 2024). See para 8 of the Preamble and Article 1, Directive 2024/1712.
42 UN press release 'United Nations: Member States Finalize a New Cybercrime Convention' (dated 9 August 2024) Available at: https://www.unodc.org/unodc/en/frontpage/2024/August/united-nations_-member-states-finalize-a-new-cybercrime-convention.html (accessed 16 March 2025). The United Nations Convention against Cybercrime (Cybercrime Convention) is

available at: https://www.unodc.org/unodc/en/cybercrime/convention/home.html (accessed 23 June 2025).

43 Article 14, Cybercrime Convention.

47 According to Statista, in April 2024, there were 5.44 billion internet users worldwide (67.1% of the global population); of this total, 5.07 billion users were social media users (62.6% of the global population) (Statista, 'Worldwide Digital Population 2024', https://www.statista.com/statistics/617136/digital-population-worldwide/, accessed 16 March 2025). In 2024, the ITU estimated that 5.5 billion people were online, which represents an increase of 227 million individuals based on estimates from 2023 (68% of the world's population) (ITU, 'Global Internet Use Continues to Rise But Disparities Remain, Especially in Low-Income Regions' (27 November 2024). Available at https://www.itu.int/en/mediacentre/Pages/PR-2024-11-27-facts-and-figures.aspx#:~:text=%E2%80%8B%E2%80%8B%E2%80%8B%E2%80%8B%E2%80%8B,International%20Telecommunication%20Union%20(ITU) (accessed 16 March 2025).

45 Due to their adoption of the Protocol 2000 (Protocol to Prevent, Suppress and Punish Trafficking in Persons, especially Women and Children, supplementing the United Nations Convention against Transnational Organized Crime).

46 Neil Boister, Transnational Criminal Law? (2003) 14(5) *Eur J Int L*, 945.

47 Sexual Offences Act 2003, section 72 (Offences outside the United Kingdom). Available at https://www.legislation.gov.uk/ukpga/2003/42/section/72 (accessed 24 July 2024).

48 Female Genital Mutilation Act 2003 (UK), section 3 (Offence of assisting a non-UK person to mutilate overseas a girl's genitalia) and section 4 (extension of sections 1 to 3A to extra-territorial acts or omissions).

49 Protocol to Prevent, Suppress and Punish Trafficking in Persons, especially Women and Children, supplementing the United Nations Convention against Transnational Organized Crime.

50 INTERPOL's role is discussed in detail in Kanae Kanki and Alexander Resch, 'Strengthening International Law Enforcement Cooperation: INTERPOL and Its Global Fight against Economic and Financial Crime' in M Meiselles, N Ryder and A Visconti (eds), *Corporate Criminal Liability and Sanctions: Current Trends and Policy Changes* (Routledge 2024), 107-127. For a detailed review of these challenges, see Lannier, S., Meiselles, M. Challenging the criminal liability of online services providers for sex trafficking – A comparison of the American and French approaches. (2025) 83 *Crime Law Soc Change* 38.

51 Whilst some view the role of digital providers as somewhat limited, arguing that digital providers 'do not initiate decisions to disseminate the content, products, or services that transverse their networks or services,' others disagree. See OECD, *The Economic and Social Role of Internet Intermediaries* (OECD 2010), 9.

52 Riordan, Jaani, 'A Theoretical Taxonomy of Intermediary Liability' in Giancarlo Frosio (ed), *Oxford Handbook of Online Intermediary Liability* (Oxford Academic 2020), 57–59, 62.

53 For a detailed discussion of corporate liability, see Arianna Visconti, 'Corporate Manslaughter and Corporate Violence Victims Rights in Italy: A Long and Winding Road' in Michala Meiselles, Nicholas Ryder and Arianna Visconti (eds), *Corporate Criminal Liability and Sanctions: Current Trends and Policy Changes* (Routledge 2024), 37–40.

54 Giancarlo Frosio, 'Mapping Online Intermediary Liability' in Giancarlo Frosio (ed), *Oxford Handbook of Online Intermediary Liability* (Oxford Academic 2020), 3–4.

55 Thomas Coendet, 'The Concept of Regulatory Arbitrage' in K Mathis and A Tor (eds), *Law and Economics of Regulation* (Springer 2021), 159–160.

56 United States Government Accountability Office, 'Report to Congressional Committees: Sex Trafficking - Online Platforms and Federal Prosecutions' (June 2021) GAO-21-385, 20–21.

57 United States Government Accountability Office, 'Report to Congressional Committees: Sex Trafficking - Online Platforms and Federal Prosecutions' (June 2021) GAO-21-385, 22.

58 United States Government Accountability Office, 'Report to Congressional Committees: Sex Trafficking - Online Platforms and Federal Prosecutions' (June 2021) GAO-21-385, 23–25.

59 Andrea Schloenhardt, *Palermo in the Pacific: Organised Crime Offences in the Asia Pacific Region* (Brill Nijhoff 2010), 6.

60 Estella Baker, 'The Legal Regulation of Transnational Organised Crime' in Adam Edward and Peter Gill (eds), *Transnational Organised Crime: Perspectives on Global Security* (Routledge 2003), 183, 189.

Bibliography

Aronowitz, AA, *Human Trafficking, Human Misery: The Global Trade in Human Beings* (Praeger Publishers 2009).

Baker, E, 'The Legal Regulation of Transnational Organised Crime', in A Edward and P Gill (eds), *Transnational Organised Crime: Perspectives on Global Security* (Routledge 2003), 183–194.

Bird, SE, 'Are We All Produsers Now? Convergence and Media Audience Practices' (2011) 25(4–5) *Cult Stud* 502.

Boister, N, 'Transnational Criminal Law?' (2003) 14(5) *Eur J Int L* 953–976.

Bossler, A, and Berenblum, T, 'Introduction: New Directions in Cybercrime Research' (2019) 42(5) *J Crime Just* 495.

Burnitis, C, 'Facing the Future with FOSTA: Examining the Allow States and Victims to Fight Online Sex Trafficking Act of 2017' (2020) 10 *U Miami Race & Soc Just L Rev* 139.

Clough, J, 'Cybercrime' (2011) 37 *Commw L Bull*, 67.

Coendet, T, 'The Concept of Regulatory Arbitrage' in K Mathis & A Tor (eds), *Law and Economics of Regulation* (Springer 2021), 159–181.

Cormode, G, and Krishnamurthy, B, 'Key Differences between Web 1.0 and Web 2.0' (2008) 13(6) *First Monday*. Available at https://doi.org/10.5210/fm.v13i6.2125 (accessed 7 March 2025).

Cunningham, S, DeAngelo, G, and Tripp, J, 'Craigslist's Effect on Violence against Women' (November 2017). Available at https://coyoteri.org/wp/wp-content/uploads/2019/01/13575_paper_QZNF9dHi-1.pdf (accessed 12 March 2025).

Delateur, MJ, 'From Craigslist to Backpage.Com: Conspiracy as a Strategy to Prosecute Third Party Websites for Sex Trafficking' (2016) 56 *Santa Clara L Rev* 530.

Dinwoodie, G, 'Who Are Internet Intermediaries?' in G Frosio (ed), *Oxford Handbook of Online Intermediary Liability* (Oxford Academic 2020), 36–56.

Frosio, G, 'Mapping Online Intermediary Liability' in G Frosio (ed), *Oxford Handbook of Online Intermediary Liability* (Oxford Academic 2020), 2–33.

Goldman, E, 'The Complicated Story of FOSTA and Section 230' (2018) 17 *First Amend L Rev* 279–293.

Goldman, E, 'An Overview of the United States' Section 230 Internet Immunity' in G Frosio (ed), *Oxford Handbook of Online Intermediary Liability* (Oxford Academic 2020).

Goswami and Gautam, 'India's Cybercrime, Cybersecurity and Cyber Regulation' in P Kulshrestha, A Singh, and R Gautam (eds), *Cyber Crime, Regulation and Security: Contemporary Issues and Challenges* (The Law Brigade Publisher 2022), 47–55.

Gross, L, 'My Media Studies: Cultivation to Participation' (2009) 10(1) *Television and New Media* 66.

Hamilton-Giachritis, H, Whittle, A-C, Pintos, M, and Beech, A, 'Technology Assisted Child Sexual Abuse: Professionals' Perceptions of Risk and Impact on Children and Young People' (2021) *Child Abuse Neglect* 1–12.

Hamilton-Giachritsis, C, Hanson, E, Whittle, H, and Beech, A, 'Everyone Deserves to Be Happy and Safe. A Mixed Methods Study Exploring How Online and Offline Child Sexual Abuse Impact Young People and How Professionals Respond to It' (NSPCC 2017).

ICMEC, 'Child Sexual Abuse Material: Model Legislation and Global Review' (2018). Available at https://www.icmec.org/child-pornography-model-legislation-report/ (accessed 16 March 2025).

Kanki, K, and Resch, A, 'Strengthening International Law Enforcement Cooperation: INTERPOL and Its Global Fight against Economic and Financial Crime' in M Meiselles, N Ryder, and A Visconti (eds), *Corporate Criminal Liability and Sanctions: Current Trends and Policy Changes* (Routledge 2024), 107–127.

Lannier, S., Meiselles, M. Challenging the criminal liability of online services providers for sex trafficking – A comparison of the American and French approaches. (2025) 83 *Crime Law Soc Change* 38.

Lennard, N, 'Law Claiming to Fight Sex Trafficking Is Doing the Opposite by Cracking Down on Sex Work Advocacy and Organizing' (13 July 2018) *The Intercept*. Available at https://theintercept.com/2018/06/13/sesta-fosta-sex-work-criminalize-advocacy/ (accessed 12 March 2025).

Mehta, D, 'Canadian Police Mixed over US Shutdown of Adult Section on Backpage.com' (12 January 2017) *The Canadian Press*. Available at https://globalnews.ca/news/3177482/canadian-police-mixed-over-u-s-shutdown-of-adult-section-on-backpage-com/ (accessed 12 March 2025).

Middleton, J, 'From the Street Corner to the Digital World: How the Digital Age Impacts Sex Trafficking Detection and Data Collection' in J Winterdyk and J Jones (eds), *The Palgrave International Handbook of Human Trafficking* (Palgrave Macmillan 2020), 467–480.

Morgan, E, 'On FOSTA and the Failures of Punitive Speech Restrictions' (2020) 115 *Nw U L Rev* 503.

Pew Research Centre, 'Social Media Use in 2021' (2021). Available at https://www.pewresearch.org/internet/2021/04/07/social-media-use-in-2021/ (accessed 12 March 2025).

Pew Research Centre, 'Teens, Social Media and Technology 2024' (2024). Available at https://www.pewresearch.org/internet/2024/12/12/teens-social-media-and-technology-2024/ (accessed 12 March 2025).

Raets, S, and Janssens, J, 'The Economics of Human Trafficking in a Digitalised Age' in O Shentov, T Rusev, and GA Antonopoulos (eds), *Financing of Organised Crime: Human Trafficking in Focus* (Centre for the Study of Democracy 2018), 85–96.

Riordan, J, 'A Theoretical Taxonomy of Intermediary Liability' in G Frosio (ed), *Oxford Handbook of Online Intermediary Liability* (Oxford Academic 2020), 57–89.

Ritzer, G, Dean, P, and Jurgenson, N, 'The Coming of Age of the Prosumer' (2012) *56(4) Am Behav Sci* 379.

Romano, A, 'A New Law Intended to Curb Sex Trafficking Threatens the Future of the Internet as We Know It' (2 July 2018) *Vox*. Available at https://www.vox.com/culture/2018/4/13/17172762/fosta-sesta-backpage-230-internet-freedom (accessed 12 March 2025).

Schloenhardt, A, *Palermo in the Pacific: Organised Crime Offences in the Asia Pacific Region* (Brill Nijhoff 2010).

Tripp, H, 'All Sex Workers Deserve Protection: How FOSTA/SESTA Overlooks Consensual Sex Workers in an Attempt to Protect Sex Trafficking Victims' (2019) 124 *Penn St L Rev* 219.

Visconti, A, 'Corporate Manslaughter and Corporate Violence Victims Rights in Italy: A Long and Winding Road' in M Meiselles, N Ryder, and A Visconti (eds), *Corporate Criminal Liability and Sanctions: Current Trends and Policy Changes* (Routledge 2024), 37.

Webster, N, 'Analysis of FOSTA's Constitutionality: How the Supreme Court Should Approach This Issue' (2020) 7 *NE L Rev* 15.

Yar, M, 'A Failure to Regulate? The Demands and Dilemmas of Tackling Illegal Content and Behaviour on Social Media' (2018) 1(1) *Int J Cybersecurity Intelligence & Cybercrime* 5.

EU

European Parliamentary Research Service, 'Understanding EU Action against Human Trafficking' (2023).

Europol

Europol, 'Intelligence Notification: Trafficking in Human Beings and the Internet' (2014) Intelligence Notification 15/2014.

Europol, 'Situation Report Trafficking in Human Beings in the EU' (2016) Document No. 765175. Available at https://www.europol.europa.eu/sites/default/files/documents/thb_situational_report_-_europol.pdf (accessed 16 March 2025).

ITU

ITU, 'Internet Use' (2023). Available at https://www.itu.int/itu-d/reports/statistics/2023/10/10/ff23-internet-use/ (accessed 2 March 2025).

ITU, 'Youth Internet Use' (2023). Available at https://www.itu.int/itu-d/reports/statistics/2023/10/10/ff23-youth-internet-use/ (accessed 2 March 2025).

OECD

OECD, 'The Economic and Social Role of Internet Intermediaries' (2010). Available at https://www.oecd.org/en/publications/the-economic-and-social-role-of-internet-intermediaries_5kmh79zzs8vb-en.html (accessed 23 June 2025).

Ofcom

Ofcom, 'Children and Parents: Media Use and Attitudes Report' (2024). Available at https://www.ofcom.org.uk/siteassets/resources/documents/research-and-data/media-literacy-research/children/children-media-use-and-attitudes-2024/childrens-media-literacy-report-2024.pdf?v=368229 (accessed 7 March 2025).

UNODC

UNODC, 'Global Report on Trafficking in Persons' (2020). Available at https://www.unodc.org/documents/data-and-analysis/tip/2021/GLOTiP_2020_15jan_web.pdf (accessed 27 March 2025).

UNODC, 'Global Report on Trafficking in Persons' (2021). Available at https://www.unodc.org/documents/data-and-analysis/tip/2021/GLOTiP_2020_15jan_web.pdf (accessed 16 March 2025).

UNODC, 'Issue Paper: Policymaking and the Role of Online Intermediaries in Preventing and Combating Illicit Trafficking' (2021). Available at https://sherloc.unodc.org/cld/uploads/pdf/Online_intermediaries_eBook.pdf (accessed 16 March 2025).

UNODC, 'Global Report on Trafficking in Persons' (2024). Available at https://www.unodc.org/documents/data-and-analysis/glotip/2024/GLOTIP2024_BOOK.pdf (accessed 16 March 2025).

United States

United States Government Accountability Office, 'Report to Congressional Committees: Sex Trafficking – Online Platforms and Federal Prosecutions' (June 2021) GAO-21-385.

US Senate Permanent Subcommittee on Investigations Report, 'Backpage.Com's Knowing Facilitation of Online Sex Trafficking' (January 2017). Available at https://www.courthousenews.com/wp-content/uploads/2017/02/Backpage-Report.pdf (accessed 16 March 2025).

Index

Note: **Bold** page numbers refer to tables; *italic* page numbers refer to figures and page numbers followed by "n" denote endnotes.